M000316790

Developing Destinies

CHILD DEVELOPMENT IN CULTURAL CONTEXT

Series Editors

Cynthia García Coll
Peggy Miller

Advisory Board

Jerome Kagan
Carol Worthman
Barrie Thorne

Developing Destinies: A Mayan Midwife and Town
Barbara Rogoff

In a Younger Voice: Doing Child-Centered Qualitative Research
Cindy Dell Clark

Immigrant Stories: Ethnicity and Academics in Middle Childhood
Cynthia García Coll and Amy Kerivan Marks

Academic Motivation and the Culture of Schooling
Cynthia Hudley and Adele E. Gottfried

Perfectly Prep: Gender Extremes at a New England Prep School
Sarah A. Chase

Forthcoming Books in the Series

Literacy and Mothering: Women's Schooling, Families, and Child Development
Robert LeVine and the Harvard Project on Maternal Schooling

Developing Destinies

A Mayan Midwife and Town

Barbara Rogoff

with Chona Pérez González
Chonita Chavajay Quiacaín
and
Josué Chavajay Quiacaín

OXFORD
UNIVERSITY PRESS

OXFORD
UNIVERSITY PRESS

Oxford University Press, Inc., publishes works that further
Oxford University's objective of excellence in research,
scholarship, and education.

Oxford   New York
Auckland   Cape Town   Dar es Salaam   Hong Kong   Karachi
Kuala Lumpur   Madrid   Melbourne   Mexico City   Nairobi
New Delhi   Shanghai   Taipei   Toronto

With offices in
Argentina   Austria   Brazil   Chile   Czech Republic   France   Greece
Guatemala   Hungary   Italy   Japan   Poland   Portugal   Singapore
South Korea   Switzerland   Thailand   Turkey   Ukraine   Vietnam

Copyright © 2011 by Barbara Rogoff

Published by Oxford University Press, Inc.
198 Madison Avenue, New York, New York 10016

www.oup.com

Oxford is a registered trademark of Oxford University Press

All rights reserved. No part of this publication may be reproduced,
stored in a retrieval system, or transmitted, in any form or by any means,
electronic, mechanical, photocopying, recording, or otherwise,
without the prior permission of Oxford University Press.

ISBN 978-0-19-531990-3

Library of Congress Cataloging-in-Publication Data is on file.

3 5 7 9 8 6 4 2
Printed in the United States of America on acid-free paper

Dedicated to the memories of the grandmothers and grandfathers,
and to the babies

Contents ⠿

Developing Destinies

1 ⠿

Beginnings:
Stability and Change

THIS BOOK EMERGES from intriguing paradoxes of stability and change in the lives of individuals as well as of communities—that is, both their destinies and developments.

The foundations of the book began 35 years ago when I met Encarnación (Chona) Pérez, the renowned sacred Mayan midwife. I was interviewing her as a prominent local expert for my research on childrearing practices in the Mayan town of San Pedro la Laguna, Guatemala. Chona and I began working on the book itself about 20 years ago. It has transformed its shape numerous times in the meantime, but the story kept insisting on being written.

Usually, when I write a book, it is a project that I have chosen. In the case of this book, though, the project chose me. It chose me and it wouldn't go away, almost like it was destined as my work. It was only after years of working on the book that I realized how central its themes were to my own learning and development as a developmental psychologist.

In part, the account needed to be written because the sacred work that was destined at Chona's birth is now calling fewer women. San Pedro's population has grown, but the number of women who follow the birth destiny of sacred midwife is decreasing. The knowledge and this way of life are being lost as more babies are delivered by doctors and by midwives who were not born with this calling. They do not have the responsibility or knowledge to read birthsigns that indicate that a baby has the "gift" of being destined to serve a spiritual calling.

Chona is eager for her life and work to be written so that there will be a record of it for future generations. Although she has never read a book, she is well aware that her life has been chronicled in fieldnotes by me, and earlier by anthropologists Ben and Lois Paul. Chona is interested in making this information available in San Pedro and elsewhere.

An important part of the book is the photographs of Chona and of life in San Pedro. Many of them were taken when Chona was a young woman of 16, by Ben and Lois Paul, and others were taken by me when Chona had reached 50 and by my daughter Luisa when Chona was in her 70s. The captions and the photographs are essential to understanding the book—so please read them in the order they appear in the book, even if you're used to skipping over photo captions. Unlike the photo captions, the footnotes can be skipped or read later without missing the flow of the book, although they contain some interesting asides that I think you'll find fascinating.

In her late 70s, Chona examines a painting of her that I had drafted for an early version of this book. The painting shows baby Chona with the birthsign veil draped over her newborn head, indicating her calling as a sacred midwife. (Photo © Salem Magarian, about 2001)

The story of the changes and continuities in the lives of Chona and San Pedro also needs to be told because it provides a window for understanding humanity. It especially helps us see the cultural aspects of life. The view through this window reveals human development as a dynamic process, in which individuals and generations transform as well as preserve the practices of earlier generations.

For example, Chona's relation to school and reading and writing has changed dramatically across her lifetime, along with the changing role of schooling across generations in San Pedro. At the same time, these changes contribute to preserving knowledge of ancient traditions in San Pedro, including the spiritual calling of midwife.

Chona Did Not Go to School, But Her Sister Did

WHEN CHONA WAS A CHILD, she thought that people who read books were insane—because "paper does not have a mouth to speak with!" She never went to school, and neither did most of the girls and many of the boys in her Guatemalan Mayan town 75 years ago. Those who did attend finished only one or two of the three grades available in town.

School was run by the national government of Guatemala and the classes were in Spanish, a language the children did not speak at home or around town. The Mayan language of San Pedro is unrelated to Spanish, except for borrowed words to label things such as airplanes, for which there were no Mayan words. The schoolteachers in those days came from Guatemala's dominant Spanish-speaking population. They were not Mayan like the people of San Pedro, whose primary identification was as *Pedranos* (people of San Pedro).

⁝

WHEN THE LOCAL CONSTABLES knocked on Chona's parents' door with their wooden staffs, searching for children to send to the school, her parents hid their children under the wooden bed just inside the door and told the constables that the children did not exist. But Chona's sister Susana, ever rebellious, leaped out from under the bed and yelled, "I am their daughter, I do exist, and I want to go to school!"

So their father assented, hoping that the teachers might be able to do something with this unruly child. Chona wanted to go to school too, but she stayed obediently on the hard-packed dirt floor under the bed, her green eyes glistening as she strained to hear the drama at her doorstep.

So Susana went to school, but Chona did not. When Susana would read her schoolwork aloud by candlelight, Chona thought Susana was having a conversation with a piece of paper—crazy!

⁛

IN THOSE DAYS, in many families it was the lazy or dull or disobedient children who were sent to the town's government-sponsored school for a few years. These children's contributions to the family's work in the fields or at home would not be missed as much while they were in class. And it was hoped that the teachers might improve the ways of the troublesome children by making them less foolish and more cooperative.[1] Nonetheless, even when Susana was a vivacious young woman of 18, her father complained that "she was always a great liar and troublemaker," disobedient and lazy around the house, fighting and dominating the younger children.[2]

Parents often kept their cooperative children out of school because their children's work was essential for contributing to the family's sustenance. Parents were also concerned that school would deprive their hardworking children of necessary knowledge and skills. They worried that school would make their diligent sons lazy and unfamiliar with planting corn and beans, in the fields several hours' walk up the sides of the volcano on which San Pedro is perched.

Regarding schooling for their daughters, parents asked, "Will it help our daughters make better tortillas?" (Paul, 1950, p. 480). Corn tortillas have been the main part of all meals for Mayan families for centuries. And for centuries, women and girls rose before dawn to grind the soaked corn kernels over and over on the grinding stone, until the dough reached a fine enough texture to hand-pat the tortillas thin and smooth.

Chona did not go to school because she was so helpful at home, anticipating what she could do to assist her parents. She was obedient and respectful, worked hard, rarely created trouble, and was properly reticent, according to Ben Paul.[3] She helped by scrubbing the family's clothes on lakeshore rocks with a ball of black homemade soap and by balancing the clay jug of cooking water on her head to carry it up the steep lava path from the lake.

These girls bring their families' cooking and drinking water from the lakeshore up to town, which was important work for the family during Chona's childhood. (Photo by Lois and Ben Paul, 1941)

By age 8 or 10, Chona tended the younger children while her mother did other work, and she was already able to weave the brightly patterned cloth for her father's waist sash and other clothes. She could make delicious tortillas, except for turning them on the hot *comal* (griddle) over the hearth fire in the lean-to kitchen attached to the adobe sleeping room.

In addition to valuing her responsibility and helpfulness, Chona's parents also kept her out of school because they worried that as she developed, a schoolteacher might become interested in her, with her striking green eyes, light complexion, and curly hair. Although she was a modest and reserved girl, schoolteachers—non-Mayan men from other regions—had a reputation for taking romantic interest in the local beauties.[4]

Chona did have a tendency to daydream, like other Mayan children with a special birth destiny. But this was not a shortcoming; rather, it was another sign that her life was to be dedicated to a sacred role. She was an admirable and responsible child, not one to waste in school, where she might learn laziness.

A Combination of Destiny and Development

CHONA IS NOW in her eighties, a strong and stately woman with a highly respected position in town as a sacred midwife. Chona followed this destined role and the associated practices that are based on centuries of tradition. At the same time, she has created and adapted new practices for taking care of pregnant women and their infants and thereby contributed to the transformation of her community's ways across history.

Striking changes across generations are widespread in San Pedro, along with continuities. For example, several of Chona's university-educated grandchildren correspond with me via e-mail in Spanish, and maintain strong ties to their Mayan language as well. Several of her grandchildren are doctors; one writes sociology articles about modernity and Mayans (see Tally & Chavajay, 2007). At least one is also destined to be a sacred midwife.

The changes and continuities of Chona's life and of San Pedro illustrate processes of destiny and development that characterize lives of individuals and communities worldwide. Destiny and development, together.

In addition to Chona's destiny being defined by signs at her birth, it was also defined by being born in San Pedro in a certain family and in a specific era. However, such destiny did not *determine* her life. Many women who were born with the birthsign indicating the destiny of Mayan midwife refuse this role, and many children born in San Pedro live a very different life than their ancestors and even their siblings and neighbors.

We all are born in a particular place and time period—circumstances that constitute a sort of destiny. At the same time, each of us and our communities modify what is "given" to us, in short and longer time spans.

This combination of destiny and development accords with the meaning of the ancient Mayan calendar destinies that apply to each person based on the *nahual* of the day that he or she is born: The *nahual* of the day that you are born indicates what you are given. But according to several San Pedro scholars, it does not determine what you will become. You can make something different of yourself, transforming what you are given.

The combination of destiny and development applies to whole communities, too. The ways of life in San Pedro, including centuries-old practices such as reference to the Mayan calendar and newer ones such as going to school, continue in some ways and change in others. Each generation builds on what it was given, and transforms it.

San Pedro Did Not Go to School, But Now It Does

(Photo of Chona © Barbara Rogoff, 1996)

CHONA CHUCKLES about her childhood views of literacy—her lips pressed together in a gentle smile that hides two missing lower front teeth—as she collaborates in the writing of this book. Her eagerness for a written account of her life and work as a sacred midwife is ironic, as she herself has never read a book. Nonetheless, she is now convinced that paper *does* speak.

Now, the town has great variation in literacy, from grandparents who use an X to sign their names to youngsters who manage the Internet. This relates to dramatic changes in the role of schooling in San Pedro since Chona's childhood. Third grade was the highest grade available in 1936, when Chona was 11, and few children attended at all.

Although school extended to sixth grade by the time Chona had several children (in 1953, when she was 28), for years, graduation from sixth grade was a considerable accomplishment. It was reached by less than 10% of the children. About two thirds of girls and one third of boys still did not go to school at all, and most of the rest attended only through first or second grade (Chavajay & Rogoff, 2002; Demarest & Paul, 1981; Rogoff, Correa-Chávez, & Navichoc Cotuc, 2005).[5]

The value of children's work in the home and in the fields was considerable, and the value of school was limited. Parents sent some of their children (more often boys) to school to learn some Spanish. Some knowledge of Spanish was useful to communicate with outsiders for such purposes as bringing cash crops to market or to be able to travel outside the region where the familiar Mayan language was spoken. Reading had little utility for most Pedranos, as almost nothing was written in their Mayan language.

In the 1970s, about the time I arrived in San Pedro, grades 7 to 9 became available, and three fourths of children went to school, usually completing third grade. Some children continued their schooling after sixth grade by going to schools in the capital or other large cities. Some of them did not return, seeking the kind of life and employment that schooling promoted.

The children in this Castellanización class are studying Spanish, which was a prerequisite for entering first grade in 1975. The teacher, Don Agapito Cortez Peneleu, was Mayan from San Pedro and could speak to the children in their home language, but the Mayan language was not supposed to be used in school. More recently, bilingual Mayan–Spanish classes have been introduced in early grades, and most of the teachers are now Mayan, from San Pedro. (Photo © Barbara Rogoff, 1975)

Now, many San Pedro young people complete 12 grades, locally or elsewhere. Their aspirations have changed from learning a little Spanish to preparing for wage-earning careers. A teacher-training school encompassing grades 10 to 12 opened in 1995, enabling many San Pedro young people to become teachers. By then, San Pedro already contributed more teachers to the state of Sololá than did all 18 of the other municipalities of the state combined (according to estimates from anthropologist Ben Paul).

A number of families have made financial sacrifices to send their children to schools in other parts of the country after sixth grade, either because they thought schooling was better elsewhere or because it provided preparation for other careers or for university study. By the late 1990s, about 100 students from San Pedro were attending universities.

In addition, about a dozen young people from San Pedro had received or were studying for PhD, law, or medical degrees—like several of Chona's grandchildren.

The first San Pedro Mayan to become a medical doctor, Felipe Quiacaín Chavajay, is shown here on his wedding day in 1976. Many of the men present were leading elders of the community. Don Antonio Chavajay, facing Felipe, was the lay leader of San Pedro's Catholic church for many years. Felipe's father stands facing the camera at the right, and Felipe's mother is at the left. (Photo © Barbara Rogoff, 1976)

⠿

THE CHANGES in San Pedro seem a century-worth in a few decades. Pedranos often turn to the topic of how much and how fast life has changed, in encounters on the street while doing errands, while waiting at a doctor's office or a bank, or as they sit on the door stoops in the cool evening. Young men and women still pair up for a private conversation or a stroll in the obscurity of the evening, avoiding the glare of streetlights that line the cobbled or paved roads now that the town has electricity. Meanwhile, many young children sit inside watching TV dramas, news, and sports along with others in their family. Unless a cellphone call disturbs the conversation, people gossip and joke and reminisce about what has been lost—and deliberate about whether the cultural changes they embrace have been worth it.

The transformations and stabilities in San Pedro and in Chona's life have provided me with valuable lessons in understanding the role of culture in human development. They have helped me see culture as the *ways of life* of a community, extending across several generations, with continual modifications by individuals and generations.

2 ::

Living Culture,
Across Generations

SEEING CULTURE as the *ways of life* of a community, with stability and change across generations, differs from how people in the United States often think about culture. In the U.S., culture is often reduced to an ethnic "box," such as "Latino," in which individuals belong. Shortly, I'll explain the "box problem" and I will suggest that focusing on how people *live*—their cultural practices—is a better way to understand the processes of culture and human development.

Then I'll show some U.S. and San Pedro examples of how cultural practices fit together, making rather cohesive patterns—*constellations* of cultural practices. These cultural constellations change dynamically, yet they have regularities that help us to understand distinct ways of life.

To conclude the upcoming section, I describe my own engagement in San Pedro to illustrate my claim that the key to understanding individuals' relation to culture is to focus on people's *participation* in cultural practices. Our own cultural participation is often not obvious to us. It often remains invisible to us unless we have the chance to see contrasts with other patterns of cultural practices, over time and place, as my years involved with San Pedro gave me the chance to do.

The rest of the book elaborates these ideas, focusing on Chona's life and work and life in San Pedro over Chona's lifetime. Chona's life has its foundations in ancient and recent ways, and her life's changes accompany changes in San Pedro that contributed to her development. At the same time, some of the changes in San Pedro developed thanks to her contributions. These cultural processes of an individual and her town are better understood by thinking of *ways of life* than by using the "box" approach to culture.

The "Box Problem"

IN THE UNITED STATES, culture is often treated as a set of static ethnic "boxes"—such as Latino, African American, Asian—that individuals "belong in." And they can belong in only one box. All the people "in" an ethnic box are assumed to be alike in an enduring and essentially in-born fashion. This is a rigid form of *pre*destination: Individuals' characteristics are defined in terms of the box they are born into.

Revisions of the U.S. Census stir up continual debates regarding which labels to put on the boxes. But the Census and people's concepts, both in academia and in everyday discussions in the United States, generally preserve the notion that culture is a static characteristic of individuals, determined by conditions set before their birth.

For example, the "Latino" box used in the United States would include Chona, her sister Susana, Chona's grandchildren, and the non-Mayan Guatemalan teachers who previously staffed the school, along with everyone in Cuba and Argentina and their relatives in the United States. The box view of culture would assume that all these folks have characteristics in common, such as speaking Spanish or being Catholic.

This obviously does not work for many of the Mayan people of Guatemala, the majority population of Guatemala. Distinct Mayan groups speak numerous Mayan languages (and may not speak Spanish) and they follow several religious traditions. It also does not apply to many Chicanos in the United States who do not speak Spanish or who differ in other ways from the characteristics ascribed to box membership.

The box approach lumps together very different communities spanning continents. It overlooks the fact that even communities in close proximity have both shared and unique practices.

For example, the Mayan towns around Lake Atitlán use two different but related Mayan languages—Tz'utujil (TSOO-TOO-HEEL) in San Pedro and nearby towns, and Kaqchikel across the lake. They have related but distinct practices and character. The inhabitants of San Pedro are often considered more "modern" than people of other Mayan towns around Lake Atitlán. At the beginning of the 1700s, the Tz'utujil people were described by the Spanish as the most arrogant and astute of the Guatemalan Mayan kingdoms (Tally & Chavajay, 2007). Pedranos have longstanding serious rivalries with people from neighboring Mayan towns, with disputes over land and water rights. Lumping them together in the same box with each other and with the people of distant nations obscures understanding of cultural processes.

Although the box approach gets in the way of understanding cultural processes, it does have real effects on people's lives. As long as people are prejudged according to ethnic or racial boxes in everyday life, and as long as their opportunities and life circumstances are determined in part by category membership, it will be important to understand and address such consequences of the box approach.

But my focus here is different: How can we understand culture? This is a question for which the box approach is not suitable. The problems with the box approach cannot be resolved simply by creating smaller boxes, because the variations within the smaller boxes would require designating still smaller boxes.

For example, it would not solve the problem simply to switch from "Latino" to much more local boxes, such as creating a "Pedrano" box for the people from San Pedro. Cultural practices within San Pedro vary. Chona did not go to school; her sister Susana did. The differences in their lives and involvement in distinct cultural practices were deep and also not unusual among people of San Pedro. Chona speaks the Mayan language Tz'utujil and continues to live in San Pedro; Susana spoke both Tz'utujil and Spanish and moved to the capital city and then settled in another Mayan town, Santiago Atitlán, where she adopted the typical way of dressing and some other practices of her new town. The sisters' lives diverged in numerous ways, although both accepted their birth destiny of becoming sacred midwives. They do not really fit in one uniform box.

Chona's sister Susana (second from the left) wears the headdress and clothing typical of Santiago Atitlán, where she lived after she married, adopting various practices distinct from those of San Pedro. The man next to Susana wears clothing characteristic of San Pedro in those days, and the other man in the front row dresses mainly as did the men from Santiago Atitlán. Lois Paul is in the back row; her clothing also demonstrates participation in cultural practices of several communities. So does the clothing of the man beside her. (Photo by Ben Paul, 1964)

Like the differences between Chona's cultural practices and Susana's, the differences between Chona's practices and those of her grandchildren are also striking. At the same time there are important cultural commonalities across the generations. Understanding cultural processes would not be aided by creating smaller boxes that maintain the idea that people within each box are destined to have certain static characteristics.

Thus I suggest that we discard the box approach when we are trying to understand culture. Instead, we can focus on changes and continuities in *how communities of people live—their cultural practices*.

Focusing on Cultural Practices

IF WE OPEN-MINDEDLY examine how people live, we can move beyond using ethnic labels that assign predetermined characteristics to people.

We can think of culture as communities' ways of living. Our focus thus becomes people's participation in cultural *practices*. This helps us understand the commonalities and differences that exist both within and among cultural communities. This approach also helps us understand individuals' and communities' changes and continuities.[6]

Chona's life story and that of her community provide a case study revealing how people revise as well as extend prior generations' ways of living. In her 80-plus years, Chona has witnessed and contributed to striking cultural changes in the lives of San Pedro children and families. At the same time, she and the other Mayan people of San Pedro have maintained cultural practices that they inherited from ancestors across centuries. Individuals and generations actively use and transform the cultural practices of their communities.

Chona's life illustrates such combined destiny and development. Chona was born with the birthsign indicating a destiny of being a sacred midwife. Her individual destiny was foretold by the midwife who delivered her, following a tradition that is centuries old. The midwife who presided over her birth whispered to Chona's mother that Chona, like the midwife herself, was born with the destiny to assist mothers and infants in the process of birth.

This is a spiritual as well as an obstetric profession, which is called *iyoom* (pronounced EE-YOME; the plural is *iyooma'* and is pronounced EE-YOH-MA) in the regional Mayan language, Tz'utujil. An *iyoom* is a divine healer who mediates between the supernatural world and the ordinary world, protecting the hazardous passage of souls as they emerge from the world of the womb. The *iyoom* also has the responsibility to reveal the destinies of some children born with special birthsigns, like the veil formed from the amniotic sac, indicating the calling of *iyoom*.

Chona was born with a specific and important destiny tying her to centuries of tradition, and she also played an active and creative role in her life direction. Chona's mother, who also was born with this destiny, did not accept it. Chona, after initially struggling to avoid this sacred calling, overcame the challenges in her path and became an honored professional whose judgment and choices were influential in her own life and the lives of her family and community. Chona's life reveals both her own active agency and the cultural staging that contributed to the opportunities and constraints available to her and others in San Pedro (and beyond).

THE CHANGING ARRANGEMENTS of San Pedro childhood, from Chona's infancy until now, make it clear that just as individuals change across eras, so do communities and their practices. Children's lives of eight decades ago, when Chona was born, in many ways seem a world away from how things are now. At the same time, continuities across the 80 years provide durable connections with the Mayan past and the Mayan future.

If people see Chona as they pass her house, many greet her with respect at her doorway by kissing the back of her hand. This continues the San Pedro practice for greeting respected elders. (Photo © Luisa Magarian, 1998).

This practice was explained by a Pedrano, in Jim and Judy Butler's San Pedro fieldnotes:

> *Those who are born to be midwives are greatly respected by the people since they say it is God who teaches them their trade, they are not self-taught. And so you must kiss her hand when you meet a midwife in the street. Even little children are taught this. (Summer Institute of Linguistics, 1978, Book 45, p. 91)*

So instead of treating culture as a synonym for ethnicity or race, as a box or static "social address" characteristic of each individual, we can think of culture as how communities of people live. We can focus on people's varied participation in practices of their overlapping cultural communities—including varied involvement in schooling, ways of making a living, showing respect to elders, and so on. Such practices relate to each other in dynamic coordinated patterns—*constellations* of features of community life.

Shifting Cultural Constellations

CULTURAL PRACTICES do not stand alone, each operating separately. Instead, cultural practices fit together in rather coherent approaches to life, in both enduring and shifting patterns that can be considered *constellations* of cultural practices (Rogoff & Angelillo, 2002). For example, in the United States across the past two centuries, many common features of childhood have changed from one constellation of related cultural practices to another. Some of the features of childhood involved in these changing cultural constellations are children's likelihood of survival, the number of their siblings and involvement with extended family, the nature of their parents' work and of the children's contributions to the family's work and social life, and children's involvement in schooling. Similar changes in constellations of cultural practices have emerged in other places, including San Pedro.

Changes in constellations of cultural practices in the United States

IN THE CURRENT CONSTELLATION of related cultural practices, most U.S. children are segregated from workplaces, have extensive involvement in schooling, and live in small families. But in the early 1800s, the constellation of cultural practices common in the United States was quite different. Most U.S. children shared in the work and social life of their large farm families and only a third of White children attended school (Demos & Demos, 1969; Hernandez, 1994). About a century later, when child labor in factories was outlawed, schooling was made compulsory and lengthened. Now U.S. children's lifecourse is commonly categorized in terms of their level of schooling, as preschoolers or being high school age, and schooling itself is treated as a "natural" part of child-hood. Children are seldom seen in workplaces, and indeed are often prohibited from them.

Across this time span, child mortality and family size dropped dramatically. In 1800, almost half of children died by age 5. The number of siblings per family dropped from more than 7 to less than 3 across the 65 years between 1865 and 1930 (Ehrenreich & English, 1978; Hernandez, 1994).

Caroline Pratt, a renowned leader in innovative schooling, illustrated other changes in the constellation of cultural practices of European American childrearing during these times. In 1948, at age 80, she reflected on the changes since her birth in the mid-1800s:

> How utterly the life of a child in this country has changed during my lifetime I would scarcely believe if I had not seen it happen. Three-quarters of a century have spanned the change: my father was a Civil War veteran; I remember the day we all went down to the store to see my mother make our first call on a telephone; I remember watching the explosive progress of the first automobile down our village street.
>
> Put it this way, as the statistics put it: before 1867, the year I was born, only one out of every six people lived in cities of more than 8,000 inhabitants, and there were only 141 such cities; by 1900, one out of three people lived in such a city, and the number of those cities was 547. . . .
>
> When I grew up in Fayetteville, New York, school was not very important to children who could roam the real world freely for their learning. We did not merely stand by while the work of our simpler world was done; I drove the wagon in haying time, sitting on top of the swaying load, all the way to the barn. At ten, my great-aunt used to say, I could turn a team of horses and a wagon in less space than a grown man needed to do it.
>
> No one had to tell us where milk came from, or how butter was made. We helped to harvest wheat, saw it ground into flour in the mill on our own stream; I baked bread for the family at thirteen. There was a paper mill, too, on our stream; we could learn the secrets of half a dozen other industries merely by walking through the open door of a neighbor's shop. (Pratt, 1948, pp. xi–xii)

Spreading cultural constellations

RELATED CHANGES in cultural constellations can be seen in other places, as schooling and other practices have spread from the colonial Western nations through the colonies, in countries like Guatemala.[7] The changing constellations are not identical in the United States and Guatemala and the rest of the world, but there are some related aspects in common. The similarities are due in part to colonial domination through schooling and related practices (Rogoff, 2003).

Dominating powers of Spain and the United States have often tried to destroy Indigenous practices with force and law, treating them as inferior and trying to replace them with their own. In addition, attractions such as movies, television shows, and commercials often portray more traditional ways as backwards. New forms of occupation that offer salaries and health insurance often require abandoning traditional practices as well, such as traditional ways of dressing and speaking. New occupations also often require credentials available only through extensive schooling. Schooling frequently deprecates Indigenous forms of knowledge and instruction, may outlaw Indigenous language use, and may encourage younger generations to look down on the wisdom and skills of prior generations of their community.

But the direction of change in places like San Pedro is not *necessarily* to become like the United States. People can at times combine approaches in new and valued ways, creating new constellations of cultural practices. For example, in a Mayan community in the Yucatán, the economy has changed from corn farming to a cash economy and paid jobs, infant mortality has dropped, and children now attend school for years, but children are still very involved in the work of the household and in learning traditional Mayan values (Gaskins, 2003).

I hope that the people of San Pedro can continue to build on the features of "Western" ways that have value in their time and place, and yet maintain valued features of Mayan ways, to create new constellations of cultural practices that serve current and upcoming generations. My hope is the same for the people of the United States—that we make good use of ideas from the constellations of cultural practices of other communities—as constellations of cultural practices endure *and* continue to change in the U.S., as in any other place. This process is best served if, rather than considering a particular cultural practice in solitude, we consider new ideas with some understanding of how cultural practices make sense together in dynamic constellations.

It is possible for people's *repertoires of cultural practices* to include those of several cultural communities (Gutiérrez & Rogoff, 2003). In fact, from a historical perspective, combining of practices is the norm. For example, people who speak English speak a language built on many other languages, people who enjoy jazz listen to music built on traditions of several continents, and people who eat pizza ingest foods developed in Mesoamerica[8] as well as Europe, in new combinations (Rogoff, 2003).

For individuals, fluency in the cultural practices of several communities has many advantages over being limited to just one constellation of practices, whichever it is. Such fluency offers new ideas for ways of life, expanded perspectives, increased likelihood of mutual understanding across varying backgrounds, and the potential to take up opportunities to engage more broadly in the world. Nonetheless, it seems that often one constellation of practices replaces another, rather than constellations of practices enriching each other.

Changes in constellations of related cultural practices in San Pedro

THE CHANGES IN THE CONSTELLATION of cultural practices in San Pedro over Chona's lifetime in some ways resemble the changes in constellations in the United States. Pedrano fathers' occupations have shifted from the usual subsistence farming of corn and beans to include cash cropping of avocadoes and tomatoes, paid jobs such as truck driver and plumber, and professions such as accountant and teacher that rely on school credentials. Mothers' occupations shifted from home-based weaving, tortilla making, and family care to include professions such as teaching.

Access to the outside world in San Pedro has exploded through access to media and travel and incursions of tourists. Instead of rowing great canoes across Lake Atitlán or walking around the lake to other Mayan towns, as people did in Chona's childhood, local people now travel in motorboats or buses or taxis that run many times a day. The primary roads are no longer a place for children to play and neighbors to exchange news; they now belong to speeding trucks, buses, taxis, and motorcycles.

Formerly, children could play freely in the streets, like the little boys here, enjoying mud puddles after a rain. The streets carried foot traffic and an occasional horse rider, but motor vehicles were rare, as the town was not yet connected with other towns by a road that was reliable for vehicles. There were only a dirt road full of boulders leading around the back of the volcano, used by infrequent buses, and numerous well-worn footpaths throughout the area to other towns. (Photo © Barbara Rogoff, 1975)

These cousins enjoyed making mudcakes in the middle of the street in front of their houses. Three decades later, this street is filled with cargo trucks, motorcycles, and taxis that slow to get around each other, but people on foot are expected to look out for themselves. A white cross by the side of this road now marks the location of a teen's fatal encounter with a vehicle. (Photo © Barbara Rogoff, 1976)

Another feature of the changing constellation in San Pedro is the number of children in a family. Across the same decades in which schooling became common, the number of children born to each mother plunged, and so did the proportion that died in infancy. In 1968, mothers on average had given birth to about eight babies, and about a third of them had died in infancy; a generation later (in 1999), mothers gave birth to about two babies, and seldom did infants die. These changes made a big difference in the number of siblings available to children—reducing from numerous siblings to often having one or no siblings.

The decreased availability of siblings, increased involvement in schooling, and other changes such as the occupations of parents have had important consequences for children's contributions to family work. Children's extensive involvement in childcare and other family work has decreased compared to prior generations (Rogoff et al., 2005).

In this 1941 photo, almost every child has an infant to tend, as they wait for a celebration. Both the little ones and the child caregivers could be where the action is. (Photo by Lois and Ben Paul)

Children's contributions to family work have been a source of pride in accomplishment for San Pedro children. In San Pedro's constellation of practices of prior generations, children were integrated in the productive lives of their family and community. They were expected to observe keenly and to pitch in and help, with the supportive assistance of their elders. In the current constellation of practices, the extent of children's involvement in schooling has reduced children's opportunities to be present to observe and participate in the mature roles of the community.

Previously, a good deal of children's time was spent contributing to household work, like this 10-year-old chopping firewood for his family's cookfire and the two boys making candles for their grandfather's shaman work and little store. (Photos © Barbara Rogoff, 1975, 1976)

Children's play in previous decades often involved emulation of adult roles. These girls are playing at making mud tortillas, with a makeshift grinding stone. (Photo © Barbara Rogoff, 1976)

Girls who were becoming interested in weaving made their own little play looms out of a blade of a local plant, sticks, and discarded threads and cloth, like the little girl in the photo. Mothers considered this play, not weaving, but they noticed when their daughters began play-weaving, and treated this as an indication that soon it would be time to help daughters with their first real weaving. (Photo © Barbara Rogoff, 1975).

I have not seen girls play-weaving in recent years, and many fewer girls are learning to weave. Formerly, all women were expected to know how to weave (according to Rosales' 1938 fieldnotes, published in 1949). But women are much less commonly weavers now that they follow other occupations and now that the men have mostly discontinued wearing the traditional hand-woven shirts and pants that were characteristic of San Pedro men's clothing until the mid-1900s. Some men began to wear factory-made clothing when it became available in the 1950s, with completion of the Pan-American Highway and the discrimination that often accompanied wearing traditional Mayan clothing while traveling to markets outside the region (Brumfiel, 2006; see the contrast in the boys' clothing in the photos on page 27).

More recently, children's play has come to include imitating TV characters, greater use of manufactured toys, and for some who can afford it, paying to play video games at a local arcade. (Photo © Luisa Magarian, 1999)

In addition to the changes in children's everyday activities, transformations in parents' lives are also important in San Pedro's emerging constellation of practices. Increasingly, mothers with extensive schooling seem to use school formats in their interactions with their own children. These may be replacing some ways of supporting children's learning that were more common in prior generations, such as including children and encouraging their contributions to the range of family and community activities.

For example, one study found that San Pedro mothers with extensive schooling more often gave toddlers mini language lessons by labeling objects and asking questions that they already knew the answer to, like, "Where is the dolly's nose?" Such language games follow the same format used by teachers when they ask questions for which they already know the answers, like, "What is the capital of the United States?" (Rogoff et al., 1993; see also Richman, Miller, & LeVine, 1992). In other studies, San Pedro parents with extensive Western schooling more often assumed a managerial, teacher-ish role with children, whereas parents with little or no schooling engaged more collaboratively with children, with each contributing as they chose (Chavajay, 2006, 2008; Chavajay & Rogoff, 2002).

⁚⁚

THESE CHANGING CONSTELLATIONS of family circumstances and ways of life underline the need to think about culture in terms of ways of living. Instead of categorizing a cultural community with a one- or two-word label referring to ethnicity, race, or social class, we can give a more fluid description of cultural constellations that coordinates each of these aspects in the historical context of the other aspects (Rogoff & Angelillo, 2002). It is significant that this approach integrates history in the understanding of culture.[9]

For example, we can describe San Pedro as a Mayan Indian community in the temperate highlands of Guatemala, where for several centuries families have spoken a Mayan language and usually depended on farming to grow their own food, and in recent generations many families have begun to speak Spanish and even English, have added cash crops and merchant and professional occupations, and have started sending their children to schools derived from European-American traditions.

This cultural description refers to multiple features of a constellation, including ethnic heritage, language, economic form, and schooling. These features are not treated as separate "factors." Instead, they are coordinated in historical and mutually defining constellations of cultural practices in which people *participate*.

Participating in Communities

THE IDEA OF *participation in communities* is crucial for a dynamic view of culture. Cultural communities are composed of generations of people engaging with each other over time. Their engagement together involves some common and continuing organization, values, understanding, history, and practices that transcend the particular individuals.

Participants in a community coordinate without having exactly the same ideas, practices, experiences, and plans. They often engage in ways that fit together rather than being identical. Indeed, their points of view or purposes may be at odds with each other, while still sharing some common ground in the process of disagreement. Individual variations— such as the differences between Chona and her sister Susana, as well as between Chona and her grandchildren—are to be expected. People's multiple, overlapping, and conflicting traditions and involvements are part of their participation in dynamic cultural communities.

People often take part in the cultural traditions of more than one national, religious, political, ethnic, and economic group, as people of San Pedro do in attending Western school and as I am doing in learning about life in San Pedro. The practices of communities change as ideas spread or are imposed from one community to another, in part through the participation of some individuals in several cultural communities.

This process is clear in the shifts and amalgamations of spiritual beliefs in San Pedro. The people of San Pedro over centuries practiced the ancestral Mayan religion; some Pedranos developed a Mayan form of Catholicism after the arrival of the Spaniards. In the 20th century, evangelical Protestantism was initiated in San Pedro by a few young men who had experience outside town and who were receptive to the visits of missionaries. Evangelical Protestantism has now been adopted by half of San Pedro's population, who have divided into about 22 churches (Tally & Chavajay, 2007).[10]

::

I EMPHASIZE PEOPLE'S *participation* in communities rather than *membership* in a community because participants in a community are not necessarily members (Rogoff, 2003). For example, I would not ordinarily be regarded as a *member* of the Mayan community in Guatemala where I have done research for over three decades. I was born to European-heritage parents in the United States.

Although I am not a member, I *participate* in the community of San Pedro. I lived in San Pedro for a year and a half in 1974–76 and have returned for several weeks about once a year since then, except for a 10-year hiatus during which a genocide was carried out against Mayan people in Guatemala and also I had young children.

My involvement in San Pedro includes continuing mutual support and obligations in a number of families, including Chona's. I also have a political role that I did not seek, based initially on being given some family funds to "do something good for San Pedro." I did not particularly want this role, because I thought that I should be trying *not* to influence life in San Pedro. (As if doing nothing was not doing something! And my presence and research activities and conversations with neighbors were indeed doing *some* thing.)

The family funding prompted me to create the town library in 1976, after consulting with local friends and with the mayor and school principal regarding what would be "something good" for San Pedro. The officials, who were local Mayan people (as was usual by that time), suggested creating a library or installing flush toilets in the municipal building for visitors' use. I couldn't imagine doing a toilet project for out-of-town visitors, especially because many families in town didn't even have access to latrines. So, with the advice of many local people, I worked on creating a library. The process embroiled me in ongoing disputes among the factions of San Pedro that wanted credit for establishing the library or tried to undermine the project.

Months later, I was discussing the library project with a leading Pedrano man who was very involved in local politics. He gave me a significant look and said, "Now you know us, Barbara!"

Indeed, the library project helped me move beyond a romantic view of people and life in San Pedro. I had for the first year been very impressed with the general congeniality of people in San Pedro, who greet each other on the street and are involved in each other's lives in ways I had not seen growing up in a couple of middle-class European-American towns. Becoming involved in a multifaceted way in San Pedro allowed me to see past my romantic first impressions and realize that San Pedro factions run deep and human relations are complex—across political groups as well as among and within families.

My view of the world has been deeply informed by participation in the community of San Pedro. My own childrearing practices, for example, were based in part on my participation in this Mayan community. To take a mundane example, I watched how mothers nurse babies in San Pedro, and how they avoid the breast milk leaking when the baby stops nursing.[11] When I became a mother, I made use of this information as I remembered how nursing mothers in San Pedro stop the milk flow by pressing the heel of their palm into their nipple. The opportunity to observe nursing is rare in the United States; when I've told people in the United States about this method to stop the milk flow, it seems that in many circles in the United States it is a new and useful technique.

Chona, a new mother, pressed her nipple to stop the milk flow, in this photo taken long before I met her. (Photo by Lois and Ben Paul, 1941)

These "lessons" from my participation in life in San Pedro have contributed to cultural change in the United States and elsewhere as I have shared this knowledge with others (including you). Such borrowing and mixing of cultural practices contributes to the continually changing ways of individuals and communities, when individuals and communities with different traditions interact (Gutiérrez, Baquedano-López, & Tejeda, 1999; Gutiérrez & Rogoff, 2003).

In turn, an in-depth account of the functioning of the town of San Pedro could likewise consider my participation over several decades in a number of families and in a few institutions (such as the town library and the newly established Internet learning center). My participation does not give me membership in the local ethnic group, but instead involves me in many of the cultural practices that make up constellations characteristic of this community over recent decades.

As a participant, I am second from the left in this photo of the organizing committee, taken at the inauguration of the Internet learning center. At the Center, Pedranos come to learn to use the Internet as well as to learn to write in Tz'utujil, to develop a love of reading (primarily in Spanish), and to learn English, math, art, music, and local history. For more information on the learning center: http://www.taapit.org/index.php

The name of the center was chosen by the organizing committee to encourage revitalization and learning of Mayan ways along with international tools and skills: "Centro de Talleres Intercultural Enseñanza Aprendizaje Taa' Pi't Kortees" [Center of Intercultural Teaching/Learning Workshops Don Agapito Cortez]. (The name includes the name of beloved teacher Don Agapito, one of the first literate Pedranos—the teacher in the classroom photo earlier in this book.)

During the inauguration ceremony for the Center, I was asked to introduce Mayan Nobel Laureate Rigoberta Menchú to the audience. After I did so, she thanked me for being part of San Pedro, which fits with my point about being a participant in this community, though I am not a Pedrana. (Photo Centro Taa' Pi't, 2006)

As generations of people participate in the practices that they inherit and that they adopt, they also modify the practices in line with current circumstances, using available resources and new ideas. As anthropologist Robert LeVine (1980) has pointed out, each generation relies on customary cultural practices that have developed historically to meet prior circumstances, such as hazards to child survival that have been historically experienced by the community. Cultural practices endure or change with the moment-to-moment and generation-by-generation participation of people.

Chona's and San Pedro's lives reveal durability of some practices and the transformation or discarding of others. The rest of this book examines the intertwining of cultural and individual processes of destiny and development, across more than 80 years of one important individual's life and across centuries in the life of her remarkable community.

3 ::

Meeting Chona and San Pedro

MY ENTRY into San Pedro in 1974 was facilitated by introductions by anthropologist Ben Paul in the mayor's office, when Ben visited Guatemala a few months before I arrived. Don Agustín Pop, the mayor, was a Pedrano whom Ben had known for many years, a friend since their youth when Ben and Lois first stayed in San Pedro, in 1941.

When I got to town, I went to the mayor's office to introduce myself and to ask permission to study children's learning and development in San Pedro. The mayor sat at his impressive wooden desk in the presence of a number of his councilmen, who were sitting solemnly in upright wooden chairs lined against the wall opposite me. I sat in one of the guest chairs and tried to be patient waiting for the mayor to address me. I waited, and waited, while the mayor seemed to be just sitting at his desk, not looking at me but not seeming to be occupied with anything else. Sitting silently for so long was difficult for me, but seemingly not for anyone else in the room. I was tempted to sit on my hands to help me stay silent, but resisted that urge.

Eventually, after many minutes, the mayor addressed me, inviting me to speak. I explained that I was interested in studying childrearing practices and children's thinking in San Pedro, for a project sponsored by the Institute of Nutrition of Central America and Panama. The mayor listened with interest and offered to show me around town. As he and the councilmen and I walked from the municipal offices through the streets, I noticed that ahead of us, wherever we went, people were sweeping the streets. I thought, "What cleanly people the Pedranos are!"

This is a street scene like I saw during my first walk through town.
(However, this photo was taken a year or so after my arrival in San Pedro.)
(Photo © Barbara Rogoff, 1976)

I later learned that the mayor was on a campaign for clean streets, and had announced, a few days before, that a government official would be coming to town to inspect the streets. Householders were responsible for cleaning the street in front of their house; people whose street was dirty would receive a hefty fine.

So Pedranos first thought I was the street inspector!

That didn't last long, however.

As people saw my interest in children's learning and child development, the identity most commonly ascribed to me was "teacher." I always tried to clarify that I was a researcher, trying to learn about children, and that I was not teaching the children but learning from them. But because there was not a local category of "psychological researcher" at that time, in the eyes of most Pedranos, I remained a teacher. Many of the children who were in my research studies referred to themselves as my students. Even now, more than three decades later, it is common for 40-year-old Pedranos to remind me or to tell someone else with pride that they are my *alumnos* (students). Some have asked me to open a "school" again like the one they went to, "because the children need it."

As I first entered the town, I was struck with the differences between San Pedro and Boston, where I had been living. In addition to being struck by the sheer beauty of the landscape, I was fascinated by the scenes of women sitting weaving vivid cloth in their patios, the small children free to play around the town as they tended smaller children, and the difficulty of the language as I tried to return greetings.

Like the Pedranos who jumped to conclusions to figure out who I was, I was also in a position of ignorance and I naturally based my perceptions on my own assumptions and experience. I felt privileged, and also apprehensive, to be living in San Pedro, and I was prone to romanticizing the Tz'utujil Mayan way of life that I was meeting. Over time, "The Tz'utujil Maya" became less exotic to me and more familiar, as I got to know and engage with individuals, the town's institutions, the language (somewhat), and the history.

The Paths of Generations

ALMOST ALL of the people of San Pedro are Tz'utujil Mayans, descendants of the people who lived in this region since before the Spanish invaded Guatemala in 1523. The Tz'utujil people were one of the independent kingdoms that the Spaniards encountered; about 2 or 3 million Indigenous people resided in their territory.

However, the population of this territory was not homogeneous and stable before the arrival of the Spanish. There were numerous contacts with a variety of cultural communities across many centuries.

Tz'utujil territory was inhabited by about 600 B.C. and hosted trade, warfare, and alliances among numerous Indigenous groups from great distances. The region was under the influence of Teotihuacan in central Mexico by about 700 A.D. Then it came under the influence of Nahuatl-speaking people from the Gulf Coast of Mexico, and by about 1000 A.D. the territory came under the influence of people linked with Toltec Chichén Itzá in the Yucatán.

About 1200 A.D., the region underwent another influx of a migrant warrior group from around Tabasco-Veracruz, via Tula/Tollan, the Toltec capital. These newcomers lost their language (which was likely Chontal) after conquering and intermarrying with Mayan people who spoke languages in the Quiché family, such as Tz'utujil (Orellana, 1984). The Tz'utujil tribe established itself on Lake Atitlán by about 1270 A.D., displacing a prior Indigenous group, the Malaj (Richards, 2003).

The arrival of the Spanish resulted in cataclysmic changes. The Indigenous population was decimated due to warfare, a rash of epidemics of introduced diseases, and labor abuses, including slavery. Some estimates place the resulting population of Mesoamerica at about 10% of what it was when the Spanish arrived.

The population of the Tz'utujil kingdom dropped to 9% of what it had been at the time the Spanish arrived, over a period of only 61 years.

When the Tz'utujil kingdom was conquered in 1524, the population was 48,000, including 12,000 male tribute-payers (heads of household). By 1585, there were only 1,005 tribute-payers (Christenson, 2001). Most of the loss occurred within the first 23 years (by 1547), when the population had dropped to 12% of what it had been (Orellana, 1984).

A Spanish colonial official and the resident priest explained in 1585 that in addition to warfare, the decimation was due to illnesses, including:

> smallpox, measles, fever, blood which ran from their noses, and other epidemics and . . . the great labors that they were required to pay, since the Spaniards used them as burden carriers in their fields and estates [and gold mines] (Betancor & Arboleda, 1964 [1585], p. 95, as translated by Christenson, 2001, p. 39)

Waves of epidemics were also fostered as the Spanish gathered the Mayans from their dispersed settlements into towns in the mid-1500s, in order to control them for labor and for religious conversion (Brown, 1998).

⁛

EVEN AS RECENTLY as the middle of the twentieth century, more than a third of the people who were born in San Pedro did not survive early childhood, according to my examination of town birth and death records. Most of the young children who did not survive died as infants of diseases related to the invasion (Magarian, 1976).

During the twentieth century, however, the population increased, in part due to vaccines against some of the introduced diseases. In 1974, when I arrived in San Pedro, the town's population of 5,000 was more than double that of 30 years before, and it has more than doubled again in the meantime.

The photos on the next pages show San Pedro across five decades: in 1941, 1975, and 1998. In each pair of photos, the top image is taken from about the same vantage point, and the bottom one shows what a few blocks of the town looked like.

The town layout, centered in a grid around the plaza with the Catholic church and the municipal offices, follows the Spanish plan for congregating dispersed hamlets; San Pedro's "congregation" had occurred by 1550 in the location of the pre-conquest Tz'utujil settlement known as Chi-Tzunún-Choy. In the process of congregation the Franciscan priests also constructed schools to teach the Tz'utujil people Spanish and how to read, write, sing, and serve in the Catholic church (Orellana, 1984).

In 1941 there was plenty of space around the one-room houses made of adobe or cane with thatched or tiled roofs, and the earthen streets carried foot traffic among playing children. The population was about 2,000. (Photos by Lois and Ben Paul)

Thirty-four years later, in 1975, there were still ample patios between houses, which now mostly had tin or tile roofs, and the cobbled roads carried an occasional truck or bus. When the rare vehicle passed, children were shooed off the street. The population was about 5,000. The level of the lake had dropped, creating more land along the shore. (Photos © Barbara Rogoff, 1975)

By 1998, houses began to extend upwards two or three levels, made of reinforced concrete. The narrow streets were the only unbuilt spaces, carrying pickups, motorcycles, trucks, and buses rushing by hapless pedestrians. The population reached about 13,000 and the lake had continued to drop, exposing even more land along the shore. (Photos © Luisa Magarian, 1998)

The growth in San Pedro (and Guatemala generally) has been in spite of a large out-migration (Loucky & Moors, 2000). In recent years, increasing numbers of Pedranos have moved to cities elsewhere in Guatemala or to the United States.[12]

In recent decades, many parents have sent their children to schools in Guatemalan cities that offer more grades or were perceived as better than schools in San Pedro. Many of these children do not move back to San Pedro as adults. They may not be equipped to engage in their ancestors' work, and there is not enough land for the increased population anyway. They aspire to jobs making use of their extensive schooling. But these do not exist in San Pedro in sufficient quantity, and are not plentiful enough elsewhere in Guatemala either (see also Ehlers, 1990). Many have trained as teachers, and although Pedranos staff a large proportion of the teaching posts in the state, there are not enough posts for all the available teachers. San Pedro now has many people certified as teachers who cannot find work as teachers.

The out-migration from San Pedro has also increased in recent decades due to economic pressures and the severe inequities of land ownership in Guatemala. In Guatemala, 5% of the population owns 80% of the land, according to the 2008 report of the United Nations Development Program (Guatemala Human Rights Commission, 2009). Most of the big landowners are of European descent; the disparities are among the worst in the Western Hemisphere.

In addition, the violence of the Guatemalan genocide against Mayan people, which peaked in 1982 in San Pedro, led some residents to leave town and to leave Guatemala. (For discussion of these issues, see Paul & Demarest, 1984; Paul, 1988.)

Some Pedranos sought refuge in the United States and Mexico. Others traveled to the U.S. seeking work to be able to support their families. Several of the 60 children who were in my dissertation study, now about age 45, have been working in the United States, and more hope to. One recently returned to San Pedro after working in construction in Los Angeles for three years to make enough money to send his children to school. He is fluent in Tz'utujil and Spanish but struggles in English, so he found many aspects of life in the United States to be a challenge.

Greetings in a New Tongue

I HAVE THE REVERSE PROBLEM with language in San Pedro. At the time of my initial interview with Chona, I had spent some months living in

San Pedro. Through everyday engagement in town events, I had begun to make sense of the unfamiliar sounds of Tz'utujil and began to understand routine conversations, but nothing complex.

My Tz'utujil was probably amusing my young companions as we sat under the town square's ceiba *tree at the weekly market where peddlers offered skirt fabric, wooden chests and tiny chairs, and coastal fruits. (Photo © Salem Magarian, 1976)*

Before I arrived in San Pedro, I had spent a few weeks at a language institute in Antigua, Guatemala, trying to learn to produce sounds that require coordination of parts of the throat that are not used for English. I also learned some greetings and a bit of grammar.

In my first days in San Pedro, the greetings that I had learned in Tz'utujil served me well in transforming some women's and children's apprehension into curiosity. There had not been many foreigners in San Pedro at the time I arrived, and often people darted away as I walked on back paths of town. But when I greeted them in Tz'utujil, they returned and addressed me, soon joined by a little crowd asking a barrage of questions. The questions were beyond my skill in Tz'utujil, but my new acquaintances helped me understand and gradually I learned more of the language.

On one occasion when I was walking up the steep road from the room I rented, I was joined by some small children who spoke with me in Tz'utujil. I had to ask them to repeat what they had said, explaining that I didn't understand, because I didn't speak Tz'utujil. They replied, "What do you mean, you don't speak Tz'utujil? You're speaking it!" They continued speaking too fast for me, perhaps not believing that an adult who spoke some of the language might not be proficient in it. In any case, their insistence and that of adults who pressed me to speak and listen in everyday Tz'utujil conversations created excellent language instruction.

These little fellows would run and meet me many mornings when I went up the hill to the center of town, catching hold of my hands, when they weren't busy gathering firewood for their mothers' cooking fires. Their insistence on speaking with me in Tz'utujil helped me learn some of the language. (Photo © Barbara Rogoff, 1976)

(Photo © Salem Magarian, 1975)

Speakers of Tz'utujil generally can understand speakers of the closest Mayan languages (such as Kaqchikel and Ki'che'), but many other
Guatemalan Mayan languages are so distinct from Tz'utujil that they
are not mutually intelligible. Tz'utujil is the ninth largest of the more
than 20 Mayan languages spoken in Guatemala, with approximately
48,000 speakers (as of 2001, Richards, 2003).

Tz'utujil is inherited and adapted from a proto-Mayan language
spoken perhaps more than 5,000 years ago (Richards, 2003). Over time,
Mayan languages have incorporated words from other Indigenous languages of Mesoamerica. In particular, words from the Nahuatl language
(of the Aztecs in what is now central Mexico) have been adopted in
Mayan languages. Nahuatl was widely used in diplomacy and com-
merce between Indigenous groups for centuries before the arrival of the
Spanish. King Philip III of Spain declared Nahuatl the official Indian

language of New Spain, a few decades after Spanish arrival (Brown, 1998). Nahuatl words can be seen in many Guatemalan place names, such as *Atitlán*, the name the Spanish authorities adopted in the 1500s for the lake, when they substituted the translation used by their Tlaxcalan allies for the Tz'utujil name *Chiya'*, which means "By the lake" (Christenson, 2001).

Spanish terms have also replaced Mayan labels. For example, in the mid-1800s the Spanish name of San Pedro la Laguna replaced the pre-conquest Tz'utujil name *Chi-Tzunún-Choy* (meaning At-the-Hummingbird-Lake), after a period of use of a transitional name, *San Pedro Patzununá* (which also refers to hummingbirds; Orellana, 1984).

Some of the Spanish terms that have entered the Tz'utujil language refer to objects or ideas that have recently been introduced, such as motorboats. More recently, some English words have joined the vocabulary, such as "dollar" and "hippie." (Spanish and English have borrowed Indigenous terms as well, such as "chocolate" and "tomato" from Nahuatl.)

I have not become fluent in Tz'utujil, unfortunately. Tz'utujil is not related to the other languages that I know (English, Spanish, and French), and the verb conjugations work very differently than in these other languages. In addition, I have been lazy, relying on Spanish rather than Tz'utujil with people who speak both. Often, I am able to follow most of what a person says in Tz'utujil and I can reply in Spanish, which Tz'utujil speakers usually understand to some extent.

I can carry on everyday conversations in Tz'utujil. However, for discussing complex topics with someone who speaks only or mostly Tz'utujil, like Chona, I work with a colleague who translates between Tz'utujil and Spanish for parts of the conversation with which I have difficulty.

Becoming Familiar with Chona and Her Life

BECAUSE CHONA is one of the foremost experts on childbirth and childrearing in San Pedro, I was very interested in interviewing her for my research during my first year in San Pedro, while I was a graduate student. One afternoon, in the sunlight angling through the doorway of a dark adobe room, I sat with Chona taking notes on her work. With sturdy hands, Chona gestured to demonstrate how she receives a newborn, aiding its slippery passage from the womb to the world outside.

I watched Chona's hands and struggled to understand her words as she explained time-tested and newly developed knowledge, in Tz'utujil. Women of Chona's generation, like Chona, often spoke only Tz'utujil (and sometimes could understand a little Spanish).[13]

In my early months of immersion in an unfamiliar language and lifeways, I strained to comprehend what San Pedro people said and did. In the interview with Chona, I relied on the assistance of a local woman who translated the difficult sections of Chona's explanation into Spanish for me.

As I watched Chona's hands, showing me how she would clean a slippery newborn, I was struck with a feeling of familiarity in the shape of her hands and her gestures.

Such a feeling of familiarity was rare in those early months in San Pedro. I was in my early 20s and found myself embedded in a life so different from my own European-American background that I bristled with new awareness of the customs I had grown up with. The strange was not yet familiar, but at the same time, the familiar ways of my own upbringing had become strange to me.

The moment of recognition as I watched Chona's hands was very welcome. I exclaimed with surprise, "Your hands are just like my mother's!" Chona, robust in midlife, responded with a warm, serene smile, "That's because I *am* your mother."

A daughter sits on the floor

SINCE THAT DAY, over three decades ago, Chona and I have adopted the roles of mother and daughter with each other. We refer to each other as mother and daughter, and have developed a closeness that feels rather like family, with some of the obligations that being related implies in San Pedro.

For example, during that first year, if Chona and I were in a place with only a few chairs, I sat on a mat on the well-packed dirt floor with the other women to make sure that Chona had a chair. At first, other people were surprised at this, because as a visitor, according to San Pedro customs, I was always offered a chair while other women would sit or kneel on a mat on the floor. I explained that I offered her the chair out of respect for my "mother." Those who knew about our "kinship" nodded approval; those who did not glanced their questions to the others.

Chona sat in the sole chair waiting for the festivities at this wedding celebration, and I sat on the pine-needle–decorated floor with the other women, who kneeled. (I rose to take this photo, with relief from my discomfort on the floor.) (Photo © Barbara Rogoff, 1976)

As I sat on the floor, people teased me about being uncomfortable. San Pedro women (*Pedranas*) were accustomed to sitting or kneeling on the ground for hours, especially while weaving brilliant cloth for men's shirts, for women's belts, and sometimes for shawls that women use in the evening cool and for religious occasions. Women of San Pedro were traditionally skilled weavers, using Mayan backstrap weaving technology that has been passed down across many centuries. For my San Pedro companions, sitting or kneeling on the floor was routine and easy—the normal posture for working as they tended their children and chatted with their sisters or sisters-in-law weaving nearby.

While weaving, women and girls adjust their posture to maintain the appropriate tension on the threads. They sit or kneel inside the backstrap that passes around their hips to anchor the lower end of the loom, with the upper end of the loom attached by ropes to a house beam, like Chona's sister in this 1941 photo. (Photo by Lois and Ben Paul, 1941)

The kneeling position and the technology of weaving have been central to Mayan women's lives since long before the Spanish invasion. This is illustrated in this drawing from the Florentine Codex, prepared in the mid-1500s describing prior Nahua/Aztec practices; the Aztecs had many practices in common with their Mayan neighbors. (Book 2, fo. 24. Reproduced courtesy of University of Utah Press)

Note also that many photos of women and girls in this book, but none of men, show them in kneeling position. If a little boy sits in this position, he may be teased for sitting like a woman (see also Brumfiel, 2006). Now, however, women's kneeling position is less common, as chairs have become widespread.

Sitting or kneeling on the floor for hours was also important for women in preparing corn for meals. Corn tortillas (and other preparations of corn) have been the main food at breakfast, lunch, and dinner for centuries, served with black beans and occasionally meat if the family could afford it.[14] Now, people also eat bread—which in Tz'utujil is called *kaxlan way* ("foreign tortilla"). (*Kaxlan* is a Mayanization of the Spanish word for Castilian, *Castellano*, the term often used in Guatemala to refer to the Spanish language.)

Preparation of tortillas has until recently required kneeling over a grinding stone to prepare the dough from soaked kernels of corn. Toasting the tortillas commonly involved kneeling on a reed mat by the griddle, which was held on three hearthstones over the wood fire on the hard-packed dirt floor.

After the corn dough was ground finely on the stone, tortillas were hand-patted and toasted with deft fingers on the hot comal *supported on the traditional three-stone hearth. In the photo, the woman kneels in the traditional position on the floor, as did most women in San Pedro in 1976 and for centuries before. Few women in 1976 had a raised hearth and none had electricity or stoves. (Photo © Barbara Rogoff, 1976)*

Now, few women cook at a fire on the floor. Many use small propane burners and toast their tortillas on a raised wood fire hearth with a built-in comal. Some who have the means or run a family restaurant have a stove, as in the photograph of Agudelina's kitchen. (Photo © Luisa Magarian, 1998)

When Chona was young, the dough for tortillas was still fully hand-ground on a grinding stone like those used by her ancestors for centuries. The women and girls of the family would rise at 4 a.m. to begin to grind the plump kernels of soaked corn into smooth dough, kneeling on the hard-packed dirt floor. They prepared the tortillas, beans, and coffee for the family's breakfast and for later in the day.

The men took tortillas in their shoulder bag, along with a gourd full of water, as they left before dawn to walk several hours to the corn *milpas*, carved out of the forest on the volcano. The roosters began to crow, displacing the fierce nighttime baying of packs of stray dogs, as the men trotted up worn dirt paths on calloused bare or sandaled feet. As they gained altitude, they could look back in the early light to see wisps of smoke wafting up from the wood fires through the chinks in the cane walls of each lean-to kitchen.

A few men would ride horseback up to their fields. (Photo © Barbara Rogoff, 1975)

Now, men and women rise later, and often men who work in the fields pay a small fee to take a truck up the volcano to work. (Photo © Luisa Magarian, 1999)

By the time I stayed in San Pedro, a half-dozen thumping neighborhood diesel-powered mills wakened the town. The women bent over the grinding stone only to bring the dough to the last fine-grind for smooth tortillas after carrying the dough back from the *molino*, where they paid to get the corn ground.

In this storefront corn mill, the owner helps his customer put her nixtamal *(hominy) corn through the diesel mill to become dough ready for a final fine-grinding on her stone at home. (Photo © Luisa Magarian, 1999)*

After the men left for the fields, the women again kneeled or sat with their legs outstretched in front of them on a straw mat, beginning their day's weaving. Those who had converted to evangelical Protestantism often accompanied their work by singing insistent religious tunes. A few transistor radios accompanied the whack and whoosh of the women's backstrap looms with marimba music and crackling news of distant places.

Thus, Pedrana women in those days were very comfortable and accustomed to kneeling or sitting on the floor. And they knew that foreigners like myself were not.

So when I insisted on sitting on the floor to give Chona a chair, the women would chuckle as I shifted position. My legs prickled with pins-and-needles and the women asked, "Barbara, are your legs getting 'ants' now?" At first I denied it and tried to act as though I was comfortable, embarrassed that I could not sit as they did in a dignified manner. But as the discomfort of my position grew, I laughed along with them at my predicament.

Weaving a family story

OVER THE YEARS, Chona has elaborated the story of how it is that I am her "daughter." Without departing from her serious and dignified demeanor, she secretly delights in the puzzlement that people show when she tells them that she gave birth to me and then had to give me away.

Chona, in public, is demure and serene. Her profession as an *iyoom* surrounds her with a powerful aura of respect. This sacred profession to which she was born requires courage and stamina and connects people with the supernatural, with their ancestors, and with their own futures.

When people pass Chona on the street, many stop to kiss the back of her hand in respect, and she responds with a gracious greeting, as in the photo on the next page of me greeting Chona. Receiving the reverential greetings of passersby can make it a slow trip for Chona to walk a few blocks.

(*Photo from video by Christine Mosier, 1986*)

In former days, people kissed the backs of elders' hands in general, but gradually the custom has eroded; it is now used primarily with the most respected elders. And for as long as I have been visiting San Pedro, the current generation of elders has bemoaned the erosion of respect among the younger generations, citing the progressive disappearance of this practice.

⁑

DUE TO THE RESPECT with which she is regarded, people take Chona seriously when she divulges soberly that she is my mother but I was given to a North American to raise. Often on market day, I spot Chona among the stalls of women calling out that their plantains are the best price or haggling over the freshness of their avocados. I have grown to expect Chona's dignified wave bidding me to join her as she stands with her puzzled acquaintances from a neighboring town.

In a serious voice, she prompts me to "tell them the truth." The visitors would look to the staid, dignified Chona as I confirmed that what she told them was true. However, unlike Chona, I have difficulty stifling the blink that signifies joking, as she explains to the bewildered visitors that the reason I am so pale and speak Tz'utujil poorly is that she had to give me up to a gringo when I was a baby. Chona tells the story with a straight face and she expects me to uphold her account.

Recently over lunch with the family, Chona told me that when people ask her if she has another daughter, a gringa named Barbara, she says yes. They ask which *iyoom* delivered this daughter, and she says it was the prominent *iyoom*, Doña María Puac. Chona recounts:

> They ask me who her father is, and I tell them, "Her father isn't
> from here, he's a foreigner, and when my daughter was born, her
> father took her away." And they ask, "Didn't your husband
> Ventura notice?" I tell them that we were separated when
> I married the foreigner and my other daughter was born. And then
> I got back together with Ventura. The people say, "She's White,
> and her father is from the United States? Does he look like her?"
> and I answer that he looks just like her.

Mischievously, I asked Chona, "What is my father's name?" She replied, straight-faced, "I can't pronounce his name; I know it, but I can't pronounce it."

Chona's appearance also makes a blue-eyed, light-brown–haired daughter more conceivable. Her hair is not jet black like most people in town but has a chestnut cast. By local standards, this makes her "blonde." Her eyes are hazel rather than the usual deep coffee-brown. She is known as *Chona Rex* (the *x* is pronounced like English *sh*): "Chona Green-Eyes."

Chona's account is shared with her grown children, who also maintain the story when someone asks if it is true. They refer to me as their sister when I am around, and speak of me as an aunt to their children. (Some people remark that I look like my "brother" Santos.)

Some of the grandchildren and great-grandchildren believed the story and were concerned about why Chona had to give me away. A few of them were upset with their grandfather upon hearing that he had made her give me to the North American man who had fathered me when Chona "was separated from" their grandfather: "Why did Grandpa do that? It's mean. Barbara is very nice." Their parents told them not to be busybodies, that this was a matter between their grandmother and grandfather.

Other grandchildren remembered that Chona's son Santos had rented a spare room to my former husband as a doctor's office when he served as the town's first resident Western doctor, the first year we lived in San Pedro.[15] The grandchildren commented to their parents that this favor must have been due to our family relationship.

Some of the youngsters were upset that when the town officials named the library I had founded, they did not include both of my surnames, only Rogoff from my father but not Pérez from Chona. Guatemalan practice is to use two surnames, the first from the father and the second from the mother. (So Chona Pérez González's two surnames are Pérez from her father and González from her mother.) The primary surname is the first one; some people abbreviate the second— so the library could have been named Biblioteca Bárbara Rogoff P., but the P. was not included when the town officials named it.

After the library spent a few decades moving between old municipal space and some rental houses, Don Agapito Cortez, who served on the Library Committee, spearheaded a petition to erect a building for the library. The mayor had this building constructed, and the president of Guatemala attended its inauguration. (Photo © Salem Magarian, 1998)

Recently I asked one of the relatives if the grandchildren still believed the story that I was born to Chona. The relative chuckled and referred to a U.S. belief: "No, it's like Santa Claus."

In any case, my relation with this family has grown over the years to one of great affection and mutual obligation, encompassing not only myself but also my children, to whom Chona also gives *consejos* (advice) as "grandchildren." Similarly, the long process of writing this book has involved many of the extended family members, who have helped Chona and me to record her destined calling and her development.

4 ⠿

Paper with a Mouth,
Recounting the Developing Destinies
of an *Iyoom* and her Community

OVER THE YEARS, Chona has given me an understanding of the sacred profession that she was born with a mandate to carry out. For my research, I was interested in how an *iyoom* cares for pregnant women, manages the birth process, and tends to babies' introduction to life.

As I got to know Chona, I also became fascinated with her destiny and how she took on the sacred role of *iyoom*. Some years later (1991), after numerous interviews on birthing practices and on her lifework for my child development research projects, I asked Chona if it would be a good idea to write a book about this. She was enthused. Chona was approaching the age of 70 and worried because there are now few *iyooma'* in San Pedro engaged in this ancient, divine calling.

Preserving a Record of a Sacred Practice

AS OF 2008, there were only about five *iyooma'* who carry this destiny from their birth, and most of them were about Chona's age. There were also about 16 *practicante* midwives who received some obstetric training as adults from personnel representing the Western medical establishment. They were not born with the destiny of *iyoom* and do not have the sacred knowledge and hallowed responsibilities of those who are born with the destiny of *iyoom*. In addition, there were about five local professional nurses and doctors who also deliver babies.

According to Chona, the reduction in number of *iyooma'* is partially due to the fact that the *practicantes* and nurses and doctors do not know the birthsigns, and they do not save the birthsign veil of a baby destined to be an *iyoom*. In addition, Chona reported that fewer *iyooma'* are being born—she had not seen any in the 5 years up to 2008. However, there are several younger women who carry this destined calling and are beginning to emerge as *iyooma'*.

Even now, most babies in San Pedro are born at home, with a midwife in attendance. The preference is still often for delivery with an *iyoom*, whose knowledge and skills are supernatural, and secondarily with a *practicante* or a nurse or doctor.[16] Generally, people from San Pedro have had less confidence in the effectiveness of those who were "merely taught" by medical personnel trained in the Western medical model[17] rather than divinely selected, with the "gift" of being an *iyoom*. In 1938, Rosales noted in his fieldnotes:

> Being an *iyoom* is one of the highest roles known [in San Pedro].
> . . . Everyone respects them as great people. . . . Being an *iyoom* is
> not work that one simply chooses—rather, it comes with birth;
> it is said that baby girls come with signs if they are to be
> midwives. The bad midwives are those who learn *por fuerza*
> [against nature, artificially]; they are greatly punished after
> they die because they acquire this work in that way. (1949 [1938],
> p. 504)[18]

The practices of the *iyooma'* are nonetheless becoming less central in San Pedro with the rise of contact with Western medicine. Another *iyoom*, Doña Jesús Quiacaín Televario, quite aged in 2004, told me that the young Western-trained *practicante* midwives are not interested in the ways of the *iyooma'*. They don't respect the old ways, the ancestors' ways, such as the need to heat the umbilical stump (so that it dries and falls off)[19] or to advise pregnant women to be careful not to sit in the doorway of the house and not to go out when there is lightning (in order to protect the unborn child from birth defects or unfortunate destinies). Doña Jesús claimed proudly that although the Western-trained *practicante* midwives discount these ideas, "That is the old way. . . . Yes, it's true, we are ancient like the rocks, ancient."

Another *iyoom*, Dolores Cumatz, age 80 in 2004 (and still working at that time), similarly complained to me that the Western-trained *practicante* midwives do not have appropriate respect for the sacred work:

> What pains me now is that the *practicantes* do not have respect for the work that we do. They feel superior to us. But now the work of receiving babies is in their hands.
>
> However, they shame us with their lack of respect for the work. One of them filmed some births and showed them on television [working with someone from the United States studying midwifery, apparently]. It showed babies emerging from their mothers' bodies, the mothers with their skirts up, showing the body and where the baby emerges, and showing the placenta. What dishonor. They are shaming the Virgin Mary, who isn't just anyone; she is the mother of God.
>
> It makes me very sad, because we *iyooma'* are very respectful; we show modesty with such things. This is why an *iyoom* is the mother of the town; one has to do the work modestly.[20]
>
> We are respectful and modest in our work, being designated by God for this work. There are very poor families; we have to be understanding with them, whether they can afford to give us just a cup of coffee or not. One must not speak badly of them in the town, because we are not all equal; some have money, others not. So one must keep this private and not speak badly of people. We *iyooma'* do not do the work for money, we do it because God has blessed us with this work. But the *practicantes* do the work for money.
>
> Also, the *practicantes*, and even the young *iyooma'*, do not show appropriate respect when they go out in town without wearing their formal shawl. They just wear their regular clothes and aprons. An *iyoom* is the mother of the town and should wear her shawl so that people respect her. That way the children that one has assisted in birth will respect one. Wearing just the apron with regular clothes, they don't respect. One must demonstrate respect in order to be respected.

Here iyoom *Dolores Cumatz is checking out the new learning center in San Pedro, pretending to use the Internet. Dolores' mother was the renowned* iyoom *Doña María Puac. (Photo © Barbara Rogoff, 2006)*

The sacred work of an *iyoom* goes beyond the obstetric practices of Western-trained *practicante* midwives. In addition to the act of delivering babies, a traditional *iyoom* mediates between the supernatural and the ordinary world and sustains traditional social values. For example, with solemn authority, an *iyoom* tells the young couple at the birth of their first child, "You see now how we are born in blood and tears; you too were born this way, and it is for this reason you must respect your mother and father" (Paul & Paul, 1975, p. 712).

⁝⁝

I WAS HESITANT about writing Chona's account because sacred information is often meant to be secret. But Chona was concerned that the knowledge may be lost altogether before long, and she reassured me that the other *iyooma'* of San Pedro would also be eager for the knowledge to be preserved in writing.

In 2004, I visited several other elder *iyooma'* to ask their permission to publish this book. They each responded with enthusiasm, thanking me for interest in the ancient ways and providing counsel for what to include in the book for the well-being of future generations. They were concerned, like Chona, about the loss of precious knowledge and the health of their community. Their comments also appear in this book, and they were pleased, like Chona, for their names to be on their words for posterity.

As Chona and I and her granddaughter, Chonita, and grandson, Josué, have worked together on this book, I have checked to be sure that Chona wants the information to be included in a book available for many people to read. (A few personal details are not included because Chona has indicated that it is better not to make them public.)

The only major part of the book that Chona hesitated to include was the account of me recognizing her hands as being like my mother's. She said that people reading it might realize there is another version of her playful story about her being my "mother." However, she agreed that that was indeed an important part of this book, and so it is here.

Chona said consistently (and Chonita and Josué supported the idea) that it was very important to make her account public so that her knowledge would not die with her: "When I am dead, there will at least be a book that tells people about all this, and my name won't die."[21] While we were looking for a publisher, Chona said that even if the book were not formally published, the process of talking about the information and writing it down is the most important.

Communicating Across Time and Place

AS THIS BOOK has developed, it has become not just the account of Chona's life and of the ways of an *iyoom*. It has expanded to become an account of the lives of San Pedro children and families, and how some of their cultural practices have changed and some have been sustained over more than 80 years.

The dramatic changes as well as the stabilities in San Pedro are intimately connected with Chona's own biography. The account of the changes and stabilities thus reveals the interrelatedness of individual lives and community history.

The account also shows connections among people and communities with distinct cultural heritages, far from San Pedro. Some of the most notable connections across communities underline the changes involved in communication itself. The transformation in Chona's views of the written word, across her lifetime, are accompanied by enormous changes throughout San Pedro in means of oral, written, and electronic communication across time and place.

Until a generation or two ago, most families had no books, or at most the Bible. In 1976 about two thirds of households had the Bible as their only book, and almost all the rest had no books. By 1999, a third of families had several books and 8% had shelves full of books. (Another 23% of households had no books and 38% had only a Bible; Rogoff, Correa-Chávez, & Navichoc Cotuc, 2005.)

Reading material, for the most part, has been in Spanish. Few books have been written in Tz'utujil, and only recently have some Pedranos begun to learn to read and write in their native language. Over many years, as Pedranos have added the Spanish language to their linguistic repertoire to be able to participate in Guatemalan markets and Western schooling and employment, the written word became more accessible.

Use of the Tz'utujil oral language continues to be remarkably stable, however. Almost everyone in San Pedro continues to speak Tz'utujil even while adding Spanish to their repertoire. In many Indigenous communities, use of the native language has eroded when a national language such as Spanish or English is added. For a short time several decades ago, a number of Pedrano families tried speaking to their young children in Spanish and avoiding Tz'utujil with them, to prepare their children for school. However, within a few years, many of them decided that children could learn both languages, and resumed speaking Tz'utujil at home.

The changes in the use of Spanish and of books are accompanied by other changes in communication with the world outside San Pedro. When Chona was a child, there was only occasional contact with other places through Spanish-language newspapers, the radio at the courthouse, and some travel (mainly by the men) to distant towns. By 1976, many families had small transistor radios and already 6% of families had a television, a year after electricity reached San Pedro households. When the household I lived in got their first television, the first program I watched with them was the Miss Universe contest. There was still no telephone; telegrams could be sent in case of emergency. For several decades now, most households have a television and San Pedro receives cable programs from different parts of the world.

San Pedro also has its own Tz'utujil cable TV station and radio station. Chona sometimes explains the sacred work of an *iyoom* on the local radio station so that the knowledge will not be lost.

To my continued amazement, I can now reach Chona from the United States on her cellphone; when I called recently to wish her a happy Mother's Day, she greeted me as *waal ixoq*, "my woman-child" in Tz'utujil. Cellphones are widespread within San Pedro; they are used to communicate not only across kilometers but also across short distances that before were traversed on foot for a visit, or a child was sent with a message.

Some of the younger generation in San Pedro now use e-mail and the Internet. Chona's grandson Josué has helped considerably with this book by answering my queries and sending me useful references via e-mail. In fact, my first access to a book via e-mail was when Josué initiated me into this use of e-mail. He and I have been able to share information and speculations about the history of various practices and the origins of several key Tz'utujil words through electronically mediated conversations as well as in-person ones.

It is my hope, and Chona's and Chonita's and Josué's, that this book provides an account that is valuable to Pedranos as well as to other readers around the world, to understand cultural practices that may be disappearing along with those that will be sustained. The writing of the book has involved taking notes in Tz'utujil, Spanish, and English, and we hope to be able to publish the book in at least these three languages.

Writing Notes

ONE DAY during my first year in San Pedro, as I was relaxing on the front stoop of a house with my clipboard in hand, an old man lumbered up the steep rocky road toward me. This was the man that my former husband and I referred to as Favorite Old Man because he always had a smile and always stopped to shake hands and chat for a moment, even with a weighty load on his back. He worked as a porter, bringing loads from the canoe dock up the hill to town.

That day, as usual he was bent forward, carrying three cases full of bottles of Pepsi, supported by his back and by a tumpline across his forehead. He stopped in front of me to chat, in no hurry, seemingly heedless of his load. Bent over, he peered out from under his hat and asked, "Are you writing me down?" He seemed to be joking, but he did not continue on his way until I replied that I would indeed write him down. From his perspective, this was my job, to write people down.

Favorite Old Man stops for a rare break as he carries his load up the steep rocky street. He was indeed noteworthy; I appreciate his showing me that my job was to write people down. (Photo © Barbara Rogoff, 1975)

⁛

IN WRITING DOWN Chona's life and work, I am relying heavily on Chona's own accounts, given to me over the 30-plus years that I have known her. I present the information that Chona personally gave me without citations. The book also includes information given by her granddaughter Chonita and her grandson Josué, and other relatives.

Chonita Chavajay Quiacaín, early in the writing of this book. Chonita contributed her own observations and ideas about the destiny of being an iyoom, *and about her grandmother Chona's life and work. (Photo © Barbara Rogoff, ca. 1993)*

In addition, the book is based on informal conversations and formal interviews with many other people in San Pedro, including other *iyooma'* and many mothers. In my years of research in San Pedro on child development and childrearing practices, I have had the privilege of visiting and revisiting about a hundred families over decades.

My understanding of life in San Pedro is also based on participant observation of family and community lives and events, both public and private. I have been involved in several community committees as well as long-term friendships and engagement with families from different parts of San Pedro, across religious and political and economic lines.

I lived in San Pedro for a year and a half in the mid-1970s. Since then I have returned for a few weeks about once per year, except during the decade of "the violence," when many Mayan people in Guatemala were being killed or "disappeared." (This was almost always perpetrated by the Guatemalan Army, which was advised and supplied by the United States.)

The book also relies heavily on the work done by Lois and Ben Paul, who began their anthropological investigations of San Pedro with a year-long stay in 1941, and made numerous visits since then. (Lois died in 1975, and Ben died at 94 in 2005. He was still doing fieldwork in San Pedro until a few years before he died.)

When I asked people from San Pedro what Ben and Lois Paul had been doing there in 1941, I was told that they were writing what goes on in the town, and what are the customs. One person added, "In those days, no one from San Pedro was writing about San Pedro." Now, a number of Pedranos—especially Don Luis Batz—have published books and articles on many aspects of life in San Pedro.

Lois and Ben published several papers on the work and training of *iyooma'*, including interviews with Chona (Paul, 1975; Paul & Paul, 1975). I have also studied their unpublished fieldnotes from over 65 years ago, which discuss these topics and include observations they made of Chona, then age 16, and her family.[22]

I refer to Lois and Ben's publications or their fieldnotes when the information comes directly from those sources. Much of what Lois Paul wrote years ago is quite consistent with the information I have received, but when information from Lois supplements my information or differs from it, I refer to Lois' writing as the source. I also recount some information that Ben Paul told me directly, noting that the information comes from him, without further citation.

Lois Paul (on the left) in 1941, with a neighbor. (Photo by Ben Paul)

Ben Paul interviewing two Mayan men from another town, no date. (Thanks to Janie Paul for the photo of her father.)

Especially valuable are Lois and Ben Paul's ethnographic photographs, most of which were unpublished before now. Before they left for Guatemala in 1941, Margaret Mead told Ben and Lois to take pictures of their new neighbors' daily life, "over the fence". (The photos in this book from 1941, 1956, and 1962 are thanks to the Pauls' photography. Other photographs, from 1998, are thanks to Luisa Magarian, and most of the remainder are my own, with those from other sources noted.)

The information spreading across about 80 years in the life of one individual provides a chance not only to understand the life and development of a leading Mayan sacred specialist. It also offers a view of the striking changes and continuities in the lives of San Pedro children and families over this period. Written sources, some of them centuries old, further extend the history of changes and continuities back hundreds of years.

This view of San Pedro lives and times can enhance an understanding of humanity, and especially how we all are participants in our communities in a particular time and place. Our lives are defined initially by where we are born and in what era—a form of destiny that contributes to how we then develop. We might move to a different place, but we cannot change our era except in the process of living.

The ways that we live are informed by experiences of prior generations of our own communities and others—sometimes informed by paper with a mouth. Our inheritance from prior generations is not simply received, but can be transformed or resisted, further contributing to the destinies of future generations, of multiple communities.

5 ::

Born to a Spiritual Calling,
Across Generations:
Cultural Heritage and Resistance

WHEN CHONA WAS BORN, May 1, 1925, her parents were very pleased to learn that she carried the sacred calling of *iyoom*. The *iyoom* who delivered her, her great-aunt Doña Josefa Yojcom, discerned Chona's destiny from a birthsign. This was a light veil draped over her head when she was born, a fragment of amniotic membrane, thin and strong like plastic wrap.

The *iyoom* warned Chona's parents that they should not tell anyone about Chona's "gift"—her sacred destiny—or her life would be endangered from supernatural risks. However, the *iyoom* did tell the neighbor woman who was recruited to wash the birthing cloths that this baby had a special birthsign. The neighbor washed the veil at the lakeshore, along with the cloths, and dried it carefully.

The *iyoom* wrapped the veil carefully, together with some chunks of clear amber-colored pine incense, in a soft white cloth. She placed these in a decorated oval wooden box for Chona's parents to safeguard. If the veil is not carefully preserved, the person will not be able to carry out her destined work as *iyoom*, and may get sick. When the veil tissue dries, it looks like strong parchment paper, translucent white. Chona showed hers to me when she was 78, saying that it was all right to show it now that it was no good anymore. The veil at 78 years was an ample piece of tissue, crumpled and stiff, but still strong. The incense had disappeared. I have seen one other *iyoom*'s birthsign veil, and it too was handled and preserved carefully, with secrecy, as befits a sacred sign.

Vitality of Spiritual Threads

WHEN CHONA WAS 20 DAYS OLD, her parents took her to the Catholic church, on the town plaza, to pray to Santa Ana, the Catholic saint who is the spiritual guide of *iyooma'*. Chona's parents appealed to Santa Ana to help Chona grow up without fear of doing her work as *iyoom*. Every 20 days during her infancy, her parents returned to pray to Santa Ana to make Chona brave enough to take on her destined work.

This statue of Santa Ana is in San Pedro's Catholic church.
(Photo © Barbara Rogoff, 1996)

The prayers combined Catholic and Mayan spiritual practices, underlining the vitality of cultural practices and creative resistance of Mayan communities. The prayers were directed to the Catholic saint Santa Ana. And they were performed each 20 days, when the baby's Mayan birth *nahual* recurs on the sacred calendar of the ancient Mayans. This calendar, still in use among some Pedranos, has 13 20-day cycles

(Nash, 1970). The *nahual*—birth destiny day—thus recurs every 20 days. The *nahual* has particular power for prayer and healing ceremonies.[23]

Chona's father, who was a shaman, also took her along as he prayed on her behalf in the Catholic church in his nearby hometown, San Juan, and in the chapels of six local *cofradías*. Each *cofradía* brotherhood of principal elders and associates and their wives were responsible for the care and veneration of particular Catholic saints. This was an honor and a great and costly responsibility that rotated among community leaders. On an annual schedule, each *cofradía* sponsored elaborate ceremonies that included processions carrying statues of the saints through the town.

The cofradías *and their ceremonies had such syncretism with Mayan practices that Catholic priests discouraged the ceremonies and the* cofradías. *By the time of this 1956 procession, San Pedro had had a foreign Catholic priest in residence for two years. In 1970, a priest from Spain managed to dismantle the* cofradía *system such that it became a shadow of its earlier prominence in the life of San Pedro. For a time, a few small-scale fiestas were reminders of the former annual cycle of fiestas and the brotherhoods that sponsored them (Paul & Demarest, 1984). Recently, however,* cofradías *have regained greater prominence among some of the Catholic population of San Pedro. (Photo by Lois and Ben Paul)*

This girl carrying a candle is in the official role of texel *as part of a* cofradía *ceremony in June 1941. Each* cofradía *had three* texeles, *who were girls or single or widowed women (Batz, 1991). (Photo by Lois and Ben Paul)*

A procession honoring several saints emerges from San Pedro's Catholic church in 1941. (Photo by Lois and Ben Paul)

The saints have Catholic names and Spanish faces. But they also have Mayan character. This combination illustrates the vitality of Mayan spirituality across the ages, at the same time as the adoption of new forms; Mayan communities have historically transformed their spiritual practices while revitalizing their spirit, resisting the simple imposition of religions from elsewhere. The European saints are fused with Mayan deities who may still have similar roles in society as they did before the arrival of the Spanish. For example, Santiago, the patron saint of the neighboring Tz'utujil town of Santiago Atitlán, has an essential role in Mayan agricultural practices that does not correspond with orthodox Catholicism (Christenson, 2001).

A theory of cultural change and continuity to explain the fusion of Mayan and Catholic deities was offered by Nicolás Chávez, a leading Mayan artist from Santiago Atitlán: When the Spanish arrived, the ancient gods and the earth died, continuing a process of death and rebirth of the world that had occurred many times. Each time, when the earth and the gods are renewed, the gods again attain their power, along with new gods:

> The saints today have Spanish names because the old earth died in the days of the Spanish conquerors. When the spirit keepers of the

world appeared again they were the saints, but they do the same work that the old gods did anciently. (Chavez, quoted in Christenson, 2001, p. 135)

The Spanish priests tried to eradicate Mesoamerican spiritual practices in order to substitute the Catholic religion. In the Tz'utujil region, between 1545 and 1550, the priests burned the Mayan idols that they found, but Mayan worship continued in secret (Orellana, 1984).[24]

Mayan and other Mesoamerican communities were skilled in keeping sensitive information from the Catholic priests. Fray Bernardino de Sahagún, who organized the writing of the Florentine Codex in the mid-1500s, worried about how easily Indians could deceive priests who did not understand their languages. The Indians honored the pre-Columbian deities in their festivals, singing and dancing the histories and deeds of their ancestors and Indigenous deities, using their native languages. They covered this up by occasionally shouting the name of God or a saint, in Spanish (Christenson, 2001; see also Orellana, 1984).

Mesoamerican people often engaged in the traditional Indigenous sacred practices at night and in secret places. A few years ago, I asked a church guide, in a Nahua town in central Mexico, what the priests think of the continuing Indigenous religious practices that the guide was describing on his tour of the church. He replied, "Oh, they don't know. We know it would bother them, so we keep it to ourselves."

⁘

IN ADDITION to Chona's father's prayers in Catholic churches and *cofradía* chapels, another shaman prayed for Chona's destiny as *iyoom* at altars hidden in the forest around San Pedro. According to Chona, the health and safety of a newly born *iyoom* or shaman were always prayed for at the Mayan shrines on the volcano. The shaman's chanted prayers invoked the spirits of ancestor *iyooma'* and other ancestors, as well as the lords of nature and of time, and the Catholic saints.

A renowned shaman, Francisco Chavajay, stands between two other principal elders of San Pedro, in 1941. (Photo by Lois and Ben Paul)

Similarities between Catholic and Mesoamerican spiritual practices and deities facilitated their fusion. The altars in the forest, where the shamans prayed, often feature a cross. The cross has both Christian and ancient Mayan spiritual significance. Mayan crosses symbolize the four sacred directions—north, south, east, and west—that form the limits of the cosmos. The cross also represents corn and the pre-Columbian world tree, on which the major Mayan deity Hun Hunahpu was hung before his resurrection, like Christ (Christenson, 2001). In various Mayan communities, the cross was a deity independent of Jesus; from the colonial period it has been addressed as a saint (Duque Arellanos, 1999; LaFarge, 1947). "Far from being converted themselves, [the Mayans] converted the Catholic saints" (Christenson, 2001, p. 135, quoting Carlsen, 1997; see also LaFarge, 1947).[25]

CHONA'S PARENTS followed the Mayan form of Catholicism, as did almost everyone in town during Chona's childhood. A few Pedranos were evangelical Protestants, following the establishment of the first evangelical congregation in about 1924, the year before Chona was born. However, evangelical Protestantism grew rapidly. By 1962 about a third of the town was Protestant (Paul & Paul, 1963), as Chona now is. She converted when her son Santos became a Protestant preacher.

The Protestants (and now some Catholics) often object to the ancient Mayan spiritual practices that are still carried out by some Pedranos. Nevertheless, even after some of the *iyooma'* became Protestant, they still followed some aspects of the syncretic Catholic/Mayan form of prayer and rituals, especially with their Catholic patients. Individually, they illustrate the melding of cultural practices to meet current needs.

The Tz'utujil people have a facility to adapt while yet maintaining their identity, addressing changes from a Mayan perspective.

> The Tz'utujils . . . readily adopt aspects of Western culture, art, and language which fit the needs of their people. . . . The Maya tend to alter external influences to fit already established indigenous cultural patterns. (Christenson, 2001, pp. 213–214)

Chona's Mother's Heritage and Resistance

CHONA'S PARENTS' PRAYERS for Chona to be courageous were especially ardent because of the danger that Chona's mother, Dolores, was running by not fulfilling her own birth destiny as an *iyoom*. It is not unusual for sacred healing roles to recur across generations in a family in San Pedro. Several other leading *iyooma'* have been daughters of an *iyoom* or shaman.[26]

Chona's mother, Dolores González Navichoc, is the third woman from the left. Here she and the other councilmen's wives were sitting along the street, waiting for a religious procession celebrating San Pedro's patron saint (Saint Peter), in 1941. (Photo by Lois and Ben Paul)

Dolores, Chona's mother, was washing gourds for serving a special ceremonial drink called maatz'—*made of corn gruel, chile, and anise—to the crowds who attended a* cofradía *celebration in 1941.*

These boys savored their drink of maatz' *in 1956. (Photos by Lois and Ben Paul)*

Dolores was a modest, hard-working, and competent woman, according to Lois Paul (1975). The problem was that Dolores did not have the courage to accept the divine power of her calling. Dolores' cultural heritage provided her with a strong mandate to fulfill the role of *iyoom*, but she rejected it.

⁝⁝

WHEN I SAY, "Dolores' cultural heritage," I am referring to the *practices* of the community that she grew up and lived in. Often questions of Mayan identity in Guatemala involve consideration of a person's involvement in contemporary Mayan practices, not just his or her ancestry.

Mayan and Ladino practices and relations

IN GUATEMALA, categorization in social groups involves how a person lives, not just the race of his or her parents. In the first epoch after the arrival of the Spanish, racial classification was central to social status.

However, racial markers weakened as offspring combined European, Indian, and African descent. Then language and cultural practices gained importance as markers of social status.

The distinctions in social status were especially important because the Spanish required tribute payment from Indians, but offspring of an Indian and a non-Indian parent were exempted. The effort to avoid the heavy tribute payments led a number of people to attempt reclassification out of the Indian category (to *Ladino*); this became an issue for the Spanish government by the late 1700s (Brown, 1998).

Currently, a person might not be considered Mayan if he or she does not claim to be Mayan and does not follow Mayan practices such as speaking a Mayan language, using a Mayan name, or dressing in characteristic Mayan clothes—even though his or her parents lived as Mayan Indians. This consideration of people's practices contrasts with the usual U.S. form of categorizing individuals (in "boxes"), which often focuses solely on the ancestry of a person's parents, treating ethnicity as an inborn characteristic of an individual.

The contrast between attention to cultural practices versus inborn ancestry can be seen in the reflections of Mexican American scholar Luis Urrieta in reference to Indigenous identity. He recalled being confused during his youth regarding his father's *pueblo* in Michoacan, Mexico, which had once been culturally *P'urhépecha*:

> I heard older relatives in Los Angeles and Michoacán saying, "When we were Indians," while at other times, "When we were more Indian." This was also made more confusing when referring to people of nearby *pueblos* in the Pátzcuaro region as being *más indios*, or "more Indian," as if being "Indian" was something that could be diluted, lessened, or changed. (2003, p. 149)

Similarly, residents of a town in the region of San Luis Potosí, Mexico, referred to the past as "when we were Indians," (Frye, 1996, p. 5). They also described people from prior times as being *indiados* (Indian-like) and *más indios* (more Indian). They used the verb *estar*, indicating a temporary condition of being, rather than *ser*, which would be used for a durable state of being (*"estaban más indiados verdad, así, más indios así"*). Frye noted, "'Indian' is not their essence, their identity, but their condition" (p. 62).

The definition of being Mayan in 1948 in Chan Com (Yucatan, Mexico) likewise focused on participation in the practices common to the town. People living in the village who had Spanish surnames were nonetheless regarded as Mayan: "They are Maya because they live just as we do. They can go into the bush, and work hard there" (Redfield, 1950, p. 73). An immigrant to the village from a distant region of Mexico, who did not speak Maya and looked White, was not regarded as White because he raised corn and lived by hard work in the same way as the Mayans of Chan Com—a White person was seen as a "softer, town-inhabiting creature" (p. 73).

In Guatemala, a *Ladino* is a person who does not live as an Indigenous person, and is not considered Indigenous, but rather follows Spanish Guatemalan customs—whether or not his or her parents and other ancestors did. Ladino is generally not exclusively a designation of race or ancestry but a category that also refers to people's cultural practices, such as speaking Spanish and not a Mayan language, and dressing Western style rather than Mayan style. "By the simple act of assuming another attitude of mind [an individual], particularly if he possesses a modicum of Spanish blood to alter his physical appearance, may, and in many cases does, become a Ladino" (LaFarge, 1947, p. 15).

Many Ladinos are *mestizos* with Mayan ancestry, although often Ladinos show strong prejudices and sometimes violence against Mayan people and practices. Although the Mayans remain the majority population of Guatemala, they still hold very little power and are subject to abuses. Indeed, the violence that pervaded Guatemalan life during the last half of the twentieth century is widely regarded as genocide perpetrated by Ladino and European Guatemalan powers against the Mayan people. Anthropologist LaFarge noted, using the gender and racial language of the United States in 1947:

> The ordinary Ladino . . . looks upon the Indians much as southern white men in the United States look upon Negroes, granting the difference inherent in the Anglo-Saxon's tendency to rationalize such attitudes upon a racial basis, whereas the Latin is far more tolerant racially and, without consciously defining it, bases the alleged superiority or inferiority rather upon class and culture. To the average Ladino, the Indians are an ignorant and inferior people—"*Indios brutos: gente sin razón*"—intended to do the heavy and dirty work and in every way to be utilized for the benefit of those who are descended from the conquerors. (p. 16)

Indigenous midwifery practices have been subject to prejudice from non-Indigenous people throughout the Mesoamerican region for centuries. Harsh ethnocentric views are shown in this 1850s account of birthing practices among the Otomí people of Querétaro, Mexico, written by the Mexican politician, professor, and acclaimed author Guillermo Prieto ("Fidel"). Ironically, he was known for being an honest and virtuous representative and minister of state, promoting justice and equality (Flores, n.d.). But he wrote:

> When the young Indian finds out that she is to be a mother, she loads herself up with pagan and Christian amulets and gives herself over to practices born of superstition and ignorance. . . . When the admirable unfolding of nature is near, she submits to examination by an old sorceress, the midwife of the town . . . .
>
> This horrible old woman, bent with years, with her bristly white hair like the mane of a horse, with her yellowish complexion and her sunken penetrating gaze, approaches the patient, and after making certain cabalistic signs, inspects the volume and shape of the belly with imprudent pressure which usually results in unfortunate mishaps, for the mother and the child.
>
> Then the sorcery of the old trickster continues; she places in front of the pregnant woman a clay brazier in which she burns aromatic herbs and throws in a little saltpeter, which upon melting shows strange capricious figures. Then the repugnant old woman, possessed with a supernatural power, intoxicated with the aromatic smoke of the herbs, and delirious like a soothsayer, pronounces her judgment according to what was observed in the melting of the saltpeter. Usually coincidence comes in support of the imprudent quackery of these miserable fortune tellers; but in any case and from these moments on, the pregnant woman remains under the dominion of the midwives, who do not abandon their victim until the birth is past. At the time of the birth, and to facilitate it, they employ the most absurd methods that ignorance and barbaric custom have been able to sanction. (quoted in León, 1910, pp. 81–82)

In Guatemala, as in Mexico, non-Indians have continued to treat Indigenous people with domination and prejudice. In his novel based on San Pedro, *Entre la Piedra y la Cruz*, Mario Monteforte Toledo (a Ladino) portrayed one view of the relations between Mayan and Ladino ways of life. He described the thoughts of an imaginary Pedrano who realized that an acquaintance was deciding to become Ladino. This was about 1939, during the time that the government forced Mayans to labor on lowland plantations belonging to foreigners or rich Guatemalans. The imaginary Pedrano considered the change in status and practices for his acquaintance becoming Ladino:

> Now [the acquaintance who was becoming Ladino] could roam the land, go to the city and become a truck driver, or even a policeman. Happy or unfortunate, at least he would not be lowered ever again to brutish servitude, flatly, without protest. He had saved himself from the [forced work] of the coast. Perhaps he would begin wearing shoes, buy a felt hat, and learn to speak loud. (1948, p. 130)

Discrimination by Ladino people against Mayan people continues to be pervasive. A young Pedrana described her experience of discrimination to me (in 2008):

> There is a lot of discrimination; others don't treat us well. Well, it's not just others. Even in San Pedro, when people talk about someone being pretty, it means that they are light-skinned.
>
> But in the capital, when I was a student at the University, it was very strong. I wore my Mayan clothes, so of course everyone knew I'm Mayan. There were 400–500 students and not very many spare seats in the classroom. The Ladina students made fun of me and they wouldn't let me have a seat by them in the classroom. The other Mayan girls couldn't stand the discrimination and so they didn't wear Mayan clothes; they wore pants.
>
> I thought, "What can I do to show the Ladina girls that we're equal?" I decided to study a lot to show them I'm their equal. After the exams, when the teachers posted the grades and the other girls saw them, all the girls asked me to sit by them. I told my younger sister to do the same, but she couldn't stand the discrimination and so she used pants. Then the Peace Accords were signed, and they included a law that Mayan people have the right to use their traditional clothes. Then my sister understood and she started using her Mayan clothes.

The domination, abuses, and prejudices of Ladino Guatemala (as well as Spain and the United States) towards Mayan people, and the resistance and vitality of the Mayans, are part of the cultural history of San Pedro and they have contributed to the current practices of Pedranos. The culture of San Pedro and of individual Pedranos is built of practices that have developed over time and in relation to other communities. In addition, many individual Pedranos themselves have family histories that combine ancestries from different backgrounds.

Combined ancestry in San Pedro

ALTHOUGH ALMOST ALL Pedranos consider themselves fully Mayan, many have some European and Ladino ancestry, stemming especially from prior generations when Spanish authorities governed the town. The Spanish, Ladino, and Mayan ancestry common among Mayan people in San Pedro can be seen in the genealogical record of part of Chona's family, pieced together from Lois and Ben Paul's 1941 fieldnotes, below.

The family ancestry of Dolores, Chona's mother, provides a window on the historical combination of ethnic backgrounds of Pedranos, going back for generations. This genealogy list reveals the combinations of ancestry in the generations before and after Dolores, starting from Dolores' earliest known ancestors, five generations before her (in "generation minus 5") until three generations after her ("generation plus 3; "Dolores is in the "zero" generation). Each of the three oldest generations includes a Spaniard or a Ladino ancestor. (Only one surname was recorded in some cases.)

> *Generation minus 5*, fifth generation back from Dolores: A Spanish man named José Antonio Mar González and a Mayan woman, Pabla Tzoc.
> *Generation minus 4*. Their daughter Rosalía González, who is listed as a "native" in the Pauls' notes, was with a Ladino priest.
> *Generation minus 3*. Their son, José Antonio González was with María Mejicana, who was a Ladina who was brought in as a servant to a priest living in San Pedro. Chona says María Mejicana came from Mexico. Another descendent of María Mejicana living in San Pedro had the habit of scolding her grandchildren by calling them "Mexicans," for reasons that may be related to this ancestor's origins but are now not known.
> *Generation minus 2*. José Antonio and María's son (Dolores' grandfather), Chema González Mejicano, had ancestry that was about 7/8 non-Mayan, although he lived as a Mayan Indian. Some of his 11 siblings and their children became Ladinos, moving away from San Pedro and ceasing to live as Mayans; Chema and most of his siblings remained in San Pedro and continued to live as

Mayan Indians. Chema's wife (Dolores' grandmother), Teresa Puzul, had a Mayan surname.

An aside from this generation: According to a story told to the Pauls by Chona's sister Susana, one morning Teresa went out before dawn with her husband Chema, and she saw two water jugs at the foot of a hill. She thought some woman had left them there, and went to pick them up to keep for the woman, but she found she could not lift them. Her husband could hardly lift them either. The moon was still up, and it was rather dark, so they lit a candle and looked in, finding both pots full of old Spanish silver coins.

It was Teresa's destiny to find these riches [due to the *nahual* of the day Teresa was born, which provides the basis of a person's character and events in her life]. Teresa and Chema hauled the pots into their house. When they put the contents into two trunks, the money filled the trunks to the top. Chema used the money to buy cattle and he became quite rich, but he began to treat Teresa very badly, beating her and taking up with another woman to whom he gave Teresa's money.

Generation minus 1. Chema and Teresa's son, Rafael González Puzul, and his wife María Navichoc. These are Dolores' parents; they have surnames that are a mixture of Spanish and Mayan names. Some of the reasons appear in prior generations.

Generation zero, Chona's parents. **Dolores** González Navichoc herself married **Marcos** Pérez Yojcom. His father (Gaspar Pérez) had a Spanish surname and his mother (Concepción Yojcom) had a Mayan surname.[27]

Generation plus 1. **Chona**'s surnames have Spanish origins (Pérez from her father and González from Dolores). Chona is Mayan, although her surnames and her green eyes and curly hair are inherited from non-Mayan ancestors. Her way of life is contemporary Mayan, which combines cultural practices from non-Mayan as well as Mayan sources, from centuries ago through the present.

Generation plus 2. Chona's children, with Ventura Quiacaín Petzey, have both a Mayan and a Spanish surname: Dolores, Santos, Abraham, and María Lidia (Linda) Quiacaín Pérez.

Generation plus 3. Chona's two daughters Dolores and María Lidia are the mothers of **Chonita** and **Josué**, whose surnames are of Mayan origin (Chavajay from each of their fathers and Quiacaín from their mothers).

This lineage shows clearly the combination of different heritages over generations in San Pedro. Nonetheless, except for a few governing individuals, priests, and teachers, almost 100% of San Pedro's inhabitants have lived as Mayan people for centuries. They have identified and been treated as Mayan Indians, following Mayan customs, speaking a Mayan language as their first language, and dressing in "typical" Mayan clothing until very recently.

What is regarded as "Mayan" changes across generations, of course. For example, "typical" Mayan clothing of today is different than the clothing worn in San Pedro a century ago—the fabrics used to be plainer, with different colors and different-length pants and skirts and aprons. Now most men do not wear Indigenous clothing, but almost all of the women still do, although most women now wear "typical" Pedrana blouses made with factory-made fabrics rather than hand-woven *huipiles*.[28] Some younger women now wear both Western and Mayan clothing at different times. Private schools sponsored by Catholic and Protestant churches require both girls and boys to wear uniforms, in the Western style.

Adapting with changes in cultural practices may itself be a stable cultural characteristic! The former principal of San Pedro's central public elementary school, Miguel Angel Bixcul García, told me that people in San Pedro have for centuries generally welcomed outsiders into San Pedro, to join in the life of this town. He noted that the common pattern of Mayan people in San Pedro having both Mayan and Spanish surnames (like his own) is evidence of this longtime pattern of combining cultures (see also Rogoff, 2003).

Combining cultural practices can yield creativity and vitality. At the same time, individuals and generations navigating the currents of cultural heritage and change also encounter challenges and risks.

Risks: Chona's Father's Warning

CHONA'S FATHER, Marcos Pérez Yojcom, like his wife, Dolores, was born to a divine calling of healing. Unlike Dolores, Marcos accepted his calling as an *ajkuum* (shaman). In 1941, there were between about 6 and 15 shamans in San Pedro who served as divine intermediaries, curing ailments and foretelling the future. Marcos specialized in curing cases of insanity.

According to the Pauls' fieldnotes, at the beginning of his career as a shaman, following a long illness, Chona's father turned to drink and displayed a hot temper. When he came home drunk from fiestas, violent arguments with his wife occurred, fueled by her complaints that he was frittering away her inheritance with his drinking debts. But later in life, Lois Paul reported that Marcos drank little and "presented a friendly, quiet-spoken, dignified demeanor" (Paul, 1975, p. 454; Paul & Paul, 1975).

Marcos worried for his wife, Dolores, when she fell very ill. Marcos' work as a shaman included predicting the future and intervening with supernatural forces to aid people. When Dolores became ill, he advised her that she might die young if she refused to do the work that her birth-sign had shown was her destiny.

Chona's father, on the left, was regarded as a strong and skillful leader in 1941. During this time, he was serving a 2-year unsalaried appointment in the municipal offices as fourth regidor *(alderman). Marcos could read and write, and held a post to help people, signing papers for people who could not write. Chona doesn't know how he learned to read and write and speak Spanish, for he grew up poor—an orphan at age 4—and did not attend school. In that era, some San Pedro men learned to read and write and speak Spanish through contact with Ladinos, while serving in the Guatemalan Army, or in selling products, making purchases, or working in other communities. (Photo by Lois and Ben Paul)*

I recently learned more about Chona's father's own risks at a lunch I invited Chona and her family to. I had noticed at a friend's house, over dinner, that Chona had regaled family and friends with stories I had never heard. Those dinner conversations gave me the idea of trying to elicit some new accounts from Chona by recreating casual dinner-table circumstances. Often I've found that listening to people's discussions with others provides insights and information that do not emerge in an interview.

So I invited Chona and some of her family to a lunch to celebrate the progress in writing this book about Chona's life and work as an *iyoom*. I also told them that I hoped some new information would emerge, to add to the book.

We met at a restaurant where we usually have celebration dinners. I got there first and chose a spot, moving the plastic tables and potted palms around on an empty part of the tile patio overlooking the lake. My goal was to arrange the scenario so that we got privacy and quiet away from other customers, and at the same time could avoid the midday sun. In the highland tropics, the midday sun can be overly warm, but in the shade, the breeze off the lake makes for springtime comfort.

I worried that the concrete stairs leading down to the patio would be too difficult for Chona to navigate, with her arthritic knees, but she insisted that the stairs were no problem. She descended regally on her daughter's arm, her hand-woven shawl draped over her shoulder in the dignified manner of traditional midwives. Right foot, left foot, both feet placed on each step, down the two flights of stairs to our table.

We greeted each other with handshakes pulling us each into cheek-kisses (a custom adopted from Ladinos in recent decades). Then Chona's family seated her beside me, facing the postcard-worthy view of the shimmering lake, and chose their own seats around the table set for eight. My little tape recorder crouched in the middle of the brilliant tablecloth. Like Chona's shawl, the tablecloth was woven of primary colors in traditional patterns like those that star in glossy calendars displaying "The Maya."

After we all exchanged greetings, and I exclaimed over how much the twins had grown, we ordered fruit smoothies and consulted each other about what we should order. As usual, we ended up with the old favorite, chicken with fries. And then, as usual, the company waited politely for me to make a little speech about how pleased I was that they could join me for lunch. I told them formally that the occasion was to celebrate progress on the book and that I was also hoping to gather more stories that would enhance the book. The company, of course, replied in kind, with thanks for the invitation and generous statements about the book—how important it is to preserve the information about *iyooma'* practices and to honor Mama Chona.

When I turned on the tape recorder in front of Chona and her youngest daughter, Linda, everyone fell silent. I felt as self-conscious as everyone else, wondering how this could become a casual conversation and not an interview. I was a bit impatient, wanting to get the conversation going before the meal arrived, when we'd be asking to have the tortillas passed, handing the salt bowl down the table, helping the twins cut their chicken, and ordering more smoothies.

I asked Chona's daughter Linda if she had any questions that she was curious about knowing about her mother's parents. Linda obliged, pausing to think of a question. She is pleased that I have been helping her son Josué to study sociology in the national university (and when he was little, passing along my kids' hand-me-downs).[29] Josué sat on the other side of me, eager to help by translating when Chona's Tz'utujil and my Spanish (and fledgling Tz'utujil) didn't get through to each other.

At a celebration meal years earlier, Chona and grandson Josué pass a plate of tamales. (Photo © Barbara Rogoff, 1991)

Josué became a sociology student at the national university; here he is a contributor at an international meeting. Psychologists Pablo Chavajay (a native Mayan of San Pedro, pictured later in this book when he was 12 years old) and Cathy Angelillo sit to his right. (Photo © Fernando García, 2007)

Linda gingerly attempted a question to Chona; it was ambiguous. It could mean "What did your parents do?" or "What were your parents like?"

Chona obliged with a brief reply: "My father harvested corn, and my mother wove and washed clothes, and cooked for us. She didn't hire anyone to cook for our fieldworkers." (Chona's mother's landholdings were large enough to need hired help.)

Josué prompted, "Was she a patient woman? Was she good, or hot-tempered?"

Chona responded,

She was good, very good. But my father, yes, he was hot tempered, very hot tempered . . . . He beat us with a belt and drank a lot.

He was a drunkard, sometimes drinking for 8 or 10 days running.

At the time we were in the Catholic religion, because when I grew up, the Evangelical [Protestant] religion didn't exist. I saw the beginning of the Evangelical religion here.

∷

ONE REASON that the Evangelical Protestant religion took hold in San Pedro, accounting for about 40% of the population even 30 years ago, was that Evangelicals were prohibited from drinking alcohol. In the Catholic religion of this region, drinking alcohol was part of the celebration of the saints and other religious occasions. Alcoholism has been a severe problem in Mayan Guatemala, as in many communities that have suffered conquest and continuing discrimination. I was told that many San Pedro wives led their husbands to Evangelism to "cure" alcoholism; however, some Protestants also suffer alcoholism.

In San Pedro, alcoholism still claims many men, and claims their earnings as well. Some have sold off their family landholdings to buy alcohol.[30] This is greatly criticized, as land is the primary form of inheritance, coming from ancestors many generations back and intended to be passed to one's children. In addition, landholdings have special meaning in Mayan understanding of how humans and the earth are intimately and spiritually connected.

Pedranos, and especially Pedranas, sometimes joke bitterly that every block has a bank where men deposit their money—a *cantina*. Many people thanked me for reducing the number of *cantinas* in town by one when I rented space for the library in a building that had been a *cantina*.

These boys are playing cantina. *The boy on the left is the bartender and the boy on the right is the customer, who pretends to have had a few drinks already. (Photo © Barbara Rogoff, 1975)*

⠶

I ASKED LINDA if she is an Evangelical like her mother. She replied,

Yes, now we are believers. It was all because of my brother Santos. He studied theology, and went with the Evangelicals. The rest of the family continued as Catholics until he graduated and became a pastor. Then my mother joined him and the rest followed too. [Pastor Santos recalls that this was in the mid-1960s.] I think it was sort of an obligation of the church for my mother to accompany my brother, changing her religion. In my case, I was small so I had to go along.

Linda had warmed up. When I asked her if she had known her mother's parents, Dolores and Marcos, she responded,

My grandmother had died, but yes, I knew my grandfather. I don't remember my grandfather very clearly, more like remembering a dream. But I remember that he would come by our house. He lived in San Juan with another woman he'd gotten together with after my grandmother died.

He would knock on the door when he was going on a trip by canoe to Santiago Atitlán and wake us up. "Get up, it's late already, it's already 6 and I'm going on a trip," he would say. So we would get up fast to greet him and kiss his hand. He wouldn't get back for three or four days, and he'd return really drunk. People would bring him to our house.

I also remember well that when my grandfather Marcos had money, he would go buy things at the San Pedro weekly market and I would go with him. He would come to the house to fetch me, and then he would buy those little dried fishes by the pound. My mother couldn't buy them by the pound, only by the ounce, because she didn't have that much money. I would always ask him to give me a little of it, "Oh, please give me a little," and he would say, "Yes, I'll give you some; yes, my little one, I'll give you some." And he would get some newspaper and wrap a handful of the little fishes in the newspaper to give me.

⁑

EVEN THOUGH her husband warned her that she would die early if she did not accept her calling, Dolores was so afraid to be an *iyoom* that she just replied, "If I die, I die." Dolores did die young, in her 50s, when Chona was 33 (about 1958).

Dolores' early death is widely regarded as a result of resisting her destiny. Chona's sister Susana reported, in a 1964 conversation with Lois Paul, that on her deathbed, Dolores called for a *palangana* (basin) and scissors—the tools of an *iyoom*. She was delirious by then, her life ending, but said she wanted to go out, to take on the role of *iyoom*.

Resisting a Risky Destiny

DOLORES HAD REFUSED her calling because she was afraid to touch blood and frightened to walk through dark roads and little alleyways at night when called to help the pregnant women in town. The rocky dirt roads and paths had only the stars and moon to light them, and most people feared the creatures and people of the night that could scare them stiff and trembling. Plus, women of good character did not go out in the night.

Dolores also feared being responsible for the lives of the mothers and infants who rely on an *iyoom* to conduct them through the perils of childbirth.[31] After all, mothers and babies often died in childbirth. This was routine in San Pedro, as expressed by Dolores' eldest daughter, Susana, who was married and pregnant at about age 18 when she worked with Lois Paul in 1941. Susana lamented the imminent departure of the Pauls at the end of their year of fieldwork: "Too bad that you won't be here when I will complete my pregnancy; you won't know whether I die or not."[32]

Even as late as 1995, maternal mortality for the state of Sololá, where San Pedro is located, was about double Guatemala's high national maternal mortality rate (Hurtado & Sáenz de Tejada, 2001). It was about eight times as high as the 1992 national average for Mexico (reported by the Secretary of Health; Sesia, 1997).[33]

An *iyoom* runs the risk of being blamed for unfortunate outcomes of a pregnancy, although many aspects are out of her control. Sometimes a baby is positioned sideways and dies during the birth process, and the *iyoom* can only hope to save the mother. Nonetheless, the blame can result in damaging gossip and legal charges against the *iyoom* in the town court.[34]

When Chona was already a renowned *iyoom*, during the course of one month three women who were Chona's patients died while giving birth. This was a source of both sorrow and worry for Chona. It was an unusual spate of deaths by then. So the town officials brought Chona into court to investigate, and they asked her and the women's families to testify. According to Chona and to the gossip that circulated at the time, the families assured the court that the deaths had not been Chona's fault and that they had great confidence in Chona's skill and treatment.

∷

IT IS NO WONDER that many women who are born to be an *iyoom* resist their destiny, especially given the risks of being responsible for others (see also Huber & Sandstrom, 2001). In the face of physical and supernatural dangers, an *iyoom* has to be decisive and ready to direct pregnant women and even to give orders to the elders and husbands who are present at delivery. Taking charge is an especially delicate issue in San Pedro, because there is a strong value of respecting the decision made by another person. People avoid forcing others to do things against their will even in medical situations. For example, rather than holding a child immobile for a medical procedure, family members may say, "She doesn't want to" (Mosier & Rogoff, 2003).[35]

An *iyoom* must also be willing to take on a role that sets her apart from others. Accepting the calling of *iyoom* exposes a woman to potential criticism and blame, especially in the first years of her practice, in this small town where malicious gossip of neighbors is feared and reputations endure for generations. Lois and Ben Paul explained resistance to becoming an *iyoom* in the context of how women lived in prior times (before 1975; women's lives are strikingly different now):

> Pedrano women are trained to keep their place, to remain in their own backyards, to shun the streets after dark except for attending church services in groups, to enter no homes except those of relatives, to assume few responsibilities outside the domestic sphere, and to refrain from interfering in the lives of others— except to criticize women who deviate from these norms. Social censure can be psychologically painful enough, but women who enjoy distinction or power or special privilege of any kind also expose themselves to *envidia* [powerful envy], which is believed to be physically dangerous, visiting death or disease upon the victim or on a more vulnerable member of the victim's family. (Paul & Paul, 1975, p. 715)

During the era when most households fetched their water from the lake or from a neighborhood tap, these places were ideal for women to catch up on events around town. With the introduction of household water supplies, these sites for community connections were removed. (Photo © Barbara Rogoff, 1975)

⁖

IN ADDITION, many husbands have not been eager for a wife to accept her destined role of *iyoom*. An *iyoom* must drop her family responsibilities at a moment's notice to attend to emergencies.

Furthermore, like other sacred practitioners, an *iyoom* must be spiritually pure, to protect the lives of her patients. This requires abstaining from sexual relations for several days before and after a birth—and an *iyoom* with a busy practice may have several deliveries per week (Paul & Paul, 1975). From the colonial period, Tz'utujil religious ceremonies have also required ritual purity, including sexual abstinence (Orellana, 1987).

Lois Paul's fieldnotes of 1974 indicate that if the *iyoom* has intercourse and then is called by a patient that night, the patient may have trouble delivering the baby. To avoid that, an *iyoom* who was called to deliver a patient after having intercourse with her husband would claim to be ill and instruct the family to call another *iyoom*.

A now-deceased *iyoom*, when she accepted her calling, was advised by an elder *iyoom* not to allow her husband to have sexual relations with her, to avoid harming her patients. When the new *iyoom* told her husband that they needed to sleep separately from then on, he told her that he had to have a woman. She said she didn't care what he did as long as he left her alone; he took up with another woman in a nearby town.

The husband of another *iyoom* is reputed to have died because he objected to his wife's practice and to her refusals to sleep with him. She attempted to get around his demands by sleeping at her patient's home for a few nights before delivery was expected.

A husband's manliness may be questioned by other men if his wife becomes an *iyoom*. Other men may also criticize a husband because his wife now brings in resources to the family when patients' families give her gifts of food or money in thanks for her services.

::

USUALLY, A woman born to be an *iyoom* refuses this destiny for a time, until grave illnesses befall her and her family members (Cosminsky, 1982; Paul & Paul, 1975). In dreams, and with the counsel of shamans, the woman and her husband learn that if she does not accept her destiny, sickness and even death are likely to result. These misfortunes may strike the woman or her husband, but often they would affect her children, as misfortune often falls on weaker members of a family.

Some women or their husbands still refuse. One husband, on being reminded that refusing to let his wife accept her destined profession would doom her, retorted, "Well, then, if she dies I'll pay the expenses of her funeral" (Paul, 1975, p. 452).

A funeral procession, carrying a woman's coffin to the cemetery.
(Photo © Barbara Rogoff, 1975)

Accepting Spiritual Persuasion and Instruction

OFTEN, HOWEVER, serious illness or premature death of family members provides the transition point to acceptance of a woman's birth destiny. The spirits of ancestor *iyooma'* aid in the acceptance of the woman's calling. Radiant in white robes, they visit the *iyoom*-to-be (and her husband) in dreams. They explain that the source of her family's illness is refusal of her destiny, and scold her or her husband for not accepting her divine calling.

In the woman's dreams, ancestor *iyooma'* also reveal the signs of pregnancy and skills of delivery, such as how to turn a fetus that is not in the correct position for delivery and how to remove a placenta that does not emerge by itself (see also Elmendorf, 1976). They teach the *iyoom*-to-be how to carry out important prayers and rituals, and reassure her that they will always be with her if she accepts her destined role.

These aspects of the process involved in accepting a divine calling are typical of a classic pattern for sacred practitioners in San Pedro, whether born to be an *iyoom* or a shaman (Paul & Paul, 1975). The Pauls recounted the development of an *iyoom* of the generation prior to Chona, whom they referred to by the pseudonym "Rosa:"

> She recalled that she was often ill and repeatedly had enigmatic dreams as a child. . . . [In her adulthood, 4 of her 12 children died young.] In 1938, at the age of forty she experienced a particularly severe and intractable illness; she was scarcely able to eat or sleep. During the illness, Rosa was visited by the spirits of dead midwives who threatened that she and her remaining children would die if she refused to help her "sisters" in childbirth. She pleaded fear and inexperience, but the spirits assured her they would teach her everything and would always be at her side during troublesome deliveries. Rosa's family finally consulted a shaman whose divination confirmed that she was indeed destined by birth to be a midwife. He warned that she must practice or perish. At that point, her mother disclosed that Rosa had indeed been born with the midwife's mantle and as proof dramatically produced the dried patch of membrane [the veil] secretly preserved since Rosa's birth.
>
> Rosa's husband balked at the idea of having his wife become a midwife. He feared that other men would question his manliness and hold him unable to support a wife, forcing her to eke out their income by going into the streets rather than running the house and weaving his clothes. Eventually these objections were overridden by the shaman's repeated warning that her illness would worsen and by the continued visits of tutelary spirits in Rosa's dreams. One day Rosa encountered a strange object in her path—a conch shell. She was afraid to touch it. That night spirits of dead midwives came to her again, rebuking her for rejecting the magic shell and directing her to go back and pick it up. The shell was her "power" (Sp., *virtud*), the spirits said. They told her to wrap it in a kerchief and keep it locked in a safe place. Another day she similarly "found" a penknife with a fish and child carved on its handle. This time she knew to pick it up. She had the shaman divine the meaning of the curious objects. He confirmed what she had been told in her dreams, that the shell was her *virtud*, and the knife the special tool of her calling used to cut the umbilical cord.

The shaman burned candles for her before the image of Santa Ana in the church and before hillside crosses at night, asking the saints and spiritual guardians of childbirth to assist and protect her.

The shaman began telling people that Rosa was a genuine midwife, and Rosa herself "found the words" to confide to a pregnant neighbor what the shaman had divined. The spirits now revisited Rosa to fulfill their promise. "The spirits instructed me how to feel for the position of the fetus, how to massage the pregnant woman, how to know when she was ready to deliver, how to cut the cord and to foretell the future children by its markings. The spirits taught me all the prayers." (Paul & Paul, 1975, pp. 710–711)

In Chona's case, her parents were eager for her to develop with the courage to carry out the destiny that her birthsign foretold. Although her mother was afraid to accept her own destiny to be an *iyoom*, she was happy that Chona had the destiny to be an *iyoom*.

Chona's life followed the classic cultural pattern described by Lois and Ben Paul for recruitment to this powerful and risky role as well as for recruitment to other sacred roles, such as shaman, in San Pedro:

birth signs, premonitory dreams, delicate health, a long illness leading to revelation by a shaman of her true destiny, show of reluctance, discovery of magic objects, dream instruction, an opportune case that demonstrates her competence, the growth of a clientele. (1975, p. 711)[36]

6 ⁚⁚

Childhood
and Where Babies Come From

CHONA'S PARENTS did not tell her about her birth destiny when she was a child. However, the *iyoom* who delivered Chona told her about her future role, in a way:

> I always went to visit the woman who delivered me, Doña Josefa Yojcom,[37] who was my father's aunt—the younger sister of his mother (Concepción Yojcom). When I was about 5 or 6 years old, she told me, "You, dear child, if you live to grow up, you will do like I do, going from house to house like I do now. That's what you will do."
>
> Only she didn't call me "dear child," but said *"atk'aamanak dyoos,"* like they did in those days.

That last phrase means "you emanate from God," and was used in the old days to show approval to a well-behaved child. Obvious praise was avoided, to keep from calling forth the evil eye on the child. In former times (and rarely now), the older people also addressed children affectionately as "my eyebrow" and "my hunk of dirt," apparently to avoid drawing the evil eye to a beloved or attractive child.

Evil eye is regarded as dangerous contact suffered by delicate people (such as babies or small children) or possessions (such as crops or domestic animals) from people who could harm them through envy of their attractiveness, or through bad intentions, "hot" states such as pregnancy or exertion, or calling the attention of dangerous spirits to their attractiveness and vulnerability.[38]

Chona told me she replied "OK" to Doña Josefa's statement that she would go house to house if she lived to grow up, like the *iyoom* herself. But Chona added, "But I wasn't thinking that what she was talking about was delivering babies; I didn't know about that." Later, when Chona was about 12, the woman who had washed her veil when Chona was born told her that she would have the work of an *iyoom*, without explaining what the work was.

Taboo Topics for Children and Youth

IN THOSE DAYS, children were not supposed to know that mothers give birth to babies, and they were not supposed to listen in on adult conversations that might have revealed the "facts of life." People of Chona's generation report that children were more respectful of their elders than currently, and if a mother was chatting with another adult and told them to go out, the children would go out and play. (However, I observed in the 1970s that children who did not call attention to themselves were often overlooked as eavesdroppers. For example, when a friend told me in secret of his marital difficulties, and asked me to tell no one, he paid no attention to the quiet and alert presence nearby of a 10-year-old neighbor boy.)

Generally, San Pedro children were sent to a relative's or a neighbor's house when a birth was occurring in their house. Lois Paul recalled,

> One evening in 1941 we had an unaccustomed visitor, the
> 7-year-old daughter of our next-door neighbor. The next morning
> she arrived to announce the big news; her mother had "bought" a
> baby the previous evening from an *extranjero* [foreigner].
> (Paul, 1969, p. 20)

The visitor, Graciela Cotuc, appears on the right in this photo, carrying a jug of water. (Photo by Lois and Ben Paul, 1941)

Where do babies come from?

WHEN SAN PEDRO CHILDREN were curious about where babies come from, adults would tell them that they buy babies from foreigners or Ladinos. The expression "buying" a baby to refer to giving birth is not just a way to fool the children; it is an ordinary figurative expression used among adults even when children are not present. They ask, "Who bought the baby?" to inquire who delivered the baby. When Lois Paul visited a mother with a newborn, "the midwife and other women continuously asked me why I don't buy a baby here and let [this midwife] buy it for me" (Paul, 1969, p. 30).

If the pregnancy was prolonged or if the mother and baby died in childbirth, Pedranos used to say, "She couldn't count her money, so she couldn't buy a baby." This practice appears in the 1973 fieldnotes of a missionary couple, Judy and Jim Butler, who had worked in San Pedro for many years:

> When the children ask their parents where babies come from they don't tell them. But what they do say to the children is: "They are

bought from the Ladinos." Everybody, whether Catholic or Protestant, says this. Now regarding the babies that die at birth the children will ask (since they don't know why a little baby would die), "How come our little baby died?" "The Ladinos killed it because we didn't have enough money," they are told. And when a woman dies in childbirth and they ask "Why did she die when she was all right yesterday?" they are told "The Ladinos killed her because she wasn't able to buy the baby. There wasn't enough money." It is the custom not to ever tell the children. (Note dated 1973, Summer Institute of Linguistics, 1978, Book 1, p. 20)

Sometimes when children ask their parents to buy something for them, the parents say "No, we don't have money." The children may respond, "Then how come we keep buying babies?"

After planes began flying overhead, the adults also told the children that airplanes bring the babies. The children would ask where the planes land, but didn't appear to figure out that this was just a story.

My colleague Marta Navichoc told of a 6-year-old, in about 1990, who wanted a baby sibling: "Mama, why don't we buy a baby?" The mother told her that airplanes bring babies. "But Mama, I call out to them but they never leave one." The mother replied, "Well, how would they drop one on the bare ground? They would need to drop it on something soft." One day when the mother was away, the child struggled to put the family's mattress out on the flat terrazzo rooftop. When the mother returned, the child was crying and the bed was in disarray. The mother said, "Where is our mattress?" and the child tearfully reported, "I put it out, but the planes haven't dropped a baby!"

Avoiding reference to pregnancy and birth with children

PREGNANCY has been an off-limits topic for children. When Marta was 13 years old, about 35 years ago, she didn't know that her older sister was pregnant. Her mother sent Marta to take special foods like green mango, fruits, and greens to her sister. (Probably the sister had food cravings.) Marta asked her mother, "Why did she marry if they don't feed her over there?" Her mother slapped her across the mouth, so Marta didn't say anything more.

Similarly, a man Marta's age reported that when he was about 12 he mentioned that a woman was going to have a baby; his grandmother slapped his mouth because children weren't supposed to talk about such things. Children were supposed to be more reserved than children are now. Now people speak openly about having babies in front of children, not in whispers. Children rub their mother's belly and ask questions. Some families no longer refer to buying babies but to giving birth.

When Marta was a child, her mother would send her out of the house when a visitor came; she gave Marta and the other children a subtle sign to go out so they would not be able to listen. Now children enter into conversation as they please, and many parents don't mind, but before, it was considered disrespectful for children to enter freely into adult conversations.

The fact that babies get born from their mothers is talked about increasingly openly and children find out. When Marta was 7 months pregnant, about two decades ago, her 6-year-old daughter's teacher told the class that some animals' babies come from the mother and other animals lay eggs. Marta's daughter asked, "So do we come from the mother? Because our mothers don't lay eggs." The teacher turned red with embarrassment but answered the girl. When the girl got home, she told her parents what she learned in school, like she ordinarily did each day. Her parents blushed, and Marta froze and couldn't say anything. But the father explained to the girl that people come from their mothers, and informed her that Marta was going to have a baby.

Still, the fact that babies come from their mothers is treated delicately. The father told Marta's daughter not to say anything about this to people, because it's a sin to talk about it. The girl was surprised but agreed that now she knew not to talk.

Adults dislike that some children joke about where babies come from or speak vulgarly in the street. It has become appropriate to congratulate a pregnant woman, but some children make fun of a pregnant woman's shape or how she got that way. This is considered a serious lack of respect and decorum.

Avoiding reference to pregnancy and birth with young adults

WHEN CHONA WAS GROWING UP, even young women were supposed to be kept in the dark about pregnancy until they were having their first baby.[39] Adults did not call attention to pregnancy; a pregnancy was spoken of in whispers among those who were already parents. One of the virtues of San Pedro women's use of a 7-yard length of cloth as a wraparound skirt is that its girth can be adjusted easily, and its thickness masks the shape underneath.

However, it seems likely, based on accounts in Lois Paul's field-notes, that young women took some notice of their mothers' and neighbors' changing shapes, even though much of the information about birth was missing or subject to the kind of misinformation that arises from speculation. In any case, girls were expected to deny having any knowledge of pregnancy until told about it when they were giving birth. (By the 1970s when I was first in San Pedro, girls who went to school learned about pregnancy in their fifth- or sixth-grade biology class, and those who didn't go to school heard about it "through the grapevine.")

The local way of referring to pregnancy makes use of the Mayan word for "sick," which some Pedranos explain was a way to keep children from knowing about pregnancy. When Chona was young, a woman pregnant with her first baby (usually about the age of 16 or 17) would be told by her mother or mother-in-law that she was "sick already" and that the *iyoom* would come and cure her. Only during labor would the young woman be told that she was going to have a baby. Lois Paul wrote,

> Strange as it may seem, primiparas frequently did not know they
> were pregnant until the very day of the delivery. . . . Older women,
> familiar with the slightest sign of pregnancy, watch the young for
> these signs. When the girl admitted that she was not menstruating,
> the mother-in-law would tell her not to worry, that she would call
> in the midwife who would "cure her and bring back her period."
> It was not uncommon for a young primipara to fear that she would
> "swell up and die" because her period had stopped. [This harks
> back to a warning sometimes given to girls when they began to
> menstruate, that if their "monthly" stopped, they would swell up
> and die.] But mothers and mothers-in-law could not overcome
> their own *vergüenza* (shame) nor did they wish to frighten the
> young girl [so they did not tell her what was happening].
> (Paul, 1969, p. 17)

During prenatal visits, the *iyoom* would reassure the first-time mother-to-be that she will "cure" her with abdominal massages. At about 5 months of pregnancy, when the girl felt movement in her abdomen "like a mouse," says Chona, she was told, "Yes, it's always like that. Your menstruation will return; don't be afraid."

The mother and mother-in-law, in addition to being too embarrassed to tell the girl about pregnancy, were also afraid that the girl would be too frightened to cooperate during the birth. Sometimes in the old days, the *iyooma'* did not tell the young woman in labor about the baby, but just told her to push. In such cases, not until the birth did the young woman know about the baby.

One way that Chona contributed to a cultural change in San Pedro was in how the process of pregnancy was communicated to first-time mothers. She departed from the custom of prior generations of Pedranas and the older *iyooma'* by informing first-time mothers what was happening to them while they were pregnant. She reassured them about the process, advising them how to take care of themselves. Lois Paul reported that this change occurred in the 1960s:

> While mothers were still unable to talk to daughters about
> menstruation or pregnancy, expanded educational curriculum in
> the local school plus a higher percentage of girls attending school
> and for a longer period of time, helped set the stage for Chona's
> new methods. With primipara patients Chona substituted
> information and reassurance for the old dependence on a
> conspiracy of ignorance. (Paul, 1969, p. 49)

A father's autobiographical account regarding a birth in about the 1950s gives a flavor of the birth experience without knowledge about the birth process. It also shows the scoldings and urging to push that formerly were common during the birth.

> Just before our first baby was born, I was very scared for my wife
> who was pregnant, since neither of us knew what happened when
> a baby was born. . . . Nothing was said to me—only just that the
> baby would soon be born. . . .
>
> [One] day the midwife must have come about three times but
> I didn't know what she had come for. . . . That night my wife got
> worse, and I really felt sorry for her, and I was getting more scared
> all the time . . . since I didn't know how a baby was born.
>
> Just a little before two o'clock in the morning, my wife had
> severe pains, and my mother-in-law said to my father-in-law,
> "You'd better go and get the midwife again." So I went with him
> to get her. But oh! It was cold. When we got back I didn't go into
> the house. I just went into the kitchen. I was scared because I heard
> the midwife say, "The time has come. Get everything ready that
> we'll need." . . .
>
> [The midwife called] "Come in, my young man. Now you'll
> see what happens during delivery. Now hold your wife and help

her a bit," she told me. But I was shaking from head to foot from fear. Then I sat down on a little chair and held my wife, and she began to deliver the child. [The midwife urged,] "Now, my dear, give it all you have. You are strong and healthy, push hard. Don't be afraid. I tell you that you are about to give birth to your child."

So my wife began to do as the midwife told her. But finally, she collapsed. She had no strength left and I was really trembling. "You'd better get rid of that boy. He's no good. He's scared stiff. Maybe there's one of you who wants to hold this girl here," she said. . . .

But my wife was tired. She didn't have any more strength left. The midwife really scolded her. "Now girl, why can't you deliver a baby? Aren't you ashamed of yourself? You have a little baby here. Aren't you longing to have your little child by the time it's light? If you had married a rough character he wouldn't mind if he took a poke at you in the face. But you're just soft. You're not used to having to take it. Understand this, if you continue on like this, you will kill your child." I saw there was lots of blood on the midwife's hand.

[Finally about 5:30, after more scolding and exhaustion, the baby was born. The midwife said] "Come and see! The baby here is dead. The mother caused it just like I told you. Quickly put a *machete* (a long-bladed knife) to heat in the fire. But fast! Maybe it will revive." So then my father-in-law quickly put a *machete* in the fire that was burning there.

I saw that the little baby down there was lying face up. It was like a little doll. It was really true. It didn't move. And there was so much blood all over it. You could hardly tell it was a little human being. Then I began to cry and think in my heart. "So that's what happens when we are born! How can we live through it?" . . .

Then they told the midwife that the *machete* was red hot. "Bring it here quickly. It's late and time is passing quickly for the child," she said. Then she took the *machete* and put it onto the long umbilical cord of the baby. "Aw, it's really dead. I told the mother to push hard. Now I'm not at fault. Maybe you will blame me for this child's death, but you all saw how I was concerned for your child. Nothing can be done for the child now." (Summer Institute of Linguistics, 1978, Book 26, pp. 73, 78–89)

Menstruation

CHONA SAYS THAT GIRLS in her time also did not know about menstruation before it happened to them. They often were frightened when they began to menstruate because they had no idea what was happening to them. When Chona had her first period, she felt blood on her legs, so she sat down on the dirt floor by the cooking fire and was afraid to get up.

> I told my mother, "Mama, I don't know what happened to me, I have a lot of blood." My mother took me to an old woman and told her, "Please counsel my daughter, because blood is coming out on her legs." So the old woman told me, "Now that you have menstruation, you must work, stay at home and don't go out, because if you go out it will not be good for you." We went home and I stayed home for 3 days.
>
> When I felt that I wasn't bleeding anymore, I told my mother, "Now I'm not bleeding, so I can go out." My mother said, "When your menstruation comes, don't go out of the house. And be careful not to be near a boy, and don't let a boy kiss or hug you, because he could leave you with a baby; an airplane will come and leave you a baby." I told my mother, "No, I don't talk with boys." That was the custom before—no young woman could be talking in the darkness with young men at 6 at night. At that hour, they closed us up in our houses and lit the candles.

Mayan mothers of Chan Kom, Mexico, similarly reported in the early 1970s that it was considered a sin to inform girls of menstruation before they had menstruated. Neither these women nor their own mothers had informed their daughters about this process. One mother reported, "Before Rosita's [her daughter's] first period she was talking about it with her cousins and asked me if it wasn't so, and I said no, it's not so, because it hadn't happened to her yet" (Elmendorf, 1976, p. 65).[40]

Sexual intercourse

WHEN CHONA WAS YOUNG, information about sexual relations was also off-limits to children and to young women before they were married. Young men began to hear about such things from each other before they married, but young women were often shocked at what their new husband suggested to them. Although they sometimes had some preview of what happens, from their friends who married early and from viewing dogs or other animals (although they were not supposed to watch them), young women were often ignorant about sexual relations.

A woman recalled her anger about her new husband's actions, when they first were married, when she was in her teens, about 1920:

I was very angry. I didn't like what he did to me. It was repulsive to me. And it scared me when he did that to me. "Why are you doing this? I'm going to tell my parents," I exclaimed.

"That would be a bad thing to do. It would be shameful. And besides that's what they did long ago," he said to me.

"Now why did he do that to me? If I had known that he would do that I wouldn't have gotten married," I thought to myself. . . .

[When I refused to call him to breakfast the next morning, my mother said,] "What's the matter? I told you not to get married. You were innocent of what happens in marriage, my dear. But men are men. That's your problem now."

[A few days later] I remarked to my mother, "That was cruel of you not to tell me. It would be different if I weren't your daughter . . ."

When I said that she just laughed at me. "You have to suffer a bit when you get married. You're just ignorant of sexual matters, girl." . . .

But I was repulsed and didn't like him any more nor did I even want to talk to him. Finally I didn't give him his meals any more. . . . And then my grandmother and mother both scolded me. "Who told you to get married? Did we order you to? Is that why it's up to us to look after him? Aren't you sorry for the poor boy that you treat him like that?"

"Even though you keep on nagging at me or even severely punish me, I haven't the slightest desire for him any more. You can talk like that because you aren't getting the treatment I am," I responded.

Then my mother tenderly gave me some advice . . . "Even if you had married another boy, he would have still treated you like that. Whether you like it or not, men always do that when you get married." So in time I slowly got over it. (Summer Institute of Linguistics, 1978, Book 37, pp. 14–18)

Another woman told me that she had thought her husband was a beast to suggest such things on her wedding night. She was about 15 and he was about 20 when they eloped. (These were the usual ages in the early 1940s.) She refused him for many nights, and cried about having run off to marry such a person. He tried to reassure her, "Everyone does it. Your mother and father, your aunts and uncles . . . Even the *gringos* do it!" After several days, while she was washing clothes at the lakeshore with friends who had also married, she learned that their husbands were also asking for this "abominable" act. Then she realized he was telling the truth, and, she reported with a chuckle and a twinkle of the eye in middle age, "I learned to like it . . ."

⠼

CHILDREN are reputed not to hear their parents having sexual relations, despite their proximity while sleeping in the same room. As of 1976, when I interviewed 60 families about where their 9-year-olds slept, almost all the families had one shared sleeping room where the whole family slept. (This was also their living space during the daytime. In addition, the families generally had a small lean-to kitchen.)

When I asked about how the parents managed their sexual relations, the parents claimed that the children slept and did not hear. They also claimed that they themselves had not heard their parents when they were children. I was skeptical of this, but I noticed that when I accompanied my then-husband on medical emergency visits in the middle of the night, it was not uncommon to find children asleep in the room where adults had congregated to aid a sick person, with candles lit and worried conversation going on. Probably, the children are often asleep. Probably they are also not always asleep, but are pretending to be.

This painting shows two small children asleep by the head of the bed in which their mother is giving birth, attended by an iyoom *and the pregnant woman's mother, mother-in-law, and sleepy husband. (The bird's-eye-view perspective in this painting was an innovation by this San Pedro Mayan artist, Juan Fermin González, and has become a widespread device in San Pedro's very successful painting tradition. Reproduction of this 1999 painting "El Parto" courtesy of Joseph Johnston, Arte Maya Tz'utuhil.)*

In a Mayan town in Mexico (Chan Kom), a researcher thought it impossible for children not to learn about sex, given the shared sleeping space. The researcher, Elmendorf, asked a mother, Anita, whether she and her husband had intercourse elsewhere or in the same room where they slept with the children, including their adolescent daughter Rosita:

Anita: We sleep here with the children.
Elmendorf: And they don't know what you're doing?
Anita: Never. When they go to sleep, they go to sleep. (She
            laughs.) They never know.

Elmendorf:	Not even Rosita?
Anita:	Not even Rosita.
Elmendorf:	And you haven't spoken to her about this?
Anita:	No.
Elmendorf:	Shouldn't you?
Anita:	No—it's a sin.
Elmendorf:	Won't she be surprised by a man sometime? . . . and she won't know what's happening. Or when she marries?
Anita:	(Laughs.) Well, when you marry it is very surprising because you don't know.
Elmendorf:	But perhaps the children would have learned from the animals. You live very closely with them.
Anita:	I don't think they pay any attention to it. They don't understand. (Elmendorf, 1976, pp. 66–67; see also LeVine, 1993)

Since I've been going to San Pedro in the mid-1970s, children in middle childhood know where babies come from; this was at first attributed to biology classes in fifth or sixth grade. And since then, of course television provides many sorts of information, and the children talk about such things in the street. One reason that the parents don't like to tell the children about pregnancy and how it may occur is that some children are rude and joke in the street about what they are told at home about serious matters.

Chona learned about sexual intercourse when she was about 13, when she had a dream in which a couple was making love, the man on top of the woman. A white-haired old woman in the dream told her, "This is what it is like when you get married. It's no good. Better not to get married; stay single."

Chona Grows Into Her Role

AS A CHILD, Chona began to have dreams that foreshadowed her future work, even though she did not understand them at the time. In one dream when Chona was a young child, she saw herself delivering a baby born to a woman wearing the distinctive clothes worn by Mayan women from the town of Santa Catarina, across Lake Atitlán. The dream was so detailed that it seemed real to her.

In the dream, Chona did all that an *iyoom* does, receiving the baby inside the kind of sweathouse that Mayan people used for bathing and for health treatments in the old days. A woman in a glowing long white robe showed her how to receive the baby in a white cloth, as it emerged, bloody, from the womb.

Chona thought that what she saw in the dream was bizarre. In the morning, she told her cousins everything she had seen in her dream. As they played together in the family courtyard, making a pretend meal of leaf tortillas on clay toy dishes, Chona regaled her chums with all the details of the birth process.

Children making a pretend meal in their courtyard. (Photo © Barbara Rogoff, 1975)

A neighbor who was weaving nearby was also listening—in those days it was common for neighbors to watch over each others' children and inform parents of their children's behavior. She was aghast that Chona was speaking of these things, since a little girl should not know where babies come from.

The neighbor sternly informed Chona's mother about what Chona had been saying to the other little girls. Chona's mother scolded her, pulling her ear to make sure she knew how dangerous it was to talk about her dream. Her mother said, "You mustn't talk about such things, because if you do, you could die." Chona had this dream five or six times during her childhood.

Chona's mother speaking with some children. (Photo by Lois and Ben Paul, 1941)

In another childhood dream, Chona saw 50 or 100 little children about 3 to 6 years old coming in a procession toward her, dressed in daz-zling white robes. They were all kinds of children—dark ones, blond ones, curly-haired ones. In the dream, the children were with a man dressed in a brilliant white robe and a lady dressed in a Mayan *corte* (wraparound skirtcloth). The man didn't say anything, but the woman told Chona that Chona would be responsible for all those children.

When Chona was about 11 years old, she had a dream in which the image of Jesus, the Sagrado Corazón de Jesús, spoke directly to her. As Chona lay cuddled on a mat on a low plank bed perched on rocks, shar-ing a wool blanket with her sister Susana, she dreamed that Sagrado Corazón de Jesús assured her, "Be calm, because I am with you." She says that His words gave her the confidence to do her work as her calling emerged.

An image of Sagrado Corazón de Jesús is at the left on this Catholic family's home altar, in back of the radio and batteries. (Photo © Barbara Rogoff, 1976; the little girl is now a teacher.)

❖

CHONA WOULD also daydream occasionally, sitting in the doorway of her house staring into space while embroidering her father's traditional hand-woven pants (Paul, 1975). Although children were usually discouraged from daydreaming, this was allowed and even expected of Chona, as a child of destiny, to show such signs of mystical inclinations.

When she was still young, Chona also came across tools for her work. This is an expected part of the preparation of a sacred professional—children with a special birth destiny find important tools for their future profession mysteriously placed in their path. Once, when Chona was delivering a clay pot full of black beans and a stack of tortillas to a neighbor, she saw a knife blade glittering at her as it lay in the road. It was shiny, shimmering like pure silver, with no handle. She thought it was a toy and picked it up and took it home, not knowing what she would use it for until years later.

❖

AS IS EXPECTED for a person destined for a sacred calling, Chona endured grave illness. When she was about 14 she became partly paralyzed for 3 months, unable to move. She lay ill in bed and didn't talk for 20 days. Her affliction worried everyone, and her family sought a cure from all possible sources. They used medicines made from plants, prayers in churches, and shamans' prayers at shrines on the sides of Volcano San Pedro, above town.

A renowned shaman, Domingo Chavajay, conducting a ceremony at a cave altar in the hills, praying with pine incense and candles. Praying in caves has been a Guatemalan Mayan practice since before the Spanish arrived, to access the spirit world of ancestors and deities of nature (Christenson, 2001). The use of pine incense is likewise an ancient practice; its rising smoke represented the clouds that bring rain (LaFarge, 1947). (Photo by Lois and Ben Paul, 1941)

Chona's father, as a shaman, told her, "You aren't going to die, Chona, my daughter. This is just a test that God is giving you. When you recover, you will do the work of *iyoom*, helping the pregnant women of our town."

He healed her with prayers and with 13 kinds of medicinal plants that he collected from the forests on the flanks of San Pedro's volcano. (The number 13 has sacred meaning in the Mayan calendar and cosmology.) The 13 medicinal herbs were boiled up, and then put on a cloth to bathe her with. She was then given a glass of the liquid to drink.

While Chona was sick, her father prayed in the Catholic churches of San Pedro and nearby San Juan, and at the hillside altars hidden in the surrounding forests. Cloaked by darkness in the deep of the night, he carried Chona, nestled in front of him on his horse. They went to shrines in the hills where they visited the ancient altars that honor the lords of nature. While she was especially weak, Chona would lay bundled in a shawl, curled on her side on a burlap bag at the foot of the stone or wooden cross.

A red cloth tied around Chona's head protected her against the cold air. When she felt better, she kneeled beside her father, arms crossed, while her father prayed to the traditional custodians of all the heavens and earth.

First he kissed the four tall white candles that he had brought along, to bless them. Then he lit the candles and burned incense.

As the smoke from the candles and pine incense surrounded them, he prayed to *Siiwaan Tinaamit*, the people of nature—all the animals, the trees, the rocks, the wind and rains. He prayed to the ancestors, "Our fathers, our mothers," and to Santa Ana and the other saints. He asked them all to pardon Chona and her relatives for anything bad they had done. Marcos promised them that Chona would accept her work of *iyoom* with a good heart. Half-heartedly accepting this calling could also be fatal.

And so Chona recovered, a young woman destined for sacred work.

7 ⚏

A Becoming Young Woman

CHONA WAS RENOWNED for her beauty, with curly hair and green eyes like her mother. Her modest bearing, gentle demeanor, self-assurance, and compassion endeared her to those around her. Chona developed a nice rounded-out figure early. As a girl of about 10, she appeared to be about 15 years old.

Chona recounts that in her early teens, she was chosen several times to compete as queen in the capital of the state of Sololá. Twice she was selected as queen in the state competition, to represent the state in the capital of Guatemala.

As an old woman, Chona reported that she had not particularly sought such distinction, but each time, the town officials would ask her to serve. After several times, her father refused to allow her to take part—but the town officials threw him in the jailroom overnight. In the morning they asked him to reconsider or to stay in jail; he agreed that Chona could take part.

⚏

AT THE DINNER TABLE of a friend one evening, Chona regaled family and friends with tales of her youth and her experiences as beauty queen. Her grandchildren leaned forward, elbows on the flowered plastic table-cloth. The girls' brows knit as Chona described walking barefoot (as was Pedrana women's custom) to reach the nearest road, to be transported to Guatemala City for the grand national fair. At that time, there were no roads connecting San Pedro with other towns, just steep rocky footpaths and canoe voyages. Chona and the state officials took a canoe across the lake, and then walked about 6 hours up a steep road from Lake Atitlán to the capital of the state. Then a truck met them and took them the rest of the way to Guatemala City.

Chona won first place among all the queens at the fair, who were both Mayan and Ladina girls. The president of Guatemala, General Jorge Ubico—famous for abuses of the Mayans—gave Chona a grand prize of 80 quetzales, an enormous amount in those days. The president danced with her, and she was treated to an airplane ride over the city.

Chona recalled that at the national fair, she saw a display of "wild" Lacandon Indians in a cage. When she described this scene, her grandson Josué, then a student of sociology at the university, gave me a significant glance. Chona commented pensively that the keepers just threw the Lacandones raw meat to eat, although "they were obviously people, with all the features of people." The Lacandones did not speak; they just looked down as the festive crowds ogled them. Chona's sympathy for the Lacandones is ironic—she and the other barefoot Mayan queens were probably themselves an exhibit at the fair.[41]

"The five southern Lacandones who were exhibited at the Guatemalan National Fair, November 1938. (Paul Royer)" (Photo and caption from Perera & Bruce, 1982, p. 51) [In 1938, Chona was 13 years old.]

An Unsuitable Suitor

CHONA'S ACCOUNT of the Lacandon Indians is doubly ironic, in that the organizer of the Lacandon exhibit at the 1938 Fair, Mario Monteforte Toledo, was one of Chona's suitors soon after. Chona mentioned his name and later her grandson Josué told me of the prominence of this suitor.

He became widely regarded as Guatemala's second most prominent author, by non-Mayan Guatemalans. He was awarded the Guatemala National Prize in Literature for his writings (Wikipedia, 2007).

Mario Monteforte Toledo, a few years before he lived in San Pedro.
(Photo: Fundación Mario Monteforte Toledo, http://www.montefortetoledo.org/)

Monteforte Toledo was a Guatemalan Ladino who had extensive experience in several Mayan communities. For a time, he lived in San Pedro, working as a notary. After courting Chona, who was not interested in him because he spoke to her in Spanish that she did not understand, he married a San Pedro woman with whom he had a daughter, Morena.

I made the connection with the Lacandon exhibit when I looked up Monteforte Toledo on the Internet and found the photo of the Lacandones.

As a younger man, he had traveled to the remote rain forest where the Lacandon Mayans were seldom seen by others. He wrote a novel about them in 1938–39, examining the dichotomy of civilization versus barbarism. He described the Lacandons ambivalently, with positive comments on many aspects of their lives while at the same time portraying them as savages and animal-like (Sitler, 1994). His attitude can be seen in his involvement in bringing the Lacandones to the national fair:

> After his initial contact with the Lacandons, Monteforte was so impressed by them, that he took five of them from their forest home to Guatemala City in 1938. His bold action suggests the degree of his fascination with this relatively isolated group of Maya. Whether the Lacandons went with the author to the city entirely voluntarily or not is not clear. What is known is that they were exhibited like animals at the Feria de Noviembre in Guatemala City in an enclosure surrounded by barb wire fencing and that one of them died as a result of the trauma before the others were returned to the forest. The author obviously greatly admired something about the Lacandon but the Ladino sense of cultural superiority may have led him to inadvertently harm those he admired. More recently, when asked about the details of these events, Monteforte is said to have responded somewhat defensively, "What is the basis of your interest in these pathetic primitives?" [Perera 282] (Sitler, 1994, pp. 123–124)

In 1979, as a "dapper, still-slender cavalier" in his 70s, Monteforte Toledo recounted that when the Lacandones visited the zoo, "they were allowed to enter the spider-monkey cages and 'play with their kin'" (Perera & Bruce, 1982, p. 281).

Monteforte Toledo's well-known novel *Entre La Piedra y La Cruz* (1948), set in San Pedro, also portrays Mayan life with ambivalence. It seems to portray Mayan life as inferior, since its protagonist is a fictional Pedrano man who eventually abandons Mayan ways and becomes Ladino. However, the book also showed admiration for some aspects of Mayan culture and protested the abuses of the Mayans by the government, foreigners, and the military (Sitler, 1994). For example, Monteforte Toledo described the horrors of the forced labor on dangerous lowland plantations and the forced conscription into the military that were inflicted on many Pedranos and Mayan people throughout Guatemala in those years: *"Los blancos defendían sus instituciones con los indios"*

(1948, p. 38). (My translation: "The Whites defended their institutions with the Indians.")

This book based on San Pedro was published while Monteforte Toledo was Vice President of Guatemala as well as leader of the National Congress, in the leftist democratic government. (He had also had served as ambassador to the United Nations; Wikipedia, 2007.)[42]

In those leadership positions, Monteforte Toledo's plan for Guatemala to become a modern nation was to bring the Mayan majority into the world of the Ladino minority (Sitler, 1994)—that is, for the Mayans to abandon their practices and become Ladino. This stance reveals a negative attitude toward Mayan life and practices, and has long been the policy in Guatemala (and also in Mexico; Bonfil Batalla, 1996; Smith, 1990). Monteforte Toledo portrayed Mayan traditional ways as an impediment to "progress."

Courtship

MONTEFORTE TOLEDO was far from alone in his interest in Chona during her teen years. Chona's many Mayan suitors courted her by the local custom, in the late afternoon after their return from work in the fields, as she gracefully carried her full water jug from the lake up the steep and rocky volcanic path to town.

The suitors would wait in the bushes beside the path to jump out, catch hold of her wrist, and tell her that they loved her. They promised to buy her fine clothes and told her that their parents were kind and would treat her well when she moved into their home, if she would assent to marry. As she stood balancing the heavy clay jug on her head, a suitor typically gave a practiced speech such as this:

> I come to court you. I love you. Let us be married. You are grown up now. It is time for you to take a husband. I will buy clothes for you; I will purchase earrings and bright shawls. My mother is a kind woman; she will not be cross with you. My father is a good man; he is not severe. We have enough corn; we have enough beans. My mother will give you whatever you need; you will get everything. Why not get married? All women get married. I am a good man; I will not get drunk and beat you. I will come with my parents to your house, and they will speak to your parents. Or if you wish, we can elope. My family will receive you well. They will

not scold you. I will buy you skirts and blouses. (Paul, 1950, pp. 483–484; see also Batz, 1991).

Chona laughs when she talks about this now that she is an old woman. She says there were so many suitors—dozens—that it took hours to get home from the lakeshore with the family's water supply. In 2006, she recalled:

> There were 48 boys who were my suitors, they were from San Juan, San Pedro, and even Ladinos among them. There were teachers and government officials who came to ask my father for my hand; they brought liquor in a suitcase and gave it to my father. I got away from them—they spoke to me in Spanish and I couldn't speak Spanish. There were 48 from San Pedro and San Juan, and of the Ladinos, 2 were officials, and 3—I don't know what their work was. They came from the capital to see me and speak with my father, as I didn't know Spanish. Of the Ladinos, I only knew Representative Monteforte Toledo.

Chona's father would get annoyed that it took her from 1 until 4 in the afternoon to bring the water. He would scold her and tell her to go fast, but there was no one else to get the water for the household, so he continued to send her. Sometimes the boys would surprise her when they jumped out of the bushes, and Chona's clay jug would fall off her head and break.

Girls would typically respond bashfully, facing away and not replying to the first speeches of a suitor. When girls had some interest, they would respond with reasons not to marry, stating that they were too young (they were usually about 15 or 16 years old, and the boys a few years older). Or they would contest the boy's claims that he is a hard worker or that his parents are kind. Such replies from a girl gave the boy encouragement, indicating that she was considering the offer (Paul, 1950; Paul & Paul, 1963).

After some weeks or months of conversation, if the suitor felt some chance of success, he would drop a symbolic gift down the back of the girl's blouse where she could not remove it until getting home. This *prenda* consisted of a little packet containing a few antique Spanish coins, which the girl was to keep if she accepted the boy's offer of marriage. Even if interested, she would show proper reserve by returning the *prendas* to the suitor's home at least the first time or two, usually via a friend or younger sibling.

When finally the girl did not return the coins, the boy knew she had accepted. Then the couple's lakeshore conversations turned to whether to elope (and how to sneak the girl away from her house) or to follow the formal approach involving negotiations and approval between the two sets of parents.[43]

Plans to marry

IN THE FORMAL APPROACH to marriage, the boy's parents along with a witness (or witnesses) met with the girl's family, to ask for the hand of the girl and to exchange gifts. The witnesses were usually respected elders who played the role of go-between.

A typical courtship, described in Jim and Judy Butler's San Pedro fieldnotes, would involve the boy and his parents and witnesses first telling the girl's parents that they want to marry, and asking permission to court the girl in her home. If her parents gave permission for the courtship, the adults advised the young couple not to listen to gossip that might malign each other's character or families, and not to hang out on the streets or flirt with others.

Then the boy would return to court the girl several evenings a week. First he would greet the parents and kiss their hands. After conversing a little with the boy, the girl's parents would leave the couple alone to chat:

"Well, my gal! What do you say! Did they punish you for agreeing to marry me?"

"No, guy. They didn't say anything. Honest. My mother did almost bawl me out when you left yesterday [after he asked permission]. But my dad said, 'Now, cut it out. Don't get upset.'"

"Yeah. I thought you'd be bawled out because of me."

"No. Nothing was really said to me. It's just that people talk."

"Never mind, gal. People always talk. Let's not worry about that. Just like they said yesterday, 'Be patient.' Don't worry if you hear anything. Just don't pay attention to it. Don't let the talk bother you. Maybe God will let us get married."

"Yes. That's what I think. I've already decided to do that."
(Summer Institute of Linguistics, 1978, Book 5, p. 81)

During the courtship, the boy would ask the girl to set a date for the wedding, to confirm her intent to marry him. He would continue wooing her:

> I'll treat you "good." We won't fight. If I were to offer you riches—well, I don't have any. As I've told you, I'm poor. There's no place for me to get wealth. If I were to coax you with money, clothes and all, then when we got together you'd feel terrible when I had nothing to offer you. And so we'd separate. However, even if we just eat greens if you really trust me you'll overlook this if this is how we live. (Summer Institute of Linguistics, 1978, Book 5, p. 88)

If the girl agreed to the marriage, a date for the union was arranged. The boy's parents and the witnesses returned to the girl's parents to formally ask permission for the marriage. The girl's parents would ask if she truly wants to marry the boy, and they would ask whether her view is without anyone swaying her opinion. Then the parents of the couple would set the wedding date, perhaps a month or two hence.

On the wedding day, the girl and her parents parted, weeping, as the girl's mother gave the boy's mother the girl's clothes to take with her (Paul, 1950; Paul & Paul, 1963). At the groom's house, the couple ate from the same dish. As they listened politely, on their knees, a respected third party gave a formal speech and advice to the couple, telling them of their duties as husband and wife, instructing them not to quarrel, and warning them not to listen to malicious gossip. This formal speech was a powerful and essential part of the ritual, and it still occurs now (Chavajay, personal communication, August 2008). Festive ceremonial foods such as tamales, meat, and chocolate were prepared during the night by the groom's relatives, and sent the next day to the bride's family and the intermediary's family, as well as to the groom's relatives.

Chona did not choose her husband

IN CHONA'S CASE, her father decided whom she would marry, taking note of which young man was hardworking and reliable. Ordinarily, the choice was made by the young couple, but sometimes the girl's parents chose.[44] Chona's father got annoyed, from when Chona was queen, with the many Ladinos who wanted to marry her and came to his house with suitcases full of liquor to ask for her hand. Chona would hide when they called out, "Queen, Queen—where are you? We want the Queen."

Her father got exasperated with all of them and decided it would be better if Chona got married, so the suitors would stop bothering them.

Chona was not enthusiastic about her father's choice of Ventura Quiacaín Petzey. At age 81, she recounted:

> Ventura went to ask my father and mother for my hand, but I said, "No, I'm not marrying him." And my father told me that I'm not in charge of this and that I had to marry Ventura. I told my parents that I didn't like it, and my father said that Ventura is good for me because he knows how to work the earth and gather the wood for the cooking fire.
>
> In those days, parents could choose for the daughters. They did this to many of us. Even if you liked someone a lot, the parents said, "Here's what you have to do." We wept and cried, "No papa, no mama, I don't like that boy." They said, "You don't but we do, and you have to marry him." They told the boys, "Come on in" and the father presented his daughter. This happened to many girls in those days, not just me. It was a custom. But my sister Susana was different—she said, "I don't want that boy, and even if you beat me, go ahead and beat me, because the boy that I love, it's because I love him, and nobody tells me what to do." That's Susana.

Chona went along with her father's choice, but Susana made her own choice of husband by eloping. Indeed, the majority of girls of that time (and still in 1976) were "stolen" by a suitor of their choice, running off together from the girl's home and hiding at the boy's home. Sometimes the girl's parents did not know which of her suitors was the guilty party, so they could not pursue until morning.

The young couple was usually discovered by the next day, when the girl's parents showed up with some of the town marshals at the boy's house. The girl's parents often filed a suit in the town court against the young couple, with the boy's parents as accomplices, especially when the girl's family disapproved of the girl's choice. The local judge sometimes jailed the couple overnight (separately) for disrespect to their elders, and exacted a fine from the groom's family to the bride's parents. Chona explained:

> If the boy's parents denied that the girl was there, the marshals had the right to search the house. If they found the girl, they would take her to jail, even if she was only 14 or 15, along with the boy.

The punishment for the girl was to sweep the street that goes all the way from the dock up to the cemetery, with her broom and her basket. Then she had to carry the trash in the basket on her head and walk through all the streets of the town, until she got back to the cemetery. This was so that the girl would feel ashamed. Then she had to carry the trash to throw it out in the part of town called Pachanay, and then sweep from Pachanay to the soccer field, and then throw out the trash there.

While the girl was sweeping, the marshals announced to the whole town that a girl was sweeping the streets, and parents would bring their children to watch what the girl had to do for disobeying her parents and running off with a boy: "Don't do like she did, because you will be ashamed." The young people came out to the streets to watch the girl sweeping.

When parents would tell their daughter, "You'll marry such-and-such boy," and the daughter said, "No, I don't like him," the parents would say, "They will take you to jail and you'll be sweeping the streets." So the daughter would respond, "OK, I'll marry him," to avoid being shamed.

Because Chona was to follow the more respected practice of marriage arranged between the families, rather than running off "stolen" with the boy, her husband-to-be worked with her father for a year before their marriage. This fits with the traditional Mayan practice in which the boy shows respect and obedience to his future in-laws by bringing loads of firewood to their home between the time that the couple becomes engaged and when they marry (Paul & Paul, 1952).

For the first 4 months, Chona chuckles now, she never spoke to her fiancé, even though he was working in her household every day. She agreed to marry him only if he would live with her parents, instead of moving in with his parents.

Usually the girl went to live with the boy's family when they became a couple, but sometimes the boy went to the girl's household, especially if the girl's family had more resources. Chona's parents also had followed this pattern—her father had moved in with her mother's family, joining their relatively well-to-do household. He had been born of poor parents in nearby San Juan, and had been orphaned young and subsequently raised in San Pedro (Paul, 1975).[45]

Now, Chona reports that the choice of husband was a good one. Chona married when she was 15, as was common in the 1940s. (Now she advises my daughters not to marry young—to wait until age 30. I asked her if she gives the same advice to Pedrana girls. She replied, "Yes, always. At 25–30 years they know what they're doing—they can think by then.") She and Ventura have been married for almost 70 years.

Ventura and Chona in their home. (Photo © Barbara Rogoff, 1996)

Bearing Children and Sorrow

CHONA AND VENTURA have had 10 children together. This is not an unusual number of births for that era. Their first child, Ana, was born when Chona was 16.

Chona nursing her first child, Ana. (Photo by Lois and Ben Paul, 1941)
Babies are nursed whenever they cry or seek the breast, and are thereby fed as well as pacified. This may have been an important way of ensuring that during this vulnerable stage of life, in a community with high infant mortality from diarrhea, the infant was well hydrated and calm (LeVine, 1980).

Although all 10 of Chona's babies survived infancy, misfortune stalked 6 of them who died in childhood. Little Ana (in the photo above) died at age 11 years, of measles. After Ana, there was Marcos, the name-sake of Chona's father, who also did not survive. Then a girl and a boy were born who lived, and three more died of measles (another Ana, who also died at about age 11, Alberto Apolonio, and Salvador, who died at about age 7). Then there was a boy who lived. Then the ninth child (another Marcos) died at about 4 years old, also of measles. The last-born child, a girl, survived.

Losing 6 out of 10 children is a heavy burden to bear. Most of San Pedro's high level of infant and child mortality involved infants dying in their first year. Chona was spared the losses of infant mortality, but the losses in childhood, when children could more easily be counted on to live, created much sorrow. At these ages, children are regarded as already fairly robust, and death was less expected. It is therefore often even harder on the parents, from what I have observed as parents tell me sadly about a child who died, adding "and he was already *kof'*—sturdy, robust, toughened up.

Chona reported on the losses from epidemics, like the measles epidemics that claimed so many of her children:

> It didn't just happen to me; it happened to lots of people. The children died from the disease called measles and they suffocated with whooping cough. In those days, ten or twelve children would die per day of those diseases.
>
> A person would become crazy with grief. One Friday, my son Salvador died, then on Sunday, another of my children died, and on Wednesday another one. I felt like I was going crazy—in one week, three of my children had died. And they were already big. My oldest boy already worked very well; he had his *machete*, his hoe, and his shoulder bag for work hanging on the wall at home. It was in the time that Pancho Yojcom was mayor. The marshals had to come get me out of a boat. I don't know where I was going, I was out of my mind.

In 1941, half or more of the children did not survive their first years (Paul, 1950). When I arrived in San Pedro in 1974, immunizations had begun, but still a third of the children born to women about a decade younger than Chona died before the age of 5 years, of diseases like measles, whooping cough, and diarrhea (Rogoff, Correa-Chávez, & Navichoc Cotuc, 2005).

San Pedro's cemetery. (Photo © Barbara Rogoff, ca. 1990)

A long history of loss

MEASLES HAD WIPED OUT large portions of the Mayan population for centuries, along with other diseases brought by the Spanish such as malaria, smallpox, influenza, yellow fever, and amebic dysentery. Within 50 years of the arrival of the Spanish among the Mayans of Central America in 1517, 75% to 90% of the population is estimated to have died. The deaths were in large part due to the newly arrived diseases, along with slaughter, forced labor and displacement, and loss of will to live.

Among the neighboring Kaqchikel Mayans, who live across Lake Atitlán, plagues killed large numbers in six epidemics between 1520 and 1601. The most severe was in 1520:

> It was truly terrible, the number of dead there were in that period . . . great was the stench of the dead. The dogs and the vultures devoured the bodies. The mortality was terrible.
> (Thompson, 1970, p. 53, citing Recinos, 1953).[46]

When I examined the tribute (tax) rolls of San Pedro from 1599, in the San Pedro office of the Academia de Lenguas Mayas, I noted that the tribute rolls included many families with no children or only one child.

::

CHONA REPORTED that when she was a young mother, there were no pills, but people used natural medicines. She knows a number of herbal remedies, and these were and are still widely used, along with the medicines now available from local pharmacies and Western doctors.

The first vaccinations became available about 45 years ago, according to Chona, when a doctor from a bigger town nearby would come to town and give shots. "But people did not go because they were afraid." By the time I got to San Pedro, people were eager for shots. In fact, they seemed to think shots were the most effective form of treatment. Some Guatemalan doctors were reputed to accede to patients who demanded a shot, by simply giving them an injection of "H-twenty"—H_2O.

In the years before vaccinations were widespread and child mortality was high, conversations like the following would have been frequent. A neighbor woman visited a family, with a customary gift of a drink made of corn gruel, trying to console the parents and grandparents over the death of a child. After greetings all around:

> "So your child died!"
> "Yes, ma'am. She died. She didn't get over the illness."
> "What a shame! Well, what's done is done, my dear. Don't cry."
> "Yes, but I can't help it. She was old enough to walk and talk."
> "Never mind, my dear. Your other children still need you. You should care for them and not let them suffer."
> [A grandparent chimes in.] "That's right, ma'am. That's what we've been telling her. We told her not to be so sad and cry so much."
> "You always are sad when you recall the good times you had with your child."
> "I remember the cute way she used to talk to me, ma'am. When she was hungry, she used to say, 'Gal, I'll have something to eat.' But now who will say that to me!"
> "Never mind, my dear. You are still young. God will probably bless you with another child."
> "That's right, ma'am. That's what we tell her."
> "Would you like some coffee, ma'am?"
> "Thank you, my dear. You did try to cure her."
> "They did their best, ma'am. But it didn't work."
> "Well, never mind. If they tried, it's not their fault then. It must have been time for her to die."

"That's exactly what we say, if they'd only realize it. But they didn't want their child to die."

"That's just how children are, my dear, just like little chickens. We need to be thankful if they come through any illness."

"That's right, ma'am. You have no say over life or death. Drink your coffee. It's getting cold."

"Thank you, my dear." (Summer Institute of Linguistics, 1978, Book 8, pp. 145–146)

The sorrow is still fresh

I LEARNED ABOUT the death of Chona's second child, Marcos, one day when I visited Chona with my little blonde daughter in tow. The three of us sat in upholstered chairs on the second floor of Chona's daughter's house. I had come equipped with a series of questions to ask Chona to clarify fine points for this book. She answered them patiently and with interest, sometimes demonstrating a move or posture to make sure that I got it right.

At one point during the interview, Chona paused for a long moment, gazing at my daughter. She took my little daughter's face between her hands, cradling each pink cheek to raise the little face to hers, and searched gravely in my daughter's eyes. My little one trustingly returned her gaze as Chona's eyes brimmed with tears. I held my breath, curious but not wanting to disturb this moment.

After a long pause Chona explained that her Marcos looked like my daughter, a beautiful child with the same celeste-blue eyes and light curly hair and the same delicate frame. Tears flowed down Chona's sun-worn cheeks as she told me about little Marcos' death at about age 4, some 40 years earlier. I thought about debates among my university students about whether people feel grief about the death of a child if they live where childhood mortality is high.

Everyone admired Marcos too much, he was such a beautiful child, Chona commented wistfully. On the day of the annual fiesta in the neighboring town of San Pablo, many Pedranos were going by canoe to enjoy the festivities and to make some small purchases from peddlers who travel from one town's fiesta to another—perhaps some fruit brought up from the coast, or holiday cookies. Some of the women might bargain for the expensive fabric for a new skirt.

Chona's mother warned her not to take the boy along. She scolded Chona, reminding her that in the crowd, he could get sick or die from evil eye—from people's envy and admiration. Pedranos avoided praising babies and handsome cornfields, to keep from calling misfortune onto them. Sometimes they explained this in terms of spirits, sometimes in terms of jealousy—either of which could be mortally dangerous.

Chona hesitated; she usually heeded her mother's counsel. But Marcos looked so adorable, dressed in a new little jacket and pants and even shoes that were a gift from Doña Luisa (Lois Paul). Chona wanted so much to take him along on the outing.

Chona clambered down the rocky path with Marcos to the planks that formed a dock, to take the great public canoe. While they were waiting for the boat, Marcos played by the shore. Many people noticed him and wondered whose child he was—they speculated that he was Chona's, or maybe that he had come with Chona but wasn't hers. Many people admired little Marcos and wanted to hold him.

They got in the canoe and headed towards San Pablo. But in the middle of the lake, Marcos fell ill. He became pale and weak. Chona recalled:

> There in the boat, my little son said to me, "Mama, I need to vomit." I replied to him, "Go ahead, vomit here." He did, and right away we turned back to San Pedro. When we got to the dock, he couldn't walk. I was terrified, breathless, running up the hill to home with him in my arms. He vomited several times, shuddered, and cried out, "Mama, I'm dying." By the time I got him home, he was dead. I laid his lifeless body down lightly on our wooden frame cot, and my mother scolded me.
>
> The lady who came to bathe my son for burial blamed me; she said I had killed my son by taking him out of the house. The pain that mothers felt in the past when a child died is the same as when mothers lose a child now.

Chona knew some herbal cures for illness caused by people's envy and admiration, but Marcos died so quickly there was no time to do anything.[47] She still felt remorse over this loss more than 40 years before.

::

NOW, THE DANGER of death in childhood is greatly reduced. A dramatic drop in both the birth rate and the mortality rate occurred within the past generation. As of the late 1990s, women averaged only about two births, and only a few of those born did not survive (Rogoff, Correa-Chávez, & Navichoc Cotuc, 2005).

Consistent with the generational changes, Chona and Ventura's four surviving children have lost very few children of their own: As of 2007, Chona and Ventura's oldest daughter lost two children and had four surviving, who in turn have had seven children between them and lost none. Chona and Ventura's other three children between them have had seven children and lost none, and these grandchildren have had four children between them and lost none. The change in child survival is dramatic, and it is accompanied by an equally dramatic reduction in the number of children that women bear.

For Chona, the memories of the illness and deaths of her children are still with her. However, how she relates the losses of her children to the timing of accepting her destined role as *iyoom* is different now than 40 years before.

8 ⸬

Changing Memories
in Changing Practices

WHEN CHONA RECOUNTED her life story many years ago, she said that losing so many of her children and her mother were part of what convinced her that she had to agree to accept her destiny as an *iyoom*.

However, over the years, some differences have appeared in Chona's account. A primary discrepancy is in regards to when she became an *iyoom*. During the past 20 years or so, since I began working on this book, Chona consistently says that she began to practice her role as *iyoom* when she made an unexpected delivery, after her own first child was born, at about the age of 17.

Chona, at about age 16, bathing her firstborn baby, Ana. (Photo by Lois and Ben Paul, 1941)

But according to Lois and Ben Paul, Chona reported that she had become an *iyoom* at about the age of 35, 2 years before their 1962 visit. This is a substantial discrepancy, spanning the beginning and nearly the end of Chona's childbearing years—almost two decades of difference in her claim of when she began to be an *iyoom*.

I asked Chona about the discrepancy when she was 78. I mentioned that I had been helping Ben go through his and Lois' fieldnotes, and that Lois had written that Chona had become an *iyoom* when she was about 35. In asking Chona about this, I referred to the time as being about when Chona's last child was born, rather than in terms of numerical age.

Chona replied confidently that the time that Lois was talking about was when Chona had first done the paperwork and gotten her license from the state to practice. She was satisfied that this accounted for the discrepancy between Lois' 1962 notes, which placed the start at about age 35, and her current account, which placed it at about age 17.

Still, there were some aspects that didn't make sense to me. If Chona began to practice at age 17, why would Lois' account have said that losing so many children and the death of her mother had led Chona to accept her role as *iyoom*? Chona still recounts that she got sick with sorrow after her mother's death, which occurred when Chona was about 33. For 15 months she was deathly ill, with her hands and legs numb, and her husband also was very sick for a long time. Lois wrote that these events were turning points for Chona and her husband accepting the call of destiny for the life work of *iyoom*.

I have considered several possible interpretations of the discrepancies in the accounts:

Translation Issues?

THERE MIGHT have been misunderstandings in translation. Both Lois and I had limited facility in Tz'utujil and usually interviewed with the help of various translators between Spanish and Tz'utujil. But I do not think that this accounts for the discrepancy in the age at which Chona began as *iyoom*, because both Lois and I interviewed Chona repeatedly, and we both could understand a fair bit of what was said in Tz'utujil. In addition, Chona can understand a little Spanish. These partial overlaps in language provide good opportunity to cross-check translators' versions.

Confusion of Ages?

COULD THERE be confusion in the reporting of ages? People of Chona's generation in San Pedro have not been used to keeping track of ages, and many of the ages referred to in Chona's account are quite approximate. Only since the 1970s has numerical age become a systematic way of reckoning lifetimes in San Pedro. In the town census that I carried out in 1974, when I asked mothers their age, they usually replied uncertainly, "Oh, I don't know, maybe 40. No, probably more like 45. Put 45." Some gestured toward their body and asked me to supply the age, "What do you think, Barbara?" Also, when I figured out their children's ages by checking the municipal birth records, the mothers' reports of the children's ages were often off by a year or two.

In Aztec chronicles of almost 500 years ago, children's phases of life were referred to in terms of the number of tortillas they would usually eat (Codex Mendoza, 1541–42). Now it is common for younger people in San Pedro to know their ages and to celebrate birthdays marking their numerical age. (Numerical age has a little longer history in the United States—about a century and a half. It became a systematic way of referring to periods of life during the bureaucratization of many industrial-era institutions, such as compulsory schooling, in the mid- to late 1800s, according to Chudacoff, 1989.)

I do not think that the approximations in reporting age can account for the discrepancy. The difference between 17 years old and 35 years old would not be confused in San Pedro. In addition, when I interviewed Chona, I seldom referred to ages but rather to events in her life, such as "when you had your first child" or "after your last child was born" or "when your mother died." Anchoring the times with events that I had previously recorded in sequence is much more reliable than dates and ages.

It may well be that from the perspective of Chona's 70s and 80s, the time between ages 17 and 35 could contract. This would make it easier to conflate events that occurred earlier and later in this period. But not as much as this.

Difficulties in Remembering the Distant Past?

ANOTHER POSSIBILITY is that Chona might have forgotten. When I interviewed Chona at age 78, she sometimes begged off a question, saying, "I am old now and my memory is not so good; back that far is like a dream." When I asked her about events that Lois had recorded, Chona indicated that she trusts what Lois wrote. Once she added, "I don't really remember, but I'm sure that what Lois wrote down is correct. It was fresh at the time, and I was young. I was sure of what I told her at that time and I still had it in mind. I had it in my head and in my heart. Not like now; I sometimes forget."[48]

But often when I told her a bit about what Lois had written, Chona filled in the rest of the account, reminded of it from my reporting a bit of what Lois had written. One time when this happened, Chona and I laughed together about Lois' papers having a mouth. Lois' notes conversed with Chona over the decades since Lois had written them and long since Lois had died.

Photographs can also talk, sparking recollections of the past. Having many photos (and even videos) of oneself may encourage people to keep track of earlier phases of their lives. Viewing the photos from time to time might prompt people in creating and rehearsing a life story that keeps track of times gone by that might otherwise be more difficult to recall. Thus photographic records of people's lives might contribute to a more systematic effort to remember one's past than in eras in which such records did not exist. Until the past couple of decades in San Pedro, photos have been rare.

A number of Pedranos have commented that the photos in drafts of this book bring to life a former time that they have forgotten, of which there are very few other photos. Here, two men of Chona's generation remember 57 years before, as they try to identify the three men in this 1941 photo, on the wall in the town library. The photo that they are scrutinizing appears in this book, like many of the others now on the library wall. This photo collection, provided by Ben Paul, Luisa Magarian, and myself, serves as reference material for many San Pedro painters. (Photo © Luisa Magarian, 1998)

Adjusting the Account
According to Who Is Listening?

CHONA MIGHT have adjusted the account to fit different circumstances. Her relationship with Lois and me (and the translators) seems to involve mutual trust, so it seems unlikely that she was trying to deceive us. However, it is well known that the telling of history (of nations, groups within nations, and families) transforms with changing politics. "We change our stories as our point of view, our ideology, or our overall understanding changes and reshapes our history." (Linde, 1993, p. 31; see also Behar, 1993).

The complications of living in a small town where people know each other's business (or think they know it) could have led to different considerations in different eras in the recounting of when Chona began practicing as an *iyoom*, especially as the accounts were addressed not only to me or to Lois but also to the local translators and in some cases intended for publication. In the interviews, from the start, Chona would have been aware of the likely spread of information at least via the translators, in a town where sharing stories is a major source of entertainment and retaliation.

In fact, Chona has decided that some minor details are not to be published in this book. For example, some names are omitted to protect the privacy of some individuals. Those details do not seem to relate to the discrepancy that puzzles me, though.

However, withheld information is responsible for the account of the first delivery coming to light only in later years: Chona told me that she could not talk about the very first delivery (when she was about 17) until after the death of a senior *iyoom*. The baby's mother was the patient of the senior *iyoom*, who was apparently inebriated at the time of the birth. Women rarely drank alcohol in those days, and a woman being drunk would have resulted in criticism and gossip. (Women's inebriation is still rare, though perhaps it has increased slightly.) The *iyoom* would have been angry with Chona if the information had become public.

The *iyoom* found out what happened because the baby's father went to her the next day and told her that the baby was a boy. The *iyoom* asked, "Who 'bought' it?" and he told her it was Chona. The *iyoom* examined the mother and baby, checking the baby's umbilical cord and so on, and said that Chona had done well and had the destiny of *iyoom*. The *iyoom* took over the care of the mother and baby after the delivery, attending to their postnatal care. Although Chona was afraid that the *iyoom* would be upset with her, and she hid when the *iyoom* looked for her, the *iyoom* was not angry. Nonetheless, Chona did not publicly talk about having aided in this delivery.

There may well be information that Chona has cast differently at different times, however, due to changing attitudes towards some practices in her family and town. For example, supernatural explanations seem to be less common now. When Chona was young, supernatural explanations involving shamans and sorcery were common in San Pedro. Now there are fewer shamans, and although talk of shamans' work and of sorcery continues in private settings, it appears to be less publicly acknowledged. (This is likely due in part to the disapproval of

Mayan spiritual traditions from both Catholic priests and Protestant sects that have become increasingly central to Pedrano life.)

It is also likely that Lois and I have introduced some of our own interpretations that change the account, as we try to make sense of bits of Chona's story that we have heard over numerous different tellings. In making an account, we probably have made adjustments in the effort to create coherence. We have each likely added our general understandings of life in San Pedro across time, as well as our understandings of life based on our own historical and cultural backgrounds prior to and since becoming a part of San Pedro. Our own understandings undoubtedly changed over time.

The Meaning of Being an *Iyoom* has Changed

ALONG WITH tellers adjusting an account as circumstances change, it is probable that the meaning of being an *iyoom* has changed. Perhaps when the first notes on Chona's becoming an *iyoom* were written, Chona (and Lois) focused on the time when Chona committed to the sacred role of *iyoom* as her life's work, at about age 35. This would involve different criteria than just helping a mother or a few mothers give birth. It may require confident practice both of the technical obstetrical skills of midwifery and the spiritual aspects of the profession, as well as a regular clientele.

The extent of commitment to the sacred calling of *iyoom* is much greater than what is required to deliver one or two babies. The required dedication is demonstrated by estimates that the two established *iyooma'* serving San Pedro in 1941 each averaged nearly three house calls per day, including Sundays and holidays (Paul & Paul, 1975). Prenatal and postnatal checkups could be limited to an hour, but births and some of the postnatal care would take far longer.

Furthermore, although the *iyoom* would generally know when a delivery is imminent, she would regard it as her sacred responsibility to respond immediately, dropping whatever she is doing whenever a patient's relative appears at her door calling her urgently when "the time has come." So the *iyoom* is constantly on call, generally without backup. (If two births happen at once, the *iyoom* goes back and forth between them, helping first one woman and then the other.) This level of life-enveloping responsibility would require great commitment and dedication as well as sacrifices by the *iyoom* and her family.

⠃⠃

THE EXPLANATION for the discrepancy probably has to do with the presence of numerous transition points in the process of "becoming" an *iyoom*. By analogy, determining when a person becomes an artist could likewise have several starting points, with varying criteria such as first thinking of oneself as doing art, first having a piece in a public show, first selling a piece, becoming recognized as an artist, and dedicating oneself to making a living as an artist. Other professions too have several transition points, such as "student doctor" while in medical school and doing medical procedures but not being fully responsible, doctor licensed to practice solo, and doctor with responsibility for the regular care of a group of patients.

A focus on the process of *becoming*, with multiple transition points relating to the contexts of change, seems valuable to apply to many other developmental transitions as well: becoming a writer, a friend, a babysitter, someone who can talk or walk or take others' perspectives. Developmental psychology in the United States has often focused on determining specific onset points for many developmental transitions (such as when a child can talk or "has" specific concepts or the ability to take another's perspective). Some issues that have troubled developmental psychology may be resolved (or dissolved) by examining multiple, contextually supported transitions in how people address a situation.

It may well be that Chona delivered a number of babies before she confronted the question of whether she was really going to accept the sacred and demanding role of *iyoom* as her lifework—to *be* an *iyoom*. This would be a different kind of "becoming" an *iyoom* than just delivering a few babies in an emergency or for relatives, which seems to be the case for the first babies Chona delivered. It also fits the situation of a few younger women in San Pedro who were born destined to be *iyooma'* but who are not yet generally regarded as having accepted and established their lifework as *iyooma'*, although they may have delivered a number of babies.

The shift away from a focus on the spiritual calling might also derive from Chona's becoming more aware of obstetrical practices used in Western medicine. Greater awareness of other approaches would derive in part from the midwifery courses required for licensure and also by the practices of Pedrana women who have become *practicante* midwives trained in practices of the Western medical establishment. Sacred aspects of Mayan midwives' roles in southern Mexico and Guatemala have decreased as their roles become increasingly secular, especially due to medicalization of their work by training of governmental and international organizations (Cosminsky, 1994, 2001a, b).

In addition, increased travel and communication among nearby towns may provide information that fuels a change of focus. *Iyooma'* in other Mayan towns on Lake Atitlán had fewer deliveries and less of a supernatural role, although they likewise have supernatural connection with Spirit-Lords and Guardians, have special objects indicating their divine calling, and show reluctance to obey their destiny until hardships urge acceptance. According to the Pauls, midwives in other Mayan towns attended an average of four or five births per year, making the work more a sideline than a profession; midwives were often poor, elderly widows; and shamans sometimes took on more of the spiritual aspects of pregnancy and birth (Paul, 1969; Paul & Paul, 1975).

::

HENCE, CHONA'S RECENT REPORTING of when she became an *iyoom* may have shifted to when she began to deliver babies (at about age 17). Her earlier accounts may have focused on when she fully dedicated herself to the sacred lifework and responsibilities of a divinely chosen professional whose duty it is to respond to the needs of women in childbirth (at about age 35).

It is consistent with this interpretation that in 1962, when Chona was 37, about 2 years after she had become established as an *iyoom*, she estimated to Lois Paul that she had delivered a total of about 30 babies, and 5 years later her clientele was over 100 families (Paul, 1974–75). This suggests that she delivered 30 babies over the first 20 years or so of her practice, including the first 2 years after she finally became established as an *iyoom*, and quickly thereafter, her practice increased dramatically.

Chona when she was about 37 and was known as an established iyoom *in the community. In this photo she appears with three of her surviving children. The eldest, Dolores, is on the left, Abraham is in front, and María Lidia is in Chona's arms. Chona's son Santos is not in the photo. (Photo by Lois and Ben Paul, and Santos Quiacaín Pérez, 1962)*

A 48-year-old Pedrana (born about 1960) spontaneously announced to me proudly in 2008 that she had been Chona's first delivery; the woman's mother confirmed this. When I asked Chona about this, she said, "No, my first delivery was a boy who would be 68 years old now, except that he died when he was 12 years old." (For some years now, Chona has been consistent in her claim that this boy was her first delivery. She has also begun to refer to ages in chronicling events. However, her estimate of her age at first delivery has crept a little younger, to age 15; a decade or two earlier her estimate was that it was at about age 17.) The 48-year-old woman's claim could be accounted for if she was Chona's first delivery after Chona became licensed or after Chona fully accepted *iyoom* as her life's work. This would be consistent with the public version of Chona's career around the time when the woman was born.

⠶

SOME OF THE DISCREPANCIES in the timing of events remain as unsolved mysteries of memory and history. Such mysteries are likely more common in all of our lives and our communities' histories than we notice. After all, memory is a process of reconstruction based on life in the present, with consideration of how the information may be used in the future, even for very recent events but especially for lifelong accounts. The changing nature of life stories is inescapable; new events occur and we make sense of them, reinterpreting prior events.

9 ::

Entry and Prominence
in a Sacred Profession

CHONA'S ENTRY into her profession seems to have followed this course of events: Chona began to deliver a few babies when she was about 17. When she was about 35, life-changing challenges prompted soul-searching regarding her willingness to accept the lifework of her destined role of *iyoom*. Her mother's premature death (believed to be due to not accepting her own destined role of *iyoom*), the deaths of six of Chona's children, and the illnesses and threatening dreams of Chona and her husband would be convincing evidence to both Chona and her husband that she must dedicate herself to her destined responsibilities or risk her own or others' deaths.

The First Births

CHONA'S FIRST DELIVERY, when she was about 17 and already married with a baby, was by chance. She had been sent to a neighbor's house to buy some *chipilín* greens to cook as an accompaniment to the usual corn tortillas and black beans. She found the neighbor at home by herself, about to give birth. The neighbor's *iyoom* hadn't arrived, because she was drunk, and in pain the neighbor asked young Chona to help her. Chona was afraid, but she delivered the baby. When she looked for something to cut the umbilical cord, there wasn't anything around. Then she remembered the shimmering knife blade that she had found years before, ran home for it, and finished tending to the newborn and the mother.

Chona didn't tell people about that delivery because she was afraid that the neighbor's real *iyoom* would get angry with her for taking over her patient. Chona didn't even tell her parents about it; she was afraid they would be furious. Her parents found out only because the woman's husband brought a gift of bread rolls to Chona's mother. When her mother asked why he was bringing this gift, he said that her daughter had done the favor of serving as *iyoom* to his wife, when her own *iyoom* had not come, and they were very grateful.

Chona's mother scolded her, "You're hardly a woman of stature already! Don't you have any *vergüenza* [humility, restraint, moral fiber]? What are you doing delivering a baby? What if the woman died in your hands? Why did you agree to do it?"

Chona's mother, Dolores (Photo by Lois and Ben Paul, 1941)

The next day, Chona's father pointed out that Chona had been born with the destiny of *iyoom*, and that she could do that work. He was grateful that his daughter had started on her life's calling, and went to the church to thank the saints.

This birth was not publicized. Only the woman's family, Chona's parents, and the *iyoom* who was supposed to have been at the birth knew about Chona's first delivery. Some other early deliveries may also have followed, with few people knowing about them.

About 5 years after the first delivery, people found out that Chona was destined to be an *iyoom* when she delivered another baby. The woman who had washed the veil that Chona was born with told everyone that it was true that Chona had been born to be an *iyoom*. She verified that Chona was a true *iyoom* with a divine calling from birth, not just someone who decided to receive babies. (It was all right to tell people about Chona's birthsign after she began her work, although if people had talked about it before, Chona could have died.)

The neighbor who washed the veil is on the right, carrying a baby (likely her new granddaughter), using her shawl like a sling. The woman on the left wears a hand-woven güipil *with an opening that facilitates nursing. Such openings are no longer seen now, especially because wearing underclothes has become the norm and most women wear a kind of blouse now that does not have a seam up the front. (Photo by Lois and Ben Paul, 1941)*

Sometimes when people would come to Chona's father as a shaman, for prayers and ceremonies having to do with pregnancy, he would also tell people that Chona was truly an *iyoom*. Gradually, the word spread about Chona being a divinely elected *iyoom*.

People in San Pedro as well as in the neighboring town of San Juan, a 30-minute walk from San Pedro, began requesting her services for births. At that time, she delivered babies only occasionally. By the time she was about 26, the pace of deliveries picked up. By the time she was 37, when Lois and Ben Paul revisited San Pedro in 1962, Chona's supernatural experiences and obstetrical skills were a frequent topic of conversation, "recounted with dramatic effects and in the lowered tones Pedranos use when speaking of awesome supernatural phenomena" (Paul, 1975, p. 457).

Harrowing Events and Convincing Supernatural Visits

HER MOTHER'S DEATH when Chona was 33 and Chona's own lengthy illness during the subsequent year prompted Chona to accept her destiny as an *iyoom* at age 35 (in 1960), according to Lois Paul's account. These events seem to have been a turning point in Chona's full dedication to this calling. This period also provided some medical education in the form of dreams. In 1975, Lois wrote that during Chona's illness (at age 34),

> She grew weak and wasted, slept only fitfully, and began having strange dreams. (Dreams are believed to represent real experiences of the spirit, not mere products of the mind.)
>
> In her dreams Chona was visited by big, fat women, all in radiant white, who explained that she was sick because she was shirking her obligation to help the women of San Pedro in childbirth. These were the spirits of dead midwives. When she tried to sleep, the spirits would appear. They would grab her ears and scold her, telling her she would die and her husband would die if she did not exercise her calling. They reminded her that she had already lost many children. She was being punished for neglecting to use the "power" (*k'orxin*, Zutuhil; *virtud*, Spanish) she was given. "If you continue to hesitate, your other children will also die. Remember that your mother died because she did not obey God's call."

When Chona protested that she was too ignorant and incompetent, that she knew nothing about the skills that a midwife must have, the spirits assured her they would instruct her. They showed her the signs of pregnancy, how to massage the pregnant woman, and to palpate the abdomen to feel if the fetus was in correct position for delivery. They demonstrated external version (turning the fetus). Vividly in her dreams she saw a woman delivering a baby. The spirits showed her how to hold the white cloth to receive the baby and how to clean the newborn infant. They showed her how to foretell the sequence of future births by reading the markings on the umbilical cord. They instructed her not to cut the cord before the placenta was presented. They showed her how the cord must be followed back up to the placenta in case the placenta does not come out, and the placenta removed manually if necessary. They told her they would always be present, though invisible, to help her at deliveries. The spirits instructed her how to bind the woman's abdomen after delivery to "hold the organs in place." "All these things I saw," Chona says. In addition to obstetrical skills, the spirits taught her prayers and ritual procedures.

When she related the dreams to her husband, he protested vehemently. He did not want her to go about the village as a midwife, neglecting the household, himself, and their children. He warned that people would talk, be critical. Finally, he too fell ill and was visited in his dreams by the women in white. They scolded him, saying he must persuade his wife to start practicing, or both would die. Eventually, Chona's father, in his capacity as shaman, was consulted about their frightening dreams. He lit candles in the house, burned incense, and performed rituals. His divination confirmed the warnings of the spirits. As dramatic proof of Chona's destiny, he produced the birth sign entrusted to him by her mother. Chona began to regain her strength and appetite. (Paul, 1975, pp. 458–459)[49]

::

SOON AFTER, Chona began to find objects of her work when walking in or near town—a bone and a small knife. The bone was skipping down the road. She was frightened and did not pick it up, but the women in white appeared in her dreams and told her to take the bone, telling her it was her "power," and not to show it to anyone, according to Lois.

The next day, Chona picked up the bone when it again appeared in her path. When she got home, the bone was no longer wrapped in her shawl, but had gotten itself into the cabinet. (In an interview about 15 years ago, Chona also confirmed this strange behavior of the bone to me.)

> Finding her objects was the final sign. Chona's father urged against further delay. He performed night-long *costumbres* this time, keeping Chona and her husband on their knees for many hours.[50] In the ritual rhetoric of shamans, he summoned and addressed the patron saints and the ancestral guardians of childbirth, the deities of hills, waters, rains, winds, the masters and spirit guardians of all domains. He begged forgiveness for all past and present sins of Chona and all her relatives, promising the supernaturals that Chona would fulfill their command willingly and with a good heart. He assured the spirits that her husband bowed to their will and would give his whole-hearted support to the selfless sacrifice she was about to make for the sake of the women of San Pedro. . . . Once Chona decided to practice, all traces of her illness quickly vanished; she regained good health and became unusually energetic. Other midwives report similar experiences. (Paul, 1975, pp. 459–60)

::

ANOTHER SAN PEDRO *IYOOM*, Doña Jesús (Rosaria Quiacaín Televario), at age 87, recounted that she began her work as *iyoom* at about age 30 when she already had five of her own children. Her husband angrily refused for her to practice, but then he reflected on it when she became very ill.

> I had to become ill, I stayed abed, my legs were trembling and even became paralyzed for a good while. This is a sign that truly one has been called by God to take up the work of *iyoom*. I never was a student; I have no academic preparation, there exists no man or woman who has trained me. In this I can see clearly that I carried this [calling] from my birth, from the time of the stars that saw me born.

When five women came to her requesting her services as *iyoom*, she agreed to it, irrespective of her husband's views:

> "Little did it matter to me," I told myself, "if we separate, let it be so." If we were to separate it would be the least important thing,

because what was so difficult was the illness. Nonetheless, since I took up my duty as *iyoom* I recuperated rapidly and had the opportunity to receive the first baby [I delivered] on Mother Earth.

Never did I have the opportunity to see, nor have I been shown how by a doctor, and nonetheless, I was able to receive the first baby; simply and beautifully [the skill] emerged from my head, my understanding. I received the baby and rubbed its chest and it calmed. After cleaning it, after cutting the thread for tying the umbilical cord, achieving all these steps I was able to see a baby, totally complete, sent by the forces of nature, with all its parts in their respective places. . . .

Of all the children that I have, I was only aided in childbirth with the first ones, because after them I began to function following my gift [destiny] and from then on I delivered [my own babies by] myself. Of course the *iyooma'* were angry with me, not reflecting on the fact that we are all passengers in this life. (pp. 185–191, Tuy Navichoc, 1999; my translation from the Spanish)

Doña Jesús complained that many new midwives these days—*practicantes*—have "simply studied," "they just want to do this work," rather than having been selected by divine forces. She mentioned a relative of hers who is practicing without a spiritual calling: "With all sincerity I tell you that she is not an *iyoom*, although she says that she is; it was I who helped her to be born. The child born protected with a veil has a gift, a mission to fulfill."

Divine selection, Doña Jesús claimed, gives an *iyoom* access to special obstetrical techniques as well as spiritual confidence. She indicated that a woman destined by birth to be an *iyoom* can situate the fetus in the correct position, as long as the mother-to-be begins prenatal care early enough, for example the third month, rather than being embarrassed and waiting until later. However, "these treatments can only be done by those who are truly assigned the work by God and by our mother Mary."

An *Iyoom* of Renown

NEAR THE TIME that Chona emerged as an *iyoom*, about 1961, she was summoned to the state capital, Sololá, for an examination connected with the requirement to become licensed. Apparently, one of the rival *iyooma'* had informed the authorities that Chona was practicing without a license.

The doctor in Sololá asked her how she knew what to do and who had taught her, and threatened her with jail if she was not qualified to practice. (The conversation was through a translator, to bridge between the doctor's Spanish and Chona's Tz'utujil.) The doctor presented Chona with a patient and asked her to determine when the woman would give birth. Chona examined the woman and diagnosed that the woman would give birth that same day about 12:30. The doctor expressed disbelief, but Chona's prediction turned out to be correct, and the doctor asked her to deliver the baby. The doctor was so impressed with Chona's skill that afterward he treated her to a meal and gave her the return fare to take a motorboat back to San Pedro.

This triumphant outcome of Chona's medical trial became another legendary chapter in local accounts of Chona's prowess, pitting her supernatural knowledge against the doctors' scientific training (Paul, 1975). In confirming this account about 10 years ago, Chona added that there were also some foreign doctors present, who were so impressed that they invited her to go with them to the United States, and that they would pay her round-trip expenses. But she was afraid to travel by plane and did not know how to speak Spanish, so she declined.

At first when the government began to require midwives to be licensed by the state medical establishment, this was apparently rather loose and just involved paying a fee. By the 1960s, new regulations for getting a license had been implemented, with required courses on midwifery given by public health officials and doctors trained in Western academic medicine.[51]

When Chona first began to attend courses given by the doctors, there were not yet Western-trained doctors with offices in San Pedro, so Chona and the other two renowned *iyooma'*, María Puac and Juana Rocché, would go to the only hospital in the region for the courses and the license. To get to the hospital, several miles above Lake Atitlán in the state capital Sololá, they first had to cross the formidable expanse of the lake (about 9 miles to the dock on the opposite shore). San Pedro government officials rowed the three *iyooma'* in a traditional canoe made of a hollowed tree trunk with sideboards, hoping that dangerous winds would not arise during the 3-hour crossing and the return.

Canoes preparing to embark from San Pedro. (Photo by Lois Paul, 1941)

Chona says that in the hospital, the three *iyooma'* just watched what the doctors did—they could not converse because the doctors did not speak Tz'utujil and the *iyooma'* did not speak Spanish. The doctors gave them several pairs of scissors and some bands for tying umbilical cords, to use in their practice.

∷

AS CHONA'S REPUTATION grew, she became one of the most sought-after *iyooma'* of the area. Sometimes she did three deliveries a day. Town records for 1973 indicated that she averaged a delivery once every 3 days that year (121 babies). She delivered more than a third (72) of about 200 babies born in San Pedro and more than half (49) of the 81 babies born in San Juan. San Juan families preferred to use midwives from San Pedro, and Chona was the *iyoom* most often called, in both towns, of the seven *iyooma'* and midwives from San Pedro and several from San Juan (Loucky, 1974; Paul & Paul, 1975). It was a tremendous responsibility.

Chona's practice, destined from her birth, developed over the years. Her way of ushering new people into the world, physically and spiritually, built on ancient Mayan ways that form part of the destiny of *iyoom*. In addition, she developed new ideas and techniques. Her contributions stemmed from her own ideas and wisdom and her experiences in the births of her own children and those she aided as *iyoom*, as well as from her experiences with *kaxlan* (foreign) ways. Destiny and development, together.

10 ⸬

Ripples

Across Generations and Nations
in Mayan Pregnancy and Childbirth

MEDICAL CARE in San Pedro derives from numerous sources, including longstanding Mayan medical expertise and spiritual practice. In addition, there have been borrowings and impositions from colonial European and modern European and North American practices, as well as from Indigenous Mexican and Caribbean influences.

Many of the prenatal, birth, and postnatal practices used by Chona and other San Pedro *iyooma'* occur in Mayan communities throughout Guatemala and southern Mexico (Cosminsky, 2001a). The survival of ancient Mayan practices is due in part to the fact that during the Colonial period, although parts of the Catholic Church and the Spanish Crown tried to eradicate "pagan" customs, few Spaniards lived in remote areas. Those who did live in Indian towns tended to respect native herbal medicine (Orellana, 1987).

Many practices in Indigenous communities—such as those involving clothing and foods—shifted towards Spanish customs following colonization. However,

> in birthing, [the Indians] remained faithful to their ancient traditions, and it seems that they endeavored to hide them from the inquisitive view of the missionary, the priest, or the ruling colonist. (León, 1910, p. 51)

Longevity of the Goddess of Midwives, Childbirth, Water, and the Moon

ALTHOUGH SPANISH MISSIONARIES intended Catholic deities to *replace* Mayan ones, it was common among the Mayans to incorporate Catholic practices into Mayan religion. They took up the European ideas and practices that "resonate with Maya concepts, . . . subtly altering them to conform with indigenous paradigms" (Christenson, 2001, p. 71).

In this process, the sun and moon gods were merged with Jesus and the Virgin Mary. Among one Mayan group, the Hail Mary prayer is recited to the moon (Thompson, 1970; see also Nájera-Ramírez, 1997; Nash, 1970).

Among present-day Mayans, including those of San Pedro, references to God and Mary may still at times refer to sun and moon deities. For example, Doña Jesús/Rosaria Quiacaín Televario, an elder *iyoom* in San Pedro, said that babies born with a supernatural healing destiny are assigned to their supernatural work by God and "our mother María," as "children of the sacred grain of maize, from Mother Lake" (Tuy Navichoc, 1999, pp. 189, 191). The reference to maize likely connects with the ancient Mayan account of humans being created from maize by the gods. The reference to Mother Lake probably relates to the ancient goddess Ixchel (Goddess O). Ixchel is the Yucatec Mayan moon deity— and guardian of childbirth, medicine, maize, weaving, and water— whose reflection is seen in bodies of water such as Lake Atitlán (Thompson, 1970).

The patron deity of midwives and the moon—Yaxper—in the neighboring Tz'utujil Mayan town of Santiago Atitlán appears to be linked to the ancient goddess Ixchel. Both Ixchel and Yaxper serve as patrons of midwives, childbirth, and the moon, and Ixchel is portrayed as a grandmother figure. Yaxper, in turn, is described as a very old, bent but powerful woman of ancient times; she is the only deity routinely referred to as grandmother in Santiago Atitlán (like the *iyooma'* themselves; Christenson, 2001).

In the light of the full moon, on the porch of the *cofradía* that houses the statue of Yaxper, the *iyoom* bathes her pregnant client, in a ceremonial cleansing late in pregnancy. The *iyoom* puts a bowl of water before the pregnant woman so that the woman can address the moon's reflection and request a healthy baby (Christenson, 2001).

Further evidence of connections between the ancient guardian of childbirth, Ixchel, and the current deity Yaxper have to do with her rainbow headdress. Ixchel's name means "Lady Rainbow" and she is portrayed wearing a serpent headdress. Yaxper's statue displayed on the *cofradía* altar wears the traditional colorful headdress of women from Santiago Atitlán—a woven ribbon wrapped many times around the head, forming a brim. (This is the headdress worn by Chona's sister Susana in the photo shown of her after she moved to Santiago Atitlán, in Chapter 2.) This headdress was reportedly first worn by Yaxper. Women from Santiago Atitlán identify the headdress as representing a rainbow serpent as well as signifying the umbilical cord tying holy women to the sky (Christenson, 2001).

The patron deities of midwives with their rainbow serpent headdresses: on the left, the statue of Yaxper from Santiago Atitlán of recent years and on the right, a drawing of Ixchel representing the lowland Mayan deity from centuries ago. (Both courtesy of Allen Christenson. The drawing is based on the Dresden Codex 39b, redrawn after Villacorta and Villacorta 1930, p. 121 of Christenson, 2001.)

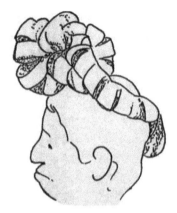

A headdress identified as a coiled serpent is also worn in some other Mayan towns. This representation is of the woven head-ribbon worn in Palín, Guatemala, as a symbol of the coiled serpent. (Drawing by Pilar Garín, courtesy of Barbara Knoke de Arathoon, 2005)

There are other connections between ancient Ixchel and Yaxper. Among her other responsibilities, Ixchel is the goddess of weaving. In turn, Yaxper is credited, along with other ancestral women, with weaving the framework of the cosmos on the backstrap loom (Christenson, 2001). The warp and woof of Yaxper's fabric is regarded as creating the structure of the cosmos, in a supporting grid network. The work of an *iyoom* is thus related to the creation of the universe.

Conception

UNTIL RECENTLY, it was expected that a couple would have children unless they had trouble conceiving. Not being able to have children was a source of sadness for those rare couples who had none.

When I was first in San Pedro, women often commented sympathetically to me on the fact that I had no children, though I had been with my husband for several years. They assumed that not having a child at this point meant that we had problems with fertility. In those days, some Pedranas used birth control methods (including the pill, IUDs, and the rhythm method) to avoid having more children after a woman had plenty—not to delay having a first child, as I was doing.

As part of her *iyoom* materials, Chona found two bones that are used for dealing with infertility—one is a woman's bone, one a man's bone. These appeared in her path when she was already an established *iyoom*. She picked them up but she didn't know what they were for, and went to ask an elderly *iyoom*, who told Chona to grate a bit of the bone and have the patient drink the bone powder in a glass of water, to treat infertility.

::

IN SAN PEDRO, as in many communities throughout the world, there were precautions to avoid conceiving twins. There are risks to mother and babies of giving birth to two babies at once; until recently, one or both babies were not expected to survive. Chona says that mothers were protected from knowing that they were carrying twins—the *iyoom* didn't tell them, even if they asked about being so big, because if they knew, they would be too frightened.

Precautions against conceiving twins are apparently no longer common. However, when I was first in San Pedro, I was warned never to laugh at the misfortune of a woman who was having twins, or I would suffer the same fate. I was also warned never to eat twin fruits, such as doubled bananas or strawberries or corn from twin cobs, to avoid having twins. I did not take this advice seriously, and ate a number of twin fruits. A few years later, I had twins, and since then the woman who most often warned me about twin fruits reminds me with a smile, "You didn't listen to me, Barbara."

The woman who warned me about eating twin fruits, Celia Bixcul (on left), stands in front of her family sweat bath—one of the few that still existed in San Pedro when I first arrived—with her mother and her daughter-in-law. (Photo © Barbara Rogoff, 1975)

Once in existence, twins are cherished in San Pedro (as are mine). They are sometimes referred to as "saints"[52] and they are treated with special care. For example, people make sure that if a toy or piece of clothing is given to one baby, an identical item is also given to the other.

These twins are two of my four namesakes in San Pedro. They are both named Bárbara (but they get called by their middle names). Some people refer to them as "the Bárbaras." (Photo ca. 1999, courtesy Inez Cotuc Yojcom)

⠶

THE FIRST person to detect that a woman has conceived is often her youngest child, according to what I was told in my first years in San Pedro. Usually, in those days, the youngest child was about 1½ or 2 years old and still nursing when the woman became pregnant with the next child. This child, who was until then the last-born—the *ch'i'p*—would become fussy and whiny in the first months of the mother's pregnancy.

This phenomenon may relate to an illness of small children provoked by a woman's pregnancy in Indigenous and *mestizo* communities in parts of Mexico (such as in Morelos in central Mexico; Mellado, Zolla, & Castañeda, 1989). The youngest child acts as if he or she senses the impending displacement, with symptoms including constant crying, loss of appetite, illness, diarrhea, and sometimes ornery aggressiveness.

This syndrome and the idea that a very young child detects pregnancy is a fine illustration of the travel and adaptation of cultural practices across time and place. The Spanish name of the condition, *chipilez*, is derived from the Nahuatl label *tzípitl* for this condition. (Nahuatl was the language of the ancient Aztec and surrounding peoples and is still spoken in some communities in central Mexico.) The idea of *chipilez* is sometimes extended to older children's or adults' childish behavior, among different language groups in three nations. Spanish- and Mayan-speaking people in Mexico, Guatemala, and the United States sometimes refer to an older child or an adult who is being demanding or self-centered as *chipi* or *ch'ip*, in a teasing critique of his or her infantile behavior.

⁙

CHONA ALWAYS knows when a woman is pregnant, according to her granddaughter Chonita. Sometimes even though a lab test indicates that a woman is not pregnant, Chona correctly diagnoses that the woman is pregnant. Chona's diagnosis is based in part on physical signs including the lack of a period, morning sickness, and headaches.

But in addition, an *iyoom* simply *knows*, based on her spiritual calling, that a woman is pregnant. According to Chona, a girl of 9 or 10 years who is destined to be an *iyoom* may say to her mother, "I saw so-and-so and she is pregnant." The mother says, "Hush. That's not something to talk about."

In her early 20s, Chonita told me that it sometimes makes her nervous how her grandmother seems to always know everything that is going on. For example, Chonita said her grandmother can just look at a young woman and know if the young woman has begun "doing something" (having sex) with her boyfriend.

An example of Chona's diagnostic skill occurred some years later, when medical personnel told Chonita that her second child would be born in mid-March. Chona insisted that the baby would be born March 31; indeed he was. (Chonita relied on medical personnel, as she then lived in a city some hours from San Pedro.)

Chona told Chonita that this baby has the spirit of Chona's father, Marcos, the baby's great-great-grandfather, and so Chonita and her husband gave the baby Marcos' name. The Tz'utujil word for namesake (*k'axeel*) also means replacement, such as when a person leaves someone else in his or her place to do a job; in some Tz'utujil settings children represent the substitute for ancestors (Christenson, 2001). Baby Marcos is expected to carry the characteristics of his namesake Marcos who preceded him, just as Chonita ("little Chona"), named after her grandmother, is expected to be like Chona in many ways. The fact that baby Marcos was born on March 31, which was a strong day in the cycle of the traditional Mayan calendar, is consistent with the strong character that he inherits from his namesake. Generational inheritances are of course modified in new generations, even as new people carry on in the fashion of their namesakes.

Requesting an *Iyoom*'s Services for Pregnancy

FOR A FIRST-TIME PREGNANCY, the mother-in-law or the mother usually contacts the *iyoom* who has served her in the past, by about the fifth month. The mother-in-law or mother requests the *iyoom* to attend the pregnant young woman who lives in her home.

The request to the *iyoom* often involves elegant formal speech, with humble and respectful words and apologies for the inconvenience and for the shortcomings of the speech and offerings. It is still the case that the mother-in-law or mother makes the request with "very pretty words" that include formally requesting the *iyoom* to do the favor of attending the pregnant woman, according to Chona:

> Please do us the favor, Ma'am, please do us the favor. My daughter is with child, please tend to her that she will be cured, that she will not die. Please excuse us, we came to you because you are an *iyoom*, we came to you because we know you are a good *iyoom*. It is for this reason that we request of you the favor of healing her.

The characteristics of Mesoamerican formal speech are a good example of a cultural practice that has endured across many centuries. Key features in formal speech, especially cyclic repetition, are "as deeply embedded in the language and culture matrix as one can go" (Hofling, 1993, p. 178, discussing a Yucatecan Mayan group; see also Martin, 1994). The structure of formal speech resembles the structure of hieroglyphic writing of a millennium ago, continuing as a rich oral performance tradition (Hofling, 1993). The cyclic repetition can be seen in the quote from

Chona, above, and among San Pedro children who continue to be taught Mayan oratory.

These boys are performing an oratory as part of a formal event (a celebration of Ben Paul's 80th birthday). Reflecting a connection of the oratory with ancient practices, they are wearing clothing that was formerly characteristic of San Pedro men, including the headcloth draped over the shoulder. Ordinarily these Pedrano boys wore Western-style clothing. (Family photo, 1991)

FORMAL SPEECHES like those of the San Pedro mothers and mothers-in-law were made centuries ago by Aztec families to entreat the midwife to accept the care of a pregnant young woman. The poetic speeches were recorded by Aztec nobles in the Florentine Codex in about 1547. Many are the echoes across the centuries:

> The mothers, the fathers of the married couple assembled one's kinsmen; and they drank, they ate. And thereafter there was consultation as to some midwife to be sought out, to be supplicated to bathe their maiden in the sweat bath and to serve as midwife. . . . First, the parents spoke with one another; they greeted, they entreated one another. One of the old men, either of the youth's people or of the maiden's people, spoke. He said:
>
> "Ye who are here present, ye who are mothers, ye who are fathers, verily, now, the child, the girl, the maiden, suffereth. For already it is thus. But behold, what hath our lord willed? Perhaps there is death. May ye help her; may ye show her to the sweat bath. . . . Place her in the lap, on the shoulders of the wise one, the skilled one, the midwife. Entreat her with a word or two." (Sahagún, 1969a, p. 149)
>
> An old woman relative . . . entreated the midwife to receive the pregnant woman whom they had left in her charge:
>
> "Here thou art seated; here our lord, the lord of the near, of the nigh, hath placed thee, precious person, our lady, noblewoman. . . . For thou understandest, thou takest heed because the baby, the girl, the maiden, hath conceived. . . . For verily our lord now wisheth to show the mercy in his heart; the lord of the earth wisheth to give a precious necklace, a precious feather; he hath wished to install a life—our lord hath wished to insert it within thy humble one. . . . And with this thou art informed that he delivereth, he placeth her in thy hands, in thy lap, upon thy shoulders. Here are the old men, the old women, the parents, those with offspring. And those who are the mothers, who are the fathers now deliver thee the child. . . .
>
> "This is all that thou acceptest, that thou hearest, O precious person, our lady, noblewoman. But be not troubled in heart, in body; be not angered. Who [else] would entreat thee? Who [else] would draw forth a word or two—would lift a clear voice, would set forth, would say the well-spoken, well-ordered [words] which thou dost accept, which thou dost heed?

The [departed] old men, the old women, those with offspring; the grandfathers, the grandmothers . . . would have entreated thee. But in their absence we perform in childish, in baby-like fashion. Stuttering, stammering are the word or two which we here deliver; ill-spoken, disordered is what we intone, what we set forth.

"With a word or two we here entreat thee. Show favor to the baby, the girl, the maiden. Perform thy task, thy duty, since thou art the skilled one, the artisan of our lord; since thou art empowered by him. This is all which thou dost grasp, which thou dost heed. Perform thy office; do thy work. Aid our lord; help him."

The midwife spoke, the one in charge of birth, the one who set the womb aright, the one who delivered. She said:

"Behold, ye who are here: our lord, the lord of the earth, hath seated you—ye who are old men, ye who are old women. . . . Verily I grasp, I accept your spirit, your words, and your weeping, your compassion with which ye weep, ye feel compassion; with which ye are anguished for the sake of your precious necklace, your precious feather, the little woman who is perhaps your second child, perhaps your eldest, or perhaps your youngest." (Sahagún, 1969b, pp. 151–153)

From the Florentine Codex: The pregnant woman responds to the orators (about 1547). (Book 6, Ch 25. Reproduced courtesy of University of Utah Press)

This account of the Aztec midwife taking on the care of a mother-to-be, about five centuries ago, has striking resonances with practices in San Pedro. The Aztec and San Pedro formal oratories entreating the midwife to help the pregnant woman share features in the structure of the speech as well as similar reverence and humility, with apologies for the inadequacy of the oratory. The social responsibilities are also similar—the older generation shares responsibility for the pregnancy and the pregnant woman.

In addition, the Aztec elders refer to the power and responsibility of the midwife being divinely selected to this role: "Perform thy task, thy duty, since thou art the skilled one, the artisan of our lord; since thou art empowered by him. . . . Perform thy office; do thy work." This spiritual calling is echoed across the centuries in the divine selection of San Pedro *iyooma'* to do this sacred work.

The Aztec midwife was careful to warn the young woman's relatives of her limitations in avoiding the mortal dangers of childbirth, as merely the assistant to "our lord." The references to "our lord" may pertain to the sun god. In ancient Mayan and related religions he was the husband of the moon goddess Ixchel, the goddess of childbirth, medicine, weaving, water, the earth, and maize (Thompson, 1970).

Chona reports that formerly in their prayers, she and the other *iyooma'* referred explicitly to *Ajau*, the Mayan name for "Lord," but now they only pray to divinities using Spanish names. The changes and continuities across centuries in these figures and their roles, visible still but transformed in today's practices, are a powerful example of the dynamic as well as persistent nature of culture.

Protecting Pregnancy

IN PRENATAL CONSULTATIONS, the San Pedro *iyoom* warns the mother-to-be how to protect the baby-to-be. This occurred even in prior decades with first-time mothers who were not told that this physical condition is due to carrying a baby.

The San Pedro *iyoom* counsels the pregnant woman and her family with many of the same protections of pregnancy as the Aztec midwife of five centuries ago. These include avoiding such negative experiences as anger or unfulfilled wants such as food cravings, in order to protect the health of the fetus and to keep from miscarrying.[53]

In San Pedro, neighbors and family members are still obliged to satisfy food cravings of an expectant mother (as well as of her youngest child if she already has children), to avoid the risk of provoking miscarriage by displeasing the fetus, from whom the food cravings arise. Even if a person is eating a banana and a pregnant woman is interested in it, the person has to give the woman what is left of the banana. Also, people often give pregnant women food and urge them to eat it even if they don't ask for it, so that the fetus will grow well. Recently a young Pedrana who was pregnant didn't know of this custom, and when a neighbor gave her some bananas, she politely declined, saying she wasn't hungry; the neighbor told her to take them home and eat them.

Protecting the pregnancy is the responsibility of the family and neighbors, not only the responsibility of the *iyoom* and the pregnant woman, who in former times might not even know what was being protected. Similar precautions were given by the Aztec midwife of nearly five centuries ago to the pregnant woman and her kin:

> And then [are told] those various things which she said to the pregnant woman, in order that she should not much hurt the baby when it was born, in order that she should be quickly delivered. Much is mentioned which is memorable—very good discourses of the sort which women say; and very good are each of the metaphors. . . .
>
> Many were the commands that the midwife left to protect the pregnant woman. . . . She said it was necessary that she should look at nothing which angered one, which frightened one, which offended one, for she would bring the same upon [the child].[54] And what the pregnant woman desired should quickly be given; it should not be delayed; for her child would suffer if what she desired were not quickly given. . . . The midwife said:
>
> "O my children, precious persons, our ladies, ye who are here: are you perchance babies? Are you perchance children? For we are the old women who consult among ourselves; you are seeing all of the mortality among us women in our wombs. Doth perchance the girl, the maiden, already know of this? Ye must take care of the girl; show special concern for her; let her yet be [the object of] your watchfulness; let her yet become [the object of] your care. . . .
>
> "Here am I, I who am called a midwife. . . . Do I perchance guard a cure for death? Shall I perchance withhold it from one if we should go to help one? Is it a cure for death which is in my hand, which I go carrying with me? For our lord can only be helped, can only be aided [by what we do]. But what we do is

only [like] fanning flies away. . . . Verily, let all of us now show our devotion; let us yet have faith in our lord, in whatsoever he is determining." (Sahagún, 1969b, pp. 151–158, bracketed words are from the original)

It is likely that the protections of pregnancy have also been greatly influenced by customs of Spain, in addition to those originating in Mesoamerica. Indeed, George Foster claimed that the pregnancy taboos in Latin America were more Spanish than Indigenous, part of the "conquest culture" resulting from the extent to which Spaniards "swarmed over America."[55] Very similar protections have been widespread in Spain, where "the food cravings of a pregnant woman must be satisfied, whatever the cost" (Foster, 1960, p. 114). In Spain, mothers' unsatisfied food cravings were believed to cause miscarriages or stillbirths because food cravings come from the unborn child, not from the mother.

Another widespread protection for pregnancy is clearly connected with ancient Mesoamerican practices, from before the arrival of the Spanish. It is common throughout many Mayan communities, including San Pedro until recently, as well as in some other Indigenous communities of Mexico, for a pregnant woman to avoid viewing an eclipse (Ingham, 1986; McClain, 1975; Mellado, Zolla, & Castañeda, 1989; Reina, 1966). In San Pedro, looking at an eclipse was believed to

> induce miscarriage or deform the developing fetus. During an eclipse women should remain indoors or wear a protective object. This may be a kerchief or belt worn about the waist or a metal item such as a key or a pair of scissors tucked into the belt. The ancient Aztecs carried an obsidian blade for this purpose. (Paul & Paul, 1952, p. 177)

A related protection is common in Latino Los Angeles as well as in Mexico: The pregnant Mexican and Mexican-heritage women often wear a safety pin in red underwear to protect the baby. This has transformed over centuries from the Aztec protection against deleterious effects of an eclipse or the full moon—wearing an obsidian blade tied over the pregnant belly with a red string (Hayes-Bautista, 2004; Mellado, Zolla, & Castañeda, 1989).[56]

Another protection in San Pedro was not to drink or eat sour lemons or sour oranges during a pregnancy, because that might lead to losing the baby. Chona herself avoided lemon when she was pregnant, but she says that now only the oldest people talk about this.

::

IT WOULD SEEM DIFFICULT in prior times to ensure that a first-time mother followed the pregnancy observances if she was not aware of pregnancy. However, the Pauls (1952) indicated that the young girls followed the instructions of their mother or mother-in-law without questions. The mother or mother-in-law could indicate that something dire would happen if the observances were not followed, without referring to pregnancy.

For example, a young Pedrano father in 1941 reported that the *iyoom* and the mother or mother-in-law told the young woman that if she craves something to eat, she should tell her mother so that it would be given to her; she must not suffer the craving unsatisfied. If she saw something good and could not buy it, she should eat a few grains of salt. The *iyoom* and the mother or mother-in-law told her that if she had an unsatisfied craving, the congealment in her abdomen would break open, but they did not tell her about the fetus.

To protect the fetus from evil eye and from unfulfilled food cravings, as well as other dangers, the San Pedro *iyoom* warned the girl simply to do what her elders told her, even though they didn't explain why:

> Since the girl doesn't know there's a baby forming inside her, the midwife will tell her, "Now, my dear, I have some advice for you. Don't get into trouble. You must remember what I say, day and night. One day you will realize what I'm saying. Don't go out walking at noon. Sit down. When your mother or your mother-in-law tell you not to go out, just say "yes." There is a reason for them why they won't allow you. If you do this, my dear, you'll find out why. But if you laugh and don't obey, you'll see what happens to you. The same is true at night. If you are told not to sit outside the house, you obey, my dear. Don't let it go in one ear and out the other. You obey. You're an adult now, you're not a child any longer. I'm dead serious." (San Pedro fieldnotes of the Summer Institute of Linguistics, 1978, Book 45, p. 152)

The *Iyoom*'s Work During Pregnancy

THE FLORENTINE CODEX of the mid-1500s described how the Aztec midwife provided prenatal care. Her treatment included administering the medicinal sweat bath and examining the fetal position and massaging the fetus into appropriate position (via external version) for head-first delivery:

And at once, of her own accord, the midwife fired, heated the sweat bath, and she put the maiden in the sweat bath, where she massaged the pregnant woman's abdomen; she placed aright [the unborn child]. She placed it straight; she kept turning it as she massaged her, as she went on manipulating her. . . . And when the pregnant woman came forth from the sweat bath, at that time she massaged her. Many times the midwife massaged the abdomen of the pregnant woman. (Sahagún, 1969b, p. 155, bracketed insertion from the original)

The Florentine Codex shows the midwife massaging the pregnant woman's abdomen to correct the position of the fetus, inside the sweat bath (about 1547). (Book 6, Ch 27, folio 130v, reproduced courtesy University of Utah Press)

THE PEDRANA *IYOOM* formerly administered the sweat bath and still uses prenatal massage and external version of the fetus in the care of the pregnant woman. Now, instead of treatments occurring in the sweat bath, usually prenatal visits are house calls to the family's home. When Chona in her 80s developed some difficulty walking, sometimes her prenatal visits took place in her own house. The prenatal visits occur approximately monthly until near the delivery, when the visits become more frequent.

During the visits, the San Pedro *iyoom* examines the pregnant woman visually and vaginally, and feels the belly. If the woman is in danger of giving birth prematurely, the *iyoom* may bind the belly snugly with a sash around the woman's waist (Summer Institute of Linguistics, 1978).

If the baby is not in the right position to emerge with the head first, Chona can often turn the baby during prenatal visits by external version, massaging the mother's belly to move the baby into the proper position. If a baby is feet-first or breech (buttocks first), Chona can usually turn it, if the pregnancy is not so far advanced that the baby is already wedged in position. Chona described this, demonstrating with her hands,

> If I can feel the baby moving with some space around it, when
> I hold my hands on both sides of the belly, I can massage the belly
> to get the baby into the right position. If the belly is tight, it is
> difficult. And if the baby is wedged sideways, it often cannot be
> shifted.

Prenatal massage has remained a widespread treatment by midwives in various parts of Mexico as well as Guatemala (Huber & Sandstrom, 2001; Mellado, Zolla, & Castañeda, 1989). In the photo, a Mayan midwife in the Yucatan (Mexico) employs prenatal massage for a pregnant woman, in the 1970s. (Note the presence of children observing in the background.) (Jordan, 1978; photo reproduced by permission)

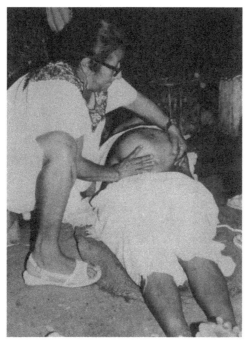

The Mayan midwife turns a fetus from breech position (bottom-first) to the appropriate head-first position, in the Yucatan. (Jordan, 1978; photo reproduced by permission)

If, despite the *iyoom*'s efforts to turn the baby to the head-down position for delivery, the baby presents in breech position or feet-first, usually the baby is born safely anyway. No special procedures are needed. But if Chona determines in a prenatal visit that the baby is firmly transverse, she sends the mother to the hospital for a cesarean section. Otherwise, the risk of the baby dying is high.

⠶

WHEN CHONA WAS YOUNG, sometimes the family refused to or could not make the arduous trip about 9 miles across the lake by canoe and about 5 miles up a steep escarpment to the hospital in Sololá. Even when I was first in San Pedro (in 1974), although there were public motorboats three times a week, these were seldom at the time of a woman's labor, and they took 2 hours to cross the lake. An express motorboat could sometimes be arranged, but at a prohibitive cost in those days. Canoes were still used to make trips to the closer lakeshore towns to bring and purchase goods at weekly markets or to attend a fiesta.

In the large canoes, people rowing paid half price. (Two of the rowers in this canoe are foreigners; photo © Barbara Rogoff, 1975)

The arrival of the three-times-a-week public motorboat was an event noticed throughout town in 1975. Children eagerly met the boat to see the action, as well as to greet returning family members and to help carry goods. (Photo © Barbara Rogoff, 1975)

Another reason that people avoided crossing the lake to the hospital was that the cold air (especially night air) of the chilly lake is regarded as a danger to sick people or those in fragile conditions. Furthermore, the hospital itself was feared because of the regularity with which people died there. (This was due to poor-quality hospital treatment as well as lack of family resources, which in turn led to people often waiting too late in the course of an illness to receive effective treatment.) In addition, in hospitals, Mayan people are often treated in a condescending manner (Cosminsky, 2001a,b) and in ways that conflict with Mayan health and social practices. Pedranos often preferred to face certain death at home than the possibility of death at the hospital, especially in past decades.

I can still clearly recall the death rattle in the throat of this young mother,
Rosita, age 36, who refused to go to the hospital for treatment of intestinal
worms because she did not want to die in the hospital. She left six young
children when she died. Here she stands in her doorway with three of her
six children, a few months before her death. (Photo © Barbara Rogoff, 1975)

Now small motor boats take about 15 to 20 minutes to cross the lake, every half-hour or less. For a nighttime delivery, chartering a boat is easier than in earlier times. In addition, San Pedro now has an ambulance (and a road to other towns) and people can charter cars. Also, some families can afford to pay for care in private hospitals, where the care is better than in the public hospitals. Thus, some of the barriers to going to the hospital on the other side of the lake have been removed.

Now families usually take the women to the hospital if needed, and a number of San Pedro babies are born in the hospital by cesarean section. In addition, C-sections are now performed in San Pedro by doctors in the recently established clinic associated with one of the Protestant churches.

Birthing

AT THE DELIVERY itself, in addition to the pregnant woman and the *iyoom*, usually the husband is present. In former times, the woman's mother and mother-in-law, and sometimes her father and father-in-law, were also present. Nobel Laureate Rigoberta Menchú (1983) explained that in her Quiché Mayan community, the presence of several other adults is important because they receive the baby to the community; the baby belongs not just to the parents but to the community.

Chona commented that in the old days, there were many people present, but it was a bother—in particular, it was embarrassing to the woman giving birth. So Chona began asking for only the husband to be present, not the rest of the family. Gradually, other midwives adopted this practice. Chona supposes that other midwives heard from their patients or their neighbors about Chona requesting for just the husband to be present, and began to follow suit.

Chona says that since she began delivering babies, she has always had her patients lie down, rather than use kneeling positions usually used by prior *iyooma'* and still by some. Previously in San Pedro, and perhaps still in other Mayan and some central Mexican communities, the customary position was kneeling or squatting (Reina, 1966; Sullivan, 1969), with the woman resting her hands or her buttocks on two small stools. Her husband would sit on a small stool behind the woman with his arms wrapped around her at the top of her abdomen and his knees pressed into her back to aid her (Paul, 1969; see also León, 1910, regarding similar practices in Mexico).

At Chona's deliveries, because the woman gives birth lying down in bed, the husband is not as involved in supporting her physically as the husband is if the woman is in the kneeling position. Instead, he sits beside his wife on the bed to help her; she sometimes grabs onto him, clasping her hands over his shoulders behind his neck as she pushes in labor.

This 1996 painting depicts a delivery in former times in San Pedro. The midwife waits on a mat with a clean cloth ready, while the mothers of the young couple tend a candle and the clay basin of boiling water. The pregnant woman's husband, father-in-law, and father support her in pushing, stand ready to assist, or look on nervously.

The woman's reclining position has been used for the last phase of delivery for perhaps six decades for at least some births in San Pedro, as near as I can tell. The artist, Pedro Rafael Gonzalez Chavajay, and Chona say that the raised position of the mother's shoulders indicates that there was some difficulty with this birth, perhaps with the position of the baby.

Pedro Rafael is one of San Pedro's most renowned painters, with paintings shown in San Francisco's Legion of Honor museum and the U.S. National Museum of the American Indian. He does considerable research on ancient ways for his paintings, gathering information especially from his grandfather, Antonio Chavajay, until he died at age 98 in 2008. The aged appearances of all the people are a mark of the style of painting for which San Pedro has become famous. (Painting "La Comadrona" reproduced courtesy of Joseph Johnston, Arte Maya Tz'utuhil)

A Mayan birth in Yucatan (Mexico), attended by a midwife who wears a mask. The pregnant woman is semi-reclining, supported by the hammock and her husband to hold onto when bearing down. (Jordan, 1978; photos reproduced by permission)

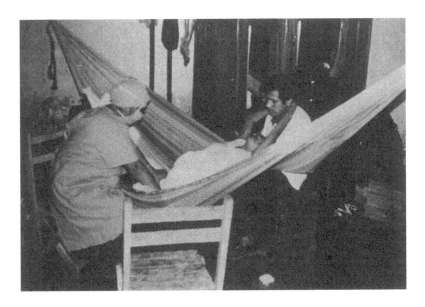

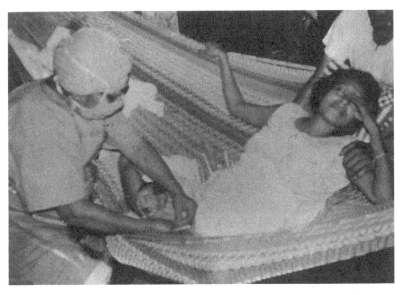

Birth activists point out that medicalization of midwives' practices has pressured midwives to use the horizontal position preferred by Western doctors, for the doctors' own accessibility to check the patient throughout labor. The traditional kneeling position, or squatting, is regarded as advantageous for ease of delivery, due to gravity, the mother's circulation and oxygen supply, and the position of the pelvic bones (Cosminsky, 2001a; Jordan, 1993).

I wondered how to understand the change from kneeling to the lying-down position in San Pedro, which Chona says works better than squatting. She reports that the doctors in midwife courses also have the patients lay down, but that she started using this position before the doctors started training San Pedro midwives.

It seems important to distinguish the position for labor from the position for the delivery itself. Chona uses the lying-down position only for the birth itself, not for labor—unlike the usual hospital labor procedure. When it is not yet time for the birth, Chona has the woman walk around, and encourages her to continue with her usual work or activities. If a family calls Chona when the birth is hours away, Chona tells the woman, "You have plenty of time, just do what you would ordinarily do."

Chona comes back when the birth is imminent. When she can tell that the time has come for the birth itself (after the water breaks and a bit of blood appears), she tells the woman to lie down. The woman lies on a clean reed mat on a bed. In former times, she would lie on a clean mat or burlap bag on the floor if the family did not have a bed, and Chona reports that sometimes people preferred the floor even if they had a bed. The floor is more secure than a bed—one time the bed broke as the baby was being born. The patient fell, hurting her back, and Chona hurt her knees as she fell, while catching the baby.

Chona's innovations illustrate the ways that individuals contribute to cultural change. She seems to have fostered use of the lying-down position in San Pedro for the final moment of delivery; it was apparently used sporadically before. She also apparently led the way for reducing the number of onlookers and for not rushing the early phases of labor and delivery.

∷

CHONA INITIATED providing a more gentle treatment of the mothers in labor. She (and others) report that previously the midwives exhorted the women to push and often scolded them, saying, "What's wrong with you? What's taking so long? Push!" The previous midwives sometimes even told the women's husbands to slap them or pull their hair to get them to exert. Rushing the birth is a practice condemned more recently by *iyooma'* as showing ignorance of the stages of labor (Paul, 1969). The women got fatigued and when it was time to push, the women had no energy for it, so the birth itself was more difficult.

Chona urges the woman to take her time, not using her forces early to push. If the baby is a long time in coming, Chona says that she simply waits, seeing that it isn't the hour for the birth yet. "The baby needs to come at its own time; one needs to be patient."

Also, rather than scolding the woman, Chona would encourage her. When Chona had newly emerged as an *iyoom*, her approach was contrasted with an "old-time midwife, well respected, whom the people were afraid of. . . . [Chona will] never despise you. She explains everything to you very carefully to reassure you" (Summer Institute of Linguistics, 1978, Book 45, p. 102).

When I asked Chona's niece, Virginia Concepción Pérez Juárez, what changes Chona has made in the cultural practices of San Pedro, she replied,

> Aunt Chona is so positive in what she does. Some midwives scold the women, "Why aren't you putting in any effort?" but Chona never gets angry with them. She speaks to them gently, saying "You can do it, *mi amor*. Little by little, *mi hija*. Everything will be fine. Your baby will come out fine. Your baby is *preciosa*. Our mother Virgin María will help you—ask Virgin María for strength." She refers to Virgin María even with patients who are Evangelical Protestants, which surprises them, since praying to Virgin María is more what the Catholics do.
>
> She doesn't force the patients, and she knows when it is time for the patient to apply effort. For example, about 4 years ago [before 2008], the mother of one of her patients told me that they had another midwife, but that other midwife pressured the woman to exert herself and she got exhausted. So about 11 a.m. that day, the family called for Chona. Chona came and said, "Rest, *hija* [daughter], you won't have a baby until tomorrow. Just do your ordinary work, you won't have your baby until 4 o'clock tomorrow afternoon. Go to the lakeshore if you want and wash clothes, whatever you usually do." The next day, Chona arrived at 3:45 p.m., and there was still no sign of a baby. Chona washed up 3:50 p.m., and still no baby. Everyone wondered what's up. But at 4:00 exactly, the baby was born, easily. (August 2008)

Chona says that she wanted to make these changes—reducing the number of onlookers, having the mother lie down for the last moments of the delivery, not rushing the labor, treating the patient gently, in addition to informing pregnant young women what was happening to them—because she was so dissatisfied with how her own first baby had been born.

Chona's own births, as learning experiences

AFTER HER FIRST BABY, Chona delivered the rest of her own babies by herself. It is common for *iyooma'* to deliver their babies alone, once they begin to practice. The *iyooma'* are often rivals and critical of each other. They may not attend each other's own births and seldom collaborate.[57]

But that is not the reason Chona gave for giving birth without an *iyoom* in attendance after the first birth. Chona was so unhappy with the way the birth of her first-born went, she preferred to give birth without an *iyoom*. Her *iyoom* had hurried and scolded her, rushing her to give birth rather than waiting patiently for the baby's time to be born. Chona explained the difficulties with the birth of her first child:

> I had labor pains for 5 days and 4 nights. The *iyoom* was with me for the 5 days and 4 nights, urging me to push. And it took me 15 months to recuperate.
>
> I didn't know that I was having a baby, they just told me to exert force so that what I had in my belly would come out. I was very scared; I had no idea what was in my belly. They told me, "You'll be done soon. Tomorrow your belly will be fine."
> But I didn't know what to think. I was exhausted, so exhausted I seemed like a drunkard.
>
> During my pregnancy, when the baby moved, I had asked my mother, "Mama, what do I have?" and she had only said, "Don't touch it, it's fine." I thought it was a mouse or something like that.
>
> During the labor, I was sitting on my husband's haunches with my thighs over his, with him pushing on my belly as they used to always do. He sat behind me on a tiny chair and clasped his arms around me. The *iyoom* sat on the floor to receive the baby.
>
> They put a rope over a roof beam for me to pull on with my hands.[58] The *iyoom* [María Puac] told me to pull on the rope with my teeth too, biting one end of the rope that went over the beam and pulling with my hands on the other end. I bit down on the

rope firmly with my teeth. But I didn't understand what I was supposed to do, and I did it wrong; I was only 16 when I had my first baby. I pulled hard with my hands *and* my teeth, on that rope. So hard that I loosened my two lower front teeth—these ones that fell out—with my first child. I was not supposed to pull with my hands and my teeth at one time; I was supposed to spell my hands for a time by using my teeth for a while.

Because I suffered so much with that first birth, I didn't want to give birth again with an *iyoom*. That's why I was afraid and I didn't tell anyone when I was about to give birth. I thought, if I die, I'll die alone, I don't want to call anyone anymore.

This photo shows Ventura and Chona just after they demonstrated Chona's birth position for me. Chona and I had recruited her husband to show how a young father would sit on one of the tiny chairs that used to be common, with his knees apart supporting the woman's buttocks and thighs. In the photo, Ventura is laughing because of the demonstration and because Chona and I had had him put on the old-fashioned headcloth, which is now seldom worn—also because the little chair was so old it was about to fall apart. (Photo © Barbara Rogoff, 1996)

I was curious as to how Chona had managed to give birth by herself. All nine of the subsequent babies were born without anyone attending her. When her older surviving daughter was born, after several other babies, Chona was alone in the house:

> It was Holy Thursday [of Easter week], and I had been losing water for 11 days before the birth, a lot of water. In those days people always made *maatz'* [the ceremonial corn gruel drink] for holidays, and I was preparing the hominy corn on the cooking fire. I was cooking the corn for the *maatz'*, and many people were arriving at my house to leave water that they had brought in jugs from the lake for the *maatz'*.
>
> And I don't know how it happened, I was stirring the corn gruel in a big clay pot on the fire, and for the time being I was by myself. Two older ladies had just left after bringing me water for the *maatz'*. I felt that something was happening to me, and I screamed, "Aaayy! Aaayy!" because I could feel that the baby was coming out. I screamed twice; it would be lying if I said I didn't scream. I screamed with the pain, since there was no one there to hear. And the baby dropped out on the hard-packed dirt floor, near the hearth. That's how I did that one alone.

Her older surviving son was premature:

> I gave birth to him alone too, but he was tiny when he was born. He was born when I hadn't yet completed 7 months of pregnancy. Tiny. I gave birth to him in the bed.

Chona's last (tenth) baby was born quickly at the end of a strenuous day. Chona had labor pains while returning in late afternoon from serving as *iyoom* for two women who had just given birth. She went to her house as fast as she could. By the time she got close to her house, the contractions were strong. As she neared her doorway, the baby came out. Chona grabbed the umbilical cord and pulled to get the placenta to come out. She pulled off her *corte* (wraparound skirt) and threw it over the baby and placenta to try to cover them up, and went into the house with only her blouse on. (Ordinarily, Pedranas were never without their skirts; they bathed and slept modestly in their skirts.)[59]

> The skirt, the baby, and the placenta, I just left them there, and went in the house, walking around with no skirt on. After a bit I realized my nakedness and grabbed a skirt to put on.

A little neighbor boy about 5 years old came to our door to ask my son to play, and I asked him to please call my neighbor Elenita. He said fine, but he was scared when he saw the baby on the ground, all bloody. The baby was crying.

Elenita arrived and asked, "What happened to you?"

"Elenita, please gather up that baby." Elenita gathered up the baby and brought her inside the house.

Elenita was afraid to touch the placenta. "What are you going to do with it? I'm afraid!"

I pulled on a corner of the *corte* to pull the placenta into the house. I picked it up and put it and the baby on a nearby mat, and began to clean up the baby and I cut the cord.

Elenita said, "Why did you do that? Why did you do it? You're going to die, because it's bad, what you did!" But I didn't realize what I was doing. I don't know if I was afraid or not; I don't know what came over me to leave a baby in the doorway like that. But that's how it was. I did it by myself.

⁚⁚

WHEN I ASKED CHONA why she began having all her patients lie down rather than kneeling or squatting, she replied that she got the idea with one of her own babies, the second one. She gave birth to him alone, lying in bed. She had been sleeping, but with labor pains for a day. She was sleeping on her side, looking at the wall, when she felt that he was coming out. She screamed, "Aaayy! Aaayy!" there by herself. Lying on her back, she grabbed hold of the posts at the head of the bed, as she has her patients do when they are bearing down, and out came the baby together with the placenta.

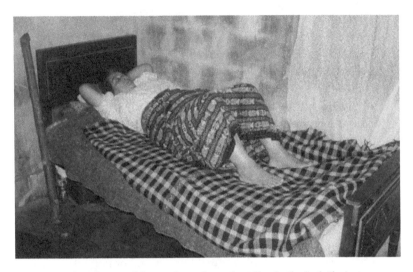

Chona demonstrated for me how the patient lies in the bed; the iyoom
would be at the patient's feet. (Photo © Barbara Rogoff, 1996)

With patience, and the woman lying down at the end of labor,
there are not problems with the placenta not coming out. I just
wait. When one urges the patient to "push, push, force yourself,
force it," before the right time, the baby pushes the placenta back
in the womb. But by putting up with the pains patiently, the
placenta comes out together with the baby. One tells the patient to
wait a little, even though they say "I'm dying, I'm dying!" I tell
them to wait a little, relax and don't push yet, and the baby brings
the placenta along. For example, with my patient last night, the
baby came and along with it came the placenta. So I wait and
I always have them deliver lying down.

The delivery of the placenta is a matter of concern. This concern
leads some other midwives to urge the woman to exert herself, as indicated by this account from San Pedro fieldnotes of the Summer Institute
of Linguistics:

When the baby is delivered the midwife says to the woman,
"Push harder, my dear. You still aren't out of the woods yet.
There's still something else that hasn't come yet. The Second
Money [another name for the placenta] hasn't come, yet." . . . The
woman will die if the Second Money doesn't come. That is why the
midwife is so insistent that the woman push harder. If the woman
hasn't any more strength left and can't push, some midwives say,

"Make her vomit by putting the ends of her hair down her throat."
Then those that are in the house do this to the poor woman so that
she'll vomit and the force of it will evacuate the Second Money.
There are other midwives who deliver it manually and thereby
save the woman. (1978, Book 3, p. 7)

A San Pedro birth connecting with pre-Hispanic Aztec practices

CENTURIES-OLD PRACTICES as well as more recent innovations can be
seen in an account of the birth of Rafael González' child, written (in
Spanish, August 27, 1941) for Ben and Lois Paul's research. Rafael was
one of the more literate men in San Pedro in 1941, with three years of
schooling; this was sufficient for him and others to work as a schoolteacher.

*Rafael founded a fine arts painting tradition for which San Pedro is now
well known (Paul & Johnston, 1998). From pre-Hispanic times, Tz'utujil
painting had been well developed; the Spanish noted the skill of the Mayan
painters, who created most of the paintings and altars in small towns
(Orellana, 1984). In 1938, Rafael was the only Pedrano who painted furniture
and refurbished the idols of antique saints (Rosales, 1949). Pedro Rafael
González Chavajay, whose painting of a delivery was reproduced earlier, is
one of his descendants who have become well-known painters. (Their paintings
and paintings of others of Rafael's descendants and other local painters can
be viewed on the website of Arte Maya Tz'utujil, http://www.artemaya.com.)
(Photo by Lois and Ben Paul, 1941)*

Rafael wrote about his wife's (Cándida's) delivery, which occurred about the same year as Chona's first baby was born, with the same *iyoom*. This was not Cándida's and Rafael's first baby, however.

At about 8 at night on the 22nd, Cándida began to feel ill. During the day, her *iyoom* María Puac came to see her and told her that she would give birth either this night or early tomorrow. And so it happened. Cándida started to have slow pains around the waist. About 10 at night they became more frequent. When I saw that the pains were coming one after another, I went to call the *iyoom* at 11 at night. I called to wake her and she didn't hear at first, but finally she woke up and we returned.

When we reached home, she examined Cándida, and told her that it wasn't time yet, and it would still be two or three more hours. She told her to walk around in the house for a while, and Cándida did so, walking for more than an hour. She told Cándida that when each pain came, she should lean against the wall and exert herself, and she did. At about 1:45, the *iyoom* saw her again and said that the time had come.

She told Cándida to deliver in the position that she was used to from when her other babies had been born. Some women, when their babies are born, lie down. Others kneel to push, with two little stools at each side, that is, one under each buttock, and that is how Cándida did it. She sat down, or rather, almost knelt, with the thighs well separated. The *iyoom* placed herself facing her and arranged a reed mat under Cándida and spread a little blanket carefully on it, and on top she put a soft cloth, to place the baby on when it was born.

But Cándida did not give birth then, because she was worn out with the previous efforts. Eventually the *iyoom* told me to sit behind her, supporting her from behind with my knees and enfolding her sturdily in my arms, and I did so. The *iyoom* also asked for an empty bottle for Cándida to blow into strongly, and she did so, blowing with force and then the baby was born. The placenta did not emerge right away; the *iyoom* says that the placenta is harder than the baby because it doesn't move on its own, but finally it came out.

Rafael noted also that he had prepared a remedy to help labor progress, made with the tail of a *wujch'* (*tacuacín* or *tlacuache*, opossum).

> I knew that when women don't give birth quickly, one gives the woman the tail of a *wujch'*. It is first toasted on the fire and then ground fine and then boiled well in a little jar. This liquid is given to the patient, and with it, she soon gives birth.

It was not clear whether Cándida was offered the opossum-tail tea during the delivery, so I considered leaving it out of Rafael's account here. But a few weeks later, I was looking through several volumes of the Florentine Codex, which is like an encyclopedia of pre-Hispanic Aztec knowledge and practices. I was looking for information on the pre-Hispanic use of some plants, and I happened by chance to open to the page about the opossum in a volume listing all the animals and their characteristics.

To my surprise, I saw that opossum-tail infusion had also been used by the Aztecs, prepared in the same fashion, over 450 years before (Sahagún, 1963, 1969c)! The odd detail I had found in Rafael's account became a key to seeing a fascinating continuity in obstetrical practices across centuries and across distinct Indigenous groups.

This illustration, from the Florentine Codex, recorded in the mid-1500s, shows a pregnant woman being given the opossum-tail medication in ancient Aztec medical practice. (Book 11, f. 171r. Reproduced courtesy of University of Utah Press)

In colonial New Spain and Guatemala and to the present, midwives have continued obstetric practices that survived since before the Spanish invasion, including "giving opossum-tail broth to a parturient to hasten labor" (Hernández Sáenz & Foster, 2001, p. 39; see also Huber & Sandstrom, 2001; León, 1910). In several towns in central Mexico as of the 1960s, for example, opossum tail was still administered for resolving delayed or difficult deliveries, although its form of preparation and administration had changed in some communities (Mellado, Zolla, & Castañeda, 1989; Sullivan, 1969).[60] There is some evidence that oxytocic chemicals in the opossum tail may produce uterine contractions (Ortiz de Montellano, 1990).

Spiritual aid during the delivery—Catholic and ancient Mayan

THROUGHOUT the delivery, Chona prays aloud to God and to Mary for the delivery to go well, requesting strength for the woman giving birth. If the family is Protestant, as Chona and half the town now are, her prayers are in the bed, facing the mother. If the family is Catholic, as Chona and everyone else in town were during Chona's youth, the prayers may be at a family altar: "Virgin, you also went through this; help her," along with standard prayers.

The Virgin Mary is connected with Ixchel, the ancient Mayan goddess of the moon and childbirth (as well as medicine, weaving, water, the earth, and maize). This may account for why Protestant *iyooma'*, as well as Catholic ones, pray to María and count themselves her daughters. In former days and still among some, the *iyoom* also prayed, in silence, to the saints, guardians of childbirth, and to the ancestor *iyooma'* (Paul, 1974–75).

Doña Jesús Quiacaín Televario, an elder *iyoom* (a Catholic), infirm in her later years and no longer practicing, told me in an audio-recorded interview in 2004 how she would pray during a birth. Her prayer contained archaic Tz'utujil terms and knowledge. Chona listened to the tape and helped me understand it, explaining that "The woman is a tree; from her emerges this flower, this fruit—that is, the child." Doña Jesús recounted:

> I call on God, saying the Padre Nuestro [Our Father] and Dios Te Salve María [Hail Mary]. "Help to loosen it [the amniotic sac and the baby], we are your daughters. Along with the 12 who are under your hands and feet [i.e., under your orders]."

I pray to God to help me, and then, to the reflections and shadows/spirits, which in spirit help to open the woman. I call them to put themselves here. First Angel Saint Michael, Saint Rafael, Saint Gabriel, Saint Vincent, Saint Gregory, Saint Augustine. These are the ones who guard over the lives of our pregnant ones. And the Virgin too. There are 12 [saints] too who help to open her, in front and behind [loosening the amniotic sac holding the baby, loosening it all around, as the *iyoom* massages the pregnant belly to loosen the baby], there are 12.

That way when the child arrives in the world it will be respectful. God is who helps us. The duty that falls to us, the children of God and of Jesus, is always through the Virgin María, to pray to the Virgin. We say to María "This is María's" and we request her aid.

After saying the Hail Mary we say "Madre María, you released and saved this your daughter. This is the good fruit, the good flower, you opened it in front and behind. Madre María we are your daughters; let it go, liberate it [the child being born]. Madre María Candelaria, María Chiantla, Monja Catalina, Monja Clara, Madre María Agosto, María Purgiria, María Salema, Monja Lucía." These are the saints; that is how it is.

Another elder *iyoom*, Dolores Cumatz (a Protestant), also reported that at the birth the *iyoom* kneels to request the help of God, the Virgin Mary, and the 12 women who protect the pregnant woman in the birth and the week following. "We women are similar to María; that is why people say that we *are* Santa María."

A midwife in a community near San Pedro reported that to encourage a speedy delivery, she prayed to Santa Ana and the *"thirteen* apostles," perhaps reflecting the importance of the thirteen numbers in the Mayan divinatory calendar. Another prayed to God and *Dios Mundo* (Lord of the World) in the case of a delayed delivery (Paul & Paul, 1975, based on Rodríguez Rouanet, 1969).

In 2005, Chona told me of a key change that had occurred years earlier in the prayers of *iyooma'* in San Pedro, shifting to the Catholic form and the Trinity. Previously their prayers involved the Mayan Lord, *Ajau*, among four deities, in keeping with the spiritual importance of the number 4 in age-old Mayan cosmology, related to the four directions and other sacred concepts:

Now the prayer is to Our Father [Padre Nuestro], in the Catholic manner. But the real prayer is to the Mayan *Ajau Dios* [Lord God]. Many years ago, rather than a trinity, there were four gods: *Ajau*, who is the Lord and guardian of everything; Great Father; Great Son, and Great Holy Ghost.

Chona noted that during birth, the mother is between life and death, so the *iyoom* prays to God, saying that she's loaning her hands to serve, but the work is God's. This resembles the statement of the midwife 450 years before, quoted in the Aztec Florentine Codex: "Our lord can only be helped, can only be aided [by what we do]. . . ." (Sahagún, 1969b, p. 158).

11 ::

Ripples
Across Generations and Nations
in Birth Destinies and Postnatal Care

AFTER THE BABY is born, the *iyoom* has further responsibilities, both spiritual and medical. At the time of birth she reads signs of the future and diagnoses special destinies carried by some infants, and she takes care of the mother and newborn as well as the placenta and the umbilical cord. During the week following the birth, she tends the mother and infant spiritually and medically. At the close of that week, the *iyoom* performs a purification ceremony and final spiritual and medical procedures and protections. If there is further need, she may return at other points in the baby's infancy to provide care.

Reading Signs of the Future

AN *IYOOM*'S SACRED KNOWLEDGE includes ways of predicting future events. She reads the spots on the umbilical cord to tell the new mother how many sons and daughters will follow the newborn, in what order and spacing. Chona reports that few families now ask her to "count" the cord. This practice was also reported to be widespread in Mexico as recently as the 1980s (Mellado, Zolla, & Castañeda, 1989).

Chona used to know the days of the ancient Mayan calendar and their meanings. However, her patients who are interested in having this information would generally consult a shaman with knowledge of the Mayan calendar to foretell the character or future of the newborn, such as whether the child would be hot-tempered or miserly or receive large amounts of money. Such a shaman has the responsibility as "day-keeper" (*ajq'iij*), tracking the cycles of the calendar and advising people regarding the portent of each day according to the ancient system.

Formerly, many Mayan people were conversant with the portent of the days of the Mayan calendar, even though those with the role of *ajq'iij* were the ones who kept track of the calendar and served as the authorities. In about 1938, most adults knew the Mayan calendar day of their own birth and that of their children, according to shaman Domingo Chavajay (interviewed by Rosales, 1949).[61] In 1975, a Pedrana grandmother told me the meaning of many days of the Mayan calendar, although she said it was necessary to consult an *ajq'iij* to determine which dates of the modern calendar the Mayan days fall on, and to know their full significance. She reported that children born on one date will always have enough corn, on another date they will have luck and plenty of everything; another date carries the destiny of being hot-tempered, while another date portends that a person will have several spouses at once (not common in San Pedro).

The Aztec practices of over 400 years ago likewise separated the role of the midwife and that of the soothsayer who told the nature of the day on which the child was born, consulting his books, paintings, and writings. The soothsayer announced whether the day sign of the baby's birth portended good or evil, revealing a destiny of being a ruler, a wealthy person, a valiant warrior, or on the other hand living a life of vice, thievery, failure, laziness, or misery (Sahagun, 1963f).

A mother consults the soothsayer in this image from the Florentine Codex, depicting pre-Hispanic Aztec practices (about 1547). (Book 6, Ch 36. Reproduced courtesy of University of Utah Press)

A few San Pedro women have been born with both the birthsign of *iyoom* and the birthsign for the shamanic destiny of *ajq'iij*. Doña Juana Rocché González was one of the few to have ever fulfilled both these birth destinies as her life work. She also carried the additional shamanic destiny of *ajkuum*, like her father Aniceto Rocché, who interpreted events and dreams and cured insanity and other illnesses (like Chona's father).[62] Doña Juana was an awesome power. I am generally not cowed by anyone, but on several occasions when I sought her professional help on behalf of some relatives, I felt that anything I was thinking would be known to her.

Doña Juana sits in front of the altar in her home, where she prays in archaic Tz'utujil, facing the statue of Jesus on the cross. (Photo © Barbara Rogoff, 1976)

The photo illustrates several changes across generations in San Pedro's practices. Doña Juana wears a recent version of San Pedro Mayan women's clothing—such as a typical blouse rather than a hand-woven güipil—*and her great-granddaughter, next to her, wears non-Indigenous clothing. Doña Juana did not attend school and did not speak Spanish, but two generations later, her grandson Pablo Chavajay (Petzey) is fluent in Spanish and English in addition to two Mayan languages, has a PhD, and is now a tenured professor in the United States. He and I have written several psychology articles together, and he provided many important suggestions for this book.*

At age 12, Pablo Chavajay, grandson of iyoom *and shaman Doña Juana, was one of the children in the first study I conducted in San Pedro (in 1974–75). He occasionally sat with me at the lakeshore. Here is a photo of him as a child, looking through a book I was reading, titled "The Maya," although he did not know English then. (Photo © Barbara Rogoff, 1975)*

In San Pedro, the use of an *ajq'iij*'s services became less prevalent in recent decades.[63] For some years, most people from San Pedro have learned their fates only by living out their lives.

Actually, I should modify that statement. Even people who learn the portent of their birth day from an *ajq'iij* need to live out their lives to learn their fates. From what I understand, the destiny foretold by a person's day of birth (or by the birthsigns seen by the *iyoom* at a person's birth) does not lead to a predetermined fate. These signs give the person particular resources and challenges, but the way the person lives life can transform these birth "gifts" in myriad ways.

Likewise, for people everywhere, many conditions of their birth—such as their country of birth, who their parents are, and the era into which they are born—constrain or channel their lives. But this "destiny" is not a rigid predestination. Individuals and generations change across their lives, building on what they were given, accepting some aspects, rejecting others, transforming destiny with development.

The Responsibility to Unveil Special Destinies

SAN PEDRO *IYOOMA'* still play their important role of reading the birthsigns of babies who are born with special destinies. Most babies do not have any special birthsign. But a few have signs showing that they have a supernatural calling, such as the veil of a newborn *iyoom* or a piece of the amniotic tissue in the shape of a shoulder bag stuck to a newborn *ajq'iij* (spiritual guide or day-keeper of the Mayan calendar). In addition, some newborns have the sign for *ajkuum*, *aj'iitz*, rainmaker, or transforming witch.[64]

An *ajkuum* is born with signs foretelling the destiny of being a shaman who can predict the future and intervene on behalf of patients' health and well-being. The destiny of *ajkuum* is indicated by a similar sign as for an *ajq'iij*.

This painting, influenced by the famous artist Juan Sisay from the neighboring Tz'utujil town of Santiago Atitlán, portrays a shaman carrying out a divination ceremony to foretell the future. [Unfortunately, the painter Juan Sisay was a victim of the violence of the 1980s, in which many Mayan people were massacred in a national wave of genocide. Santiago Atitlán was the site of a well-known massacre in the early 1990s. San Pedro did not suffer as many deaths or disappearances as many towns but lost over 20 people to "the violence"; a large proportion of San Pedro families lost one or several members (see Paul, 1988; see also Ehlers, 1990).] (Painting by Diego Pop Ajuchán, "Sajorín de Chichicastenango," 1957; courtesy of Joseph Johnston, Arte Maya Tz'utuhil)

A baby with the destiny of being a sorcerer who casts evil spells (an *aj'iitz*) is born with small worms held tightly in one hand. A few years back, Chona told me that she has delivered only one *aj'iitz*. His left hand was held strangely, away from his body, with the thumb enclosed inside the fingers in a fist, with worms inside. This birth occurred at a distance from San Pedro, by the plantation on the lakeshore around the volcano. The baby died before a year had passed. People say this was because his grandmother told everyone that he was to grow up to do evil spells; it is dangerous for a child if people tell about the birth destiny. The family may have been relieved that they were no longer raising an *aj'iitz*.

Some babies have been born destined to be rainmakers (*b'anol jab'*) who go to the mountains and the sky to bring gentle rains and ferocious storms. Opinion varies regarding which birthsigns identify a rainmaker (a tissue shaped like a cape or some other sign). There is also some change in how their destiny is interpreted now that fewer people depend on agriculture and hence on the rains.

Rainmakers are famous in old San Pedro stories—the welfare of the community for centuries depended on the rains for the success of the corn and bean crops that were Pedranos' sustenance. Droughts and torrents are common concerns in this highland tropical land, and the rainmakers' exploits in the mountains were a serious matter.

A Tz'utujil tale of a boy's transformation into a rainmaker is retold in English in Michael Richards' book "The Rainmaker" (1997), based on a traditional story from San Pedro and Santiago Atitlán. (Illustration courtesy of Angelika Bauer)

The following is a telling of the traditional rainmaker story, in 1941, written out by young Agustín Pop (page 3,769 of Ben and Lois Paul's fieldnotes; Don Agustín years later became the mayor whom I met when I first arrived in San Pedro):

They say that before, in this town, there were two young brothers—the older was a rainmaker, and the younger did not know that his elder brother had this 'virtud' [destiny, gift]. Every day they went to their work in the fields, and the older brother would tell the younger to look for firewood while he goes to take a little walk. When the elder brother returns, it is raining hard but he isn't wet. He always brings fruit that grows down on the coast [over the mountains]—bananas, platanos, cacao—but the little brother doesn't know where the big brother brings these from.

So it is said that one day the brothers went to their work and they each did their tasks and they finished at 3 in the afternoon, in the place that is called Xequistul. The older brother said to the younger to go on home because it is going to rain, "I'm going to take a little walk."

But the younger one planned to go see where his brother went, and followed him. When a cloud appeared over a hill, the elder went in that direction, and the younger one followed him secretly. Finally he arrived at a house in the hill, and the younger brother saw that the older brother and some other companions were dressing there inside the hill. There were many closets holding the clothes for the lightning, the rain, and the storm rain called Xocomil which creates floods—those ones are black, very black.

The older brother and his companions went up in the clouds, and there was a fierce rainstorm and they were making lightning. The younger brother wanted to do the same, and so he entered the house in the hill and picked out some clothes that were new and black. When he had put them on, he went outside and then up into the sky. Then a huge Xocomil storm began, stronger than ever before seen, which even lifted rocks and pulled up trees.

The rainmakers immediately returned to the hill, frightened. "Who has come among us? Now we will die," they said. They went to capture the Xocomil, and finally they grabbed him, and they saw that it was the younger brother of one of them, who had dressed in black.

Their leader, who is guardian/owner of the hill, said to the older brother, "Well now you've really messed up. Now you won't be able to continue. Instead your younger brother will take your post." The elder brother began to cry, because he would die and not continue his post. But they told him it was his fault for not hiding from his brother when he came to the hill.

Then they all returned to their homes, and when the next day dawned the older brother was dead. The younger lived many years after. But they say that the elder didn't altogether die, but instead went to the hill where he became the leader of them all and stayed forever.

::

ANOTHER DESTINY detected by *iyooma'* from birthsigns is a transforming witch (*q'iisoom;* guardian of the night, guardian of darkness) who changes into a cat or pig, horse or rat at night. Transforming witches do a somersault and become an unnatural animal, dangerous and feared. It is their destiny to go out in the dark and frighten people who are out at dusk or later, paralyzing them with terror.[65]

Babies destined to be transforming witches are born all wrapped up in the amniotic sac like a cabbage, with their little fingers holding their eyelids wide open as if to scare people. When the *iyoom* removes them from the sac, they cry out in a frightening way, as fits their destiny.

People in San Pedro report that transforming witches are not so active anymore. They explain that the town's acquisition of electric lights has discouraged the transforming witches from going out at night in the form of cats or pigs or other animals to frighten people. (But some report that a neighboring town with fewer street lights still has plenty of active transforming witches.)

Some Pedranos are skeptical of the existence of transforming witches, and others are confident that they exist. One prominent forward-thinking Pedrano many years ago (long before electric streetlights) explained to anthropologist Ben Paul how he came to believe that transforming witches do indeed exist. This man, who was at the forefront of some changes to San Pedro such as the advent of Protestantism and the use of Spanish, did not believe in transforming witches until he saw one.

One evening, at dusk, he was somewhat late in returning home from checking his fields. As he walked the shadowy dirt road back to town, an enormous pig crossed the road and scared him so much that he trembled and could hardly move, paralyzed with fear. Then he knew that there was really such a thing as transforming witches. When Ben Paul asked the man how he knew that the pig was a transforming witch, the man scoffed, "Well, I'm not afraid of a *regular* pig!"

When I myself first heard about transforming witches, in my first year in San Pedro, I too was skeptical. But then on occasion, I found myself doing things to protect myself from them. And late at night, when I heard little footsteps scurry across my tin roof, I hoped that I wouldn't have to go out into the coffee grove to the latrine in the dark. Most of the time I remain skeptical, but I cannot forget the times when the existence of these strange beings seemed to make sense, to explain events that happened to me that were otherwise difficult to explain.

When a baby is born with the destiny of transforming witch or sorcerer, or of *iyoom* or shaman or rainmaker, the parents accept their child's birth destiny as simply a fact, like whether a child is born a girl or a boy. Although they may not be happy with the news if the child is destined to be a transforming witch or sorcerer, a special destiny is simply the way things are—what this child brings in life.

Care of the Newborn, the Placenta, and the Umbilical Cord

ONE OF LOIS PAUL'S 1941 informants reported that his first child was "born dead" but the *iyoom* revived her. The *iyoom* heated a *machete* in the fire and used the hot blade to singe the umbilical cord. At that point, the baby "awakened" and started moving her limbs.

If a newborn does not need emergency care, the *iyoom* receives the baby on a cloth and wipes it clean. After the placenta emerges, the *iyoom* cuts the cord, washes the baby, and puts wax and a dressing on the end of the umbilical stump.

The *iyoom* dresses the baby and swaddles it loosely in a soft sash— or at least this was the custom 30 years ago, and before that. By about 1990, swaddling became optional though still usual.[66] By 2009, it was reported not to be common.

Swaddling is a practice that seems to swing in and out of favor worldwide. In the U.S. colonial era, people believed that swaddling was essential to encourage the growth of straight legs, and swaddling kept the baby from kicking off covers or rolling off surfaces. Colonial U.S. midwives pulled the newborn's arms and legs to straighten them, and kept the limbs straight by swaddling them tightly with strips of linen. About the time of the American Revolution, middle-class U.S. parents stopped swaddling babies, to promote their freedom of movement (Calvert, 2003). By the time that my children were born, U.S. hospitals were again advising parents to swaddle infants, and they taught us how to wrap them (not so tightly) in baby blankets so they would be cozy and feel held and supported.

The revitalization of some cultural practices such as swaddling suggests that cultural change is not a linear sort of "progress" but rather a matter of building and adapting what is provided by prior generations, in light of new circumstances as well as ideas from other places. This would involve some spiraling around, with some practices "recycling" in a new form. This is similar to the cyclical view of time involving death and rebirth of practices, expressed by Nicolás Chávez, the Mayan artist from Santiago Atitlán quoted earlier. Whereas some practices may die and be reborn, other practices may simply continue, show ruptures in use across generations, or undergo total makeovers.

The care of the placenta has changed across generations in San Pedro. Until a few decades ago, the *iyoom* wrapped the placenta in a special cloth and buried it in the house under the hard-packed dirt floor, with ritual prayers to Santa Ana and the other saints of childbirth and the spirits of dead *iyooma'*. But now that cement or tile floors have been installed in most homes, this custom has changed. Now, the father usually buries the placenta, wrapped in a cloth, in the earth outside the house. The *iyoom* simply tells him, "Go bury it. God gave it to us, and our mother María. And your wife has come out all right." These continuities and changes in recent decades continue a dynamic cultural process of current generations adapting the previous generations' traditions.

Some of these changing and continued practices can be seen in Rafael González's account of how the *iyoom* took care of his newborn baby, his wife Cándida, and the placenta, in 1941:

> Once everything had come out, we reclined Cándida on a reed mat while the baby was being bathed. First the *iyoom* cleaned its little face and its whole body with a soft cloth, and afterwards, she cut the umbilical cord with a little metal knife that she always uses. This she had found and picked up on her path; she carries it in a little box with her remedies and other instruments that she carries wrapped in cloths. She tied the cord with a white thread and then bathed the baby in warm water with fragrant soap. After the bath, she warmed the umbilicus with a little oiled cloth and then put this cloth, well warmed, over the umbilicus and tied it on with another cloth. Then she dressed the baby and put it in the bed.
>
> Then the *iyoom* asked for a wide sash to bind Cándida's abdomen, and then she washed her legs well with warm water, changed her clothes, and put her to bed.

Afterwards, she gathered up the placenta in a cloth, wrapped it up well and tied it with a cord, and told me to dig a hole. So I dug a hole in the corner of the house, about three handspans deep. Then she herself put the bundle in the hole and covered it with earth and water, and throughout this, she prayed to all the Virgin Saints and all the spirits of the ancestor *iyooma'*. I had told her that it would be better if I buried the placenta, but she told me no, because it is a sin [for someone other than the *iyoom* to bury the placenta], and the children would turn out damaged or would even die, if the placenta wasn't well disposed of.[67]

Centuries ago, Aztec midwives also buried the placenta in the corner of the house. They saved the umbilical cord, which was dried and entrusted to the warriors to bury in the battlefields to ensure that a boy baby would go forth in war or to bury by the hearth to ensure that a girl baby would "go nowhere." As the midwife cut the cord, she used ceremonial words to tell a baby boy of the difficulties of his life as a warrior and to tell a baby girl that her duty was "in the heart of the home, . . . thou art to provide water, to grind maize, to drudge; thou art to sweat by the ashes, by the hearth" (Sahagún, 1969d, p. 172).

The Florentine Codex provides this illustration of the Aztec midwife addressing the baby (apparently still within the sweat bath). (Book 6, Ch 30. Reproduced courtesy of University of Utah Press)

The Aztec midwife of the 1400s or early 1500s also gave the baby a purifying bath, with many practices resembling those of Cándida's *iyoom*. As she did so, the Aztec midwife prayed under her breath to the goddess of the water, entreating her to cleanse the child to be able to rise above the impurities with which it had been born. In her intervention on behalf of the baby, to be able to develop beyond inheritance from the prior generation, she addressed the newborn:

> May she receive thee! May she wash thee, may she cleanse thee! May she remove, may she transfer the filthiness which thou hast taken from thy mother, from thy father! May she cleanse thy heart; may she make it fine, good! May she give thee fine, good conduct! (Sahagún, 1969e, p. 175)

The Aztec midwife quietly addressed the goddess of the water with her prayer regarding the baby's destiny and development:

> Lady, [it is not known] the nature of that given [the baby] in the beginning, the nature of that which he came bearing, the attributes with which he came wrapped, with which he came bound. But behold, perhaps he cometh laden with evil; who knoweth the manner in which he cometh laden with the evil burdens of his mother, of his father? With what blotch, what filth, what evil of the mother, of the father doth the baby come laden? He is in thy hands. Receive him, cleanse him, wash him, for he is especially entrusted to thee, for he is delivered into thy hands. . . . May his heart, his life be good, may they be fine, may they be purified in order that he may live on earth peacefully, calmly. (Sahagún, 1969e, pp. 175–176)

As she bathed the baby, the Aztec midwife breathed on the water and had the baby taste it, touching the baby's head and chest with it. Then she addressed the baby, again referring to developing beyond the inheritance from the prior generation:

> My youngest one, . . . May the lord of the near, of the nigh, wash thee, cleanse thee. May he remove from thee the [evil] which was assigned thee, with which thou wert vested in the beginning. May he put to one side the evil burdens of thy mother, of thy father, and that which is the vice of thy mother, of thy father. (Sahagún, 1969e, p. 176)

After the Aztec midwife bathed the baby, she swaddled it, addressing the baby: "Precious necklace, precious feather, precious green stone."

She told the baby of the sorrow and suffering of the earth, and concluded, "Rest, settle on the ground. May our lord, the lord of the near, of the nigh, provide for thee, advise thee." (Sahagún, 1969e, p. 177)

Then in a vigorous voice, the Aztec midwife praised the newly delivered mother, telling her that she had labored bravely against death as an eagle warrior, an ocelot warrior, who was now exhausted from battle. She exhorted the relatives regarding the baby, who is "the chip, the flake of those who have already gone to reside in the beyond," whom the lord creator Quetzalcoatl had placed in their hands. She warned that they must:

> Sigh, sorrow: how may [the lord master] will? Perhaps that of which
> we here dream, that which we see in dreams, will endure—the
> precious necklace, the precious feather. And perhaps he will grow
> strong, perhaps he will live for a little time. (Sahagún, 1969f, p. 181)

Or perhaps not. She exhorted the new mother and family not to go constantly bragging of the birth, and reminded them of the fragility of the baby's life:

> Do not presume, do not take credit for it, do not consider that ye
> are worthy of this baby, [for] our lord will discover thy feelings.
> He will deal with us [because of] our desire for the child; he will
> unclasp from you his precious necklace, his precious feather.
> (Sahagún, 1969f, pp. 181–182)

The San Pedro *iyoom* now apparently does not say a prayer while bathing the baby. However, afterward, after she bathes the mother and binds her abdomen with a sash to support her organs for the first weeks postpartum, the *iyoom* kneels by the mother's bed and prays. She thanks God and María that the mother and baby are fine.

Care of Mother and Newborn
During the Lying-in Period

THE SAN PEDRO *iyoom* continues to have daily responsibility for the mother and baby for a week after the birth. This is the period in which the mother is prohibited from working and must stay in bed.

During the lying-in period, relatives and neighbors visit, bringing gifts. The visitors bring ceremonial foods such as Mayan hot chocolate, bread rolls, and a spicy corn drink. The corn drink, contained in a large decorated gourd in prior eras, is to stimulate the mother's milk to come in. Formerly, the mother receiving these gifts would remember what each person brought her, and when they in turn had a baby, the woman reciprocated their gifts in kind. Now, the gift is often baby clothes, and the mother does not necessarily reciprocate the same gifts.

The woman at the left is whipping hot chocolate, spinning the wooden tool between her hands so that its paddles beat the chocolate. Behind her on the hearth, corn is soaking in preparation for making tortillas or tamales. (Photo © Barbara Rogoff, 1975)

Chocolate is one of the foods contributed to the world by Indigenous people of the Americas; it has been an important substance to the Tz'utujiles since before the Spanish arrived. Cacao beans were used as money and were a primary form of tribute paid to the Tz'utujil lords, and then to the Spanish rulers. The Tz'utujiles cultivated cacao on the lowland coastal side of the volcanoes (Zamora Acosta, 1976).

Ajtuuj: *One who uses the sweat bath*

THE MOTHER during the lying-in period is referred to as *ajtuuj* in Tz'utujil, meaning "one who uses the sweat bath." This refers to the former practice in which the mother was treated by the *iyoom* in the sweat bath during this time to encourage lactation and the return to health. During the lying-in period, the *iyoom* examines the mother and adjusts the sash that binds her abdomen. When I asked Chona what she does if the mother's perineum has torn during the birth process, she reported that this never happens.

Bathing in the sweat bath, as well as in lakes and rivers, was a widespread therapeutic and cleanliness method throughout Indigenous Guatemala when the Spanish arrived. Spanish priests tried unsuccessfully to stop frequent bathing—bathing was infrequent in sixteenth-century Europe (Orellana, 1987). Colonial Guatemalan religious leaders were also suspicious of the sweat bath because inside it, a person was regarded as encountering goddesses connected with healing, midwifery, and the earth (Few, 2002).

In the ancient Aztec tradition, the sweat bath's curative powers were extolled, especially during pregnancy and soon after birth:

> Then one who has become pregnant, whose abdomen is already
> large, also enters there. There the midwives massage them; there
> they can place the babies straight in order that they will not extend
> crosswise nor settle face first. Two, three, four times they massage
> them there. And there those recently confined also bathe
> themselves; there, having delivered, having given birth, they
> strengthen their bodies. [The midwives] bathe them once, twice;
> and there they cleanse their breasts, that their milk will be good,
> and that they will produce a flow. (Sahagún, 1963, p. 191)

In San Pedro, use of the sweat bath by women who had recently given birth was apparently common in the early 1900s. In 1938 field-notes, Rosales (1949) wrote that starting 2 days after the birth, the mother bathed about every 3 days in the sweat bath, and the heat helped her milk come in; not until 20 days after the birth could the mother bathe in the cold water of the lake.

However, by 1941, the 1-week purification ceremony only sometimes included the *iyoom* bathing the mother in the sweat bath. This depended on whether the mother wanted it and which *iyoom* attended her, according to one of the *iyooma'* interviewed by Lois Paul. Use of the sweat bath had died out by the 1960s, prohibited by the government, according to an informant of Lois Paul's (1969).

By the time I arrived in 1974, there were only a few sweat houses remaining in town. More recently, the space that had been occupied by most of the few remaining family sweat houses is now used for new housing for the growing population. Several of the elder *iyooma'* told me that they used to bathe the pregnant woman in the sweat bath, but now that there are almost no sweat baths, this practice is not continued. However, in some other Mayan communities of Guatemala, the sweat bath is still widely used by midwives for giving prenatal and postnatal baths and massages (Cosminsky, 1982; Hurtado & Sáenz de Tejada, 2001).[68]

This photo from 1941 shows a sweat bath in San Pedro in the process of being re-roofed; bundles of thatch lean against it. The children around the sweat bath are watching a procession. (Photo by Lois and Ben Paul)

In former times, Chona would apply cooked wild herbs to the mother's chest in the sweat bath so that the mother's milk would come in. For the first 3 days after birth, it used to be common for a neighbor who was nursing her own infant also to nurse the newborn, until the mother's milk came in; now only a few do this. Others give the baby water with sugar during this time. Until recent decades, all babies were fed by nursing. Now, if the mother works outside the home, the baby often gets a bottle, and babies of some mothers who do not work outside the home do too.

Medical and spiritual attention to the newborn

DURING THE LYING-IN period, Chona changes the dressing on the baby's *muxu'x* (umbilical stump), warming the *muxu'x* daily with a cloth that she heats over hot coals from the fire. The umbilical stump dries and falls off in 3 or 4 days.

Lois Paul described a visit she made in 1941, bringing a gift of bread and chocolate to a woman who had given birth 2 days before. The *iyoom* was tending to the mother and baby when she arrived, so Lois had this opportunity to witness newborn care.

> They handed me the baby which I kissed on its cheek [as is the custom] and called "little hunk of dirt," arousing gales of laughter. I had learned that praise can endanger the infant's life and the local idiom for getting around this danger.
>
> When I handed the infant to the midwife she unwound the sash in which it was swaddled, took off its little skirt and belly band. There were small strips of absorbent cotton placed in the cracks at the top of the legs. The midwife removed the small folded square of cloth from the navel, but not the piece of wax [sealing the umbilical stump]; warmed the cloth over some burning coals on a piece of broken pot at her feet, about ten times, touching it first to her cheek to test the heat and then placing it over the navel. Finally she replaced the cloth and clothing and bound up the infant again. Babies always wear caps or handkerchiefs on their heads to protect them from *aire* [cold air, regarded as bringing illness and especially dangerous for people who are weak or ill]. This one had a kerchief tied like a cap. (Paul, 1969, pp. 30–31)

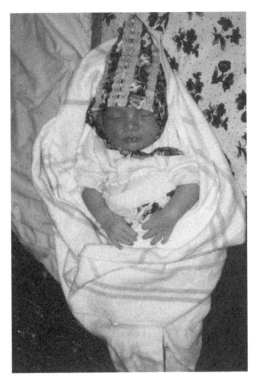

Sleepy little Santiago, a few days old, is wrapped loosely and wears a cap to protect him from aire. (Photo © Barbara Rogoff, 1996)

Formerly, the *iyoom* would put the hot coals under the bed where the mother and baby lay, after using the embers to warm the cloth used to treat the *muxu'x*. This is still often done. However, some people do not want it done anymore, as the hot coals are messy and might damage their floor, so they just throw out the coals. Previously, homes had hard-packed earthen floors, which are easier to clean and repair.

Putting the coals under the bed was believed to help the *muxu'x* dry up and fall off. This practice may be related to longstanding Mesoamerican treatment of the newborn. Among the ancient Quiché Mayans, the Grandfather and Grandmother gods prohibited removing the fire from a house of a newborn until a specific amount of time had gone by; in precolonial Mexico, a fire was kept going for 4 days in the room with a newborn, to strengthen the life force (*tonalli*) of the newborn (Orellana, 1987).

If a baby is born with the umbilical cord looped around the neck, the *iyoom* may carry out a spiritual ceremony to protect the child from the increased risk (according to local knowledge) of a previously healthy infant being found dead when the family wakens in the morning. The local knowledge accords with epidemiological data in the United States that indicates that babies who are born with the umbilical cord around the neck are at increased risk of sudden infant death syndrome (SIDS; Lipsitt, 2003).

One possible explanation for SIDS is failure of some babies' defensive reflexes to remove occlusions limiting respiration. It is interesting in this light that San Pedro babies born with the cord around their necks were supposed to be swaddled differently than ordinary babies—during the night, their arms were not to be swaddled at their sides, but left out of the swaddling cloth so that they could protect themselves when their spirit was returning to earth.

To prepare for the ceremony to protect a baby born with the cord around its neck, which is rarely done now, the *iyoom* directs the baby's father to gather leaves of specific trees, secretly in the night. Other family members are to prepare implements that correspond with the child's gender—a small *machete* and tumpline (forehead carrying strap) for a boy or weaving sticks and spindle for a girl (Paul & Paul, 1975).

The *iyoom* places the leaves and the implements in a shoulder bag for a boy or a basket for a girl. In the presence of the mother, she carries the baby and the container to each of the four corners of the room, where she prays to the spiritual guardian of each of the four corners. This prayer connects with centuries-old practices not only by addressing the spiritual guardians but also in the emphasis on the four cardinal directions. The four directions are of great spiritual importance in the ancient Mayan worldview, representing the corners or limits of the universe, according to the sacred book *Popul Vuh* (Christenson, 2001). The four corners of the house reproduce the structure of the field of maize, the community, and the cosmos (Miller & Taube, 1993).

The *iyoom* tells the looped-cord baby's spirit, which is regarded as linked to a star, not to wander about in the sky but to come straight home, and when the spirit returns (as a falling star), to come directly down into the container cushioned with leaves. This protects it from falling on the roof or a rock, which would cause the baby's death. After this ritual, the basket or bag (and contents) are put out of sight in the eaves of the house to protect the baby. The idea that the baby's spirit is connected with a star is reminiscent of longstanding Mesoamerican ideas of individuals having an associated *nahual* spirit.[69]

Purification and Protection Ceremony
to Conclude the Lying-in Period

A WEEK AFTER the birth, the San Pedro *iyoom* performs a ceremony to complete the lying-in period.[70] This ceremony, purifying and protecting the mother and baby, links with both pre-Hispanic Mesoamerican and longstanding Spanish practices.

George Foster (1960) attributed the use of a lying-in period, common in Mesoamerica, to the Spanish custom in which the mother is confined to home for 40 days (the *cuarentena*) to protect her health and that of the baby and because she was considered unclean. In Spain, the confinement ended with the mother, usually together with the midwife, taking the baby to a purification mass in the church.

To end the San Pedro 1-week ceremony, the *iyoom* bathes the mother's head, washing her hair and purifying her to conclude the period of staying in bed and avoiding the usual work routine. Formerly, this ritual was carried out in the sweat bath. When sweat baths were no longer routinely used, the purification ceremony often took place semi-publicly in the extended family's courtyard; now it occurs in private in the family home if the home is big enough.

The renowned iyoom *Juana Rocché performed a cleansing ceremony in 1941 to complete this mother's week of confinement following the birth of her baby, washing the mother's hair in a courtyard. The baby's toddler sister is watching closely. (Photo by Lois and Ben Paul)*

The San Pedro ceremony includes the *iyoom* washing the baby in a bowl of warm water that contains rue leaves, to protect the baby against the dangers of evil eye. Rue is a medicinal herb originating in Europe that has antimicrobial properties (also known as herb of grace, *Ruta graveolens*; Medical Economics Staff & Gruenwald, 2000).

Chona bathes a newborn. (Family photo, about 2001)

Lois and Ben Paul related Pedrano practices of 1941 to the ancient Aztec midwife's purification and naming ceremony, conducted in the courtyard at dawn on a propitious day, about 4 days after the consultation with the soothsayer who predicts the infant's future (Sahagún, 1969g). When the Aztec boy of almost five centuries ago was named, he might be given the name of one of his ancestors, in order to raise his fortune to the lot of the person whose name he received, as sometimes occurs in San Pedro. Paul and Paul described the San Pedro ceremony that was common in 1941:

> Washing the baby, [the San Pedro *iyoom*] performed a kind of baptismal rite. She raised the child four times, once in each direction, and offered it to the heavens. She presented a set of sex-linked implements to the child, lecturing it on its future duties. The implements for a boy among the warlike Aztecs—miniature arrows, a bow, and a shield—differed from those the Pedrano midwife uses in the [umbilical cord around the neck] ritual, but the objects for a baby Aztec girl were similar: a little reed basket, a spinning whorl, a loom shuttle. (Paul & Paul, 1975, p. 720)

These images are from the Florentine Codex, describing pre-Hispanic Aztec practices: 29. Bathing the boy, with symbols of manhood nearby. 30. The symbols of womanhood. 31. Placing the baby in the cradle. [The scrolls emanating from mouths symbolize speech.] (Book 6, Ch. 37–38. Reproduced courtesy of University of Utah Press)

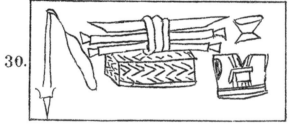

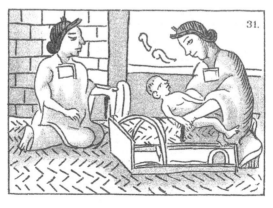

The San Pedro *iyoom*, as of about 1938, put the baby boy's implements on his back and told him, "Here is what you will use when you are big" and she whipped the implements with a belt; with a baby girl, the *iyoom* placed the weaving implements on the baby's head and told her, "Here is what you will use when you are big and you get married" (Rosales, 1949, p. 349).

After bathing the baby, the *iyoom* dresses the infant and may swaddle it. Then the baby would be given to the mother to nurse, and if the baby was a girl, her ears were then usually pierced for little earrings.

The San Pedro *iyoom* traditionally places the infant for its first time in the hammock that is used as a cradle during the daytime, hung in a central place in the house. Through their baby's infancy, mothers often would sit nearby weaving and could pull on a rope to rock the infant in the hammock, until recent decades when weaving has become much less common.

Before placing the baby on soft cloths in the hammock, however, the *iyoom* would whip the hammock with a belt or a switch. As she did so, she prayed for the spiritual guardians of the hammock to take good care of the baby, protecting it from dangers:

> Listen to me, guardian of the hammock; take good care of this baby; let nothing happen to it when it sleeps; don't let it fall out of the hammock; don't let evil spirits frighten the child. (Paul & Paul, 1975, pp. 709–710; also Paul, 1969)

Chona reported in 2008 that in recent years only a few families want her to whip the hammock and pray "Take care of the baby, that it may live," to the guardian (*ajau*) of the hammock. "Now, most families say that is worthless." Sometimes, before, when whipping the hammock, the *iyoom* also whipped the next-oldest child, telling the child also to let the baby live.

This 4-year-old rocks her cousin in the hammock. It was routinely the job of the next-older sibling (usually about 2 to 4 years old) to rock the baby in the hammock (as of 1938; Rosales, 1949). Still in about 1990, almost all families used the hammock: Of 24 families who had babies about 1990, only 2 did not use the hammock with the babies. By twenty years later, however, few families used a hammock with their babies. (Photo © Luisa Magarian, 1998)

The 1941 San Pedro practices with the hammock hearken back to practices of the Aztec midwife of nearly five centuries ago. After she washed the baby girl or boy and prayed in a low voice for its purification from vice and evil, the Aztec midwife swaddled the baby and then took it into the house and placed it in the cradle. As she did so, she called out to the spiritual guardian of the cradle:

> Thou who art mother of all of us, . . . who possessest cradling arms, thou who possessest a lap, the baby hath arrived. . . . It is yet left with thee; thou wilt strengthen it. . . . [Thou who art] its mother, receive it! Old woman, do not do anything to the baby; be gentle to it. (Sahagún, 1969h, p. 206)

The Pauls (1975) noted that, in addition to resembling ancient Mesoamerican practices, the San Pedro custom of whipping the hammock might also derive from medieval European traditions to exorcise evil.

Decades ago, the San Pedro *iyoom* used incense at this ceremony, thanking the spiritual protectors of childbirth for having been with the mother all week to guard her. "The people say, 'The masters of the people (i.e., Spirits) have come'" (Summer Institute of Linguistics, 1978, Book 3, p. 72). The *iyoom* waved the incense burner into the four corners of the one-room house and knelt to pray at the bed,

> in a manner reminiscent of the midwives among the ancient
> lowland Maya who knelt in worship before an image placed under
> the parturient's bed—the image of Ix-Chel, goddess of childbirth,
> weaving, divination, and medicine. (Paul & Paul, 1975, p. 710)

Now Chona uses incense with only a few families, usually where there are elders who request it. She reports that many others, including Catholics as well as Protestants, say, "What good is incense?" During the ceremony that concludes the lying-in period, Chona prays simply and quietly in thanks that everything went well, "because we always have to talk with God."

Safeguarding the baby's muxu'x *and the baby's future*

BY THE TIME of the 1-week ceremony, the baby's *muxu'x* (umbilical stump) has fallen off. The *iyoom* wraps it in a cloth and gives it to the family. Previously, the family safeguarded the *muxu'x* carefully, but now when Chona gives it to them, some do not save it. Those who do save the *muxu'x* now may treat it similarly whether the baby is a boy or a girl.

However, in former times in San Pedro, the boy's *muxu'x* was placed in a chest or in a corncrib, or sometimes taken to the fields, to ensure industriousness. The girl's *muxu'x* was put in a crack in the kitchen wall or buried under a hearthstone of the cooking fire to ensure that she will always come home quickly and will stay in San Pedro when she is grown (Paul, 1969). In nearby San Juan, a boy's *muxu'x* is traditionally taken to the fields and hung in a tree to ensure that the boy will do his work, and a girl's *muxu'x* is buried in the kitchen so she will stay home and cook.[71]

Similar practices surrounding the umbilical cord occurred among the Aztecs in what is now central Mexico almost five centuries ago. The Florentine Codex reported that the Aztecs buried the umbilical cord of a boy in the battlefields to ensure bravery and that of a girl near the hearth to ensure that she would stay home and work in the kitchen (Sahagún, 1969d).

A Pedrana mother, Marina Chavajay Petzey, who is the first female lawyer from San Pedro, told me that she doesn't want to limit her daughter to the kitchen. Because she doesn't know what kinds of careers her children will have, she just saved the *muxu'x* of her sons and her daughter in the attic of her house.

Marina Chavajay Petzey when she ran for mayor of San Pedro—the first woman in the region to run for mayor. With a university law degree, Marina's schooling is far greater than that of her own mother, who completed only first grade, and her grandmother, Doña Juana Rocché, the iyoom *who appears in the photo a few pages before, performing a cleansing ceremony. (Photo © Luisa Magarian, 1999)*

The changing practices regarding the *muxu'x* reflect the dramatic decrease in predictability of occupations over recent generations. Three decades ago, I asked 60 9-year-old Pedrano children what they wanted to do when they grow up. Almost all the girls aspired to cook and weave and the boys aspired to work in the fields—like their parents were doing.

As it turned out, however, about a fourth of the girls and more than half of the boys grew up to follow new, paying occupations such as teacher, accountant, factory worker, and doctor.

They also usually continued far longer in school than they had expected. When they were 9, almost all of them told me that they thought they would complete 3 to 6 grades of schooling, but a third of the girls and half of the boys ended up completing at least 12 grades.

The predictability of occupations is further reduced for even more recent generations of children, compared with three decades before. The children of the 60 former 9-year-olds gave quite different answers than their parents had at about the same age. Less than a third of the girls aspired to cook and weave, and fewer than a third of the boys aspired to work in the fields. Most of the rest wanted to go on in their studies and work in specialized careers such as teacher, accountant, pastor, and doctor; half aspired to complete at least 12 years of schooling (Rogoff, Correa-Chávez, & Navichoc Cotuc, 2005).

The changes in occupation across the decades are revealed in the generations of Chona's family. In Chona's generation and before, the men have been farmers, raising the traditional corn and beans for the family, and the women have run the household, including weaving many of the family clothes. Some have also had spiritual callings like Chona and her father.

Chona's children have a mixture of traditional and new occupations: Chona's older daughter runs a household and the younger is a teacher. One of her sons is a farmer and the other is a Protestant pastor and businessman.

Of Chona's grown granddaughters, in 2006, the eldest runs a household, two are teachers, one is a doctor, and one is studying computers. Her grandsons are a teacher, a doctor, an engineer, and a sociology student from the university.

It is no wonder that mothers now question where to put their newborn's *muxu'x*. The shifts in treatment of the *muxu'x* provide a telling example of cultural change, in a constellation associating this practice with changes in occupations, gender roles, contact outside of Indigenous communities, and Western schooling.

Related differences in following traditional Mesoamerican practices surrounding disposal of the umbilical cord have occurred across three communities in distant Guadalajara, Mexico: In a town identified as Indigenous a generation ago, almost all mothers recently reported burying or keeping the umbilical stump, often referring to the traditional rationale of encouraging the child's appropriate role development and attachment to the place. In contrast, mothers from families that had moved from rural areas to Guadalajara in the past generation and now were highly schooled did not bury the umbilical stump. Most of them kept it, but without connecting this with Indigenous practices; most of them said that they did not know why they kept the stump. In turn, Guadalajara mothers from professional families that had been urban and highly schooled for three generations simply threw out the umbilical stump, and attached no significance to it (Najafi, Mejía Arauz, & Rogoff, 2005).

Reference to the umbilical cord "grounding" people in their birthplace occurs even further away, in California. One sometimes hears a Mexican immigrant caller on Spanish-language radio identifying the small town or region of their birth by saying, "that is where I left my umbilicus."

Concluding the lying-in ceremony

IF THE *IYOOM* has put the coals under the mother's bed during the lying-in week, she carries out one further act of purification. She sweeps under the bed and around the room, and throws out the ashes along with any remains of food or other trash that has accumulated during the week.

If several babies in a row have died in the family, the *iyoom* may also do a ceremony with the new baby's surviving next-older sibling to protect the newborn from the older child's presumably hostile spirit. Nowadays the ceremony is rare, done mostly in households where elders request it: "Ma'am, we have a small pullet, please do us the favor of doing the chicken treatment."

> She wraps a pullet in a cloth and makes the older child carry the bundled chicken while accompanying the midwife as she tours the four corners of the room to offer prayers. [One midwife told Lois in 1941 that formerly the ceremony required the child to walk in the streets with the chicken on its back, to the four corners of the town.] Then privately and out of sight of the new infant, she beats the chicken to death on the back of the older child. After this act of punishment, the sacrificed chicken is cooked in a savory broth and served exclusively to the older child, who must eat it all even if it takes several meals to finish the task. The midwife lectures the child as he eats, seated behind closed doors or beside the

hammock containing the week-old infant: "Now that you have another little brother [or sister] you are not to eat him; eat this chicken instead; its meat is like the flesh of your little brother; you must take good care of him and never frighten him." (Paul & Paul, 1975, p. 709)

Pedranos are aware of differing beliefs and customs in towns around the lake. For example, in nearby San Juan, a ceremony requested by families that have lost several babies is that the *iyoom* throws out the next-older child with the ashes swept from under the bed. The *iyoom* sweeps up the debris onto a small reed mat; the next-older child is put on top of this and the *iyoom* tosses the child and the debris onto the refuse heap in the yard. The frightened and crying child must come back to the house by himself or herself, and then is seated with the *iyoom* at a table spread with food, and the two of them eat.

This twist on customs arouses gales of laughter in San Pedro when an *iyoom* recounts it. It is a good example of cultural differences that call into question the "box approach" to considering culture. San Juan is less than a kilometer from San Pedro, people also speak the Mayan language Tz'utujil, and there is some intermarriage. However, there are clear distinctions as well as numerous similarities in cultural practices between these two Mayan populations.

Cultural processes are obscured by treating culture as a uniform set of individual characteristics, determined by the individual's ethnic label (such as "Latino," as people from both San Pedro and San Juan, as well as the whole country of Guatemala and the surrounding countries would be classified in the United States). Instead, progress in understanding culture will come from focusing on how people live and examining how their practices are both shared and distinct across (and within) related as well as distant communities.

Some features of centuries-old Mesoamerican and European customs are seen in Rafael Gonzalez' account of what the *iyoom* did at the 1-week ceremony for his wife Cándida and newborn baby in 1941:

First she took off the baby's clothes and bathed him with warm water with rue leaves. Then she dried him well and warmed the navel and dressed him and put him in the bed.

In the meantime she beat the hammock with a switch or a belt, and I asked her why she beats the hammock. She told me that it was a custom—because if one doesn't beat the hammock, the little ones won't go to sleep in it, because many of them have been ruined in the hammock, so the little ones are frightened and can't get to sleep. Then she went to get the baby from the bed and put him in the hammock, wrapping it well and covering him. [A shawl is often wrapped around the hammock, enclosing the baby in a warm, dark cocoon.]

Then she washed Cándida's hair with warm water and soap, and combed out her long hair. Then she shook out the bedclothes and made the bed for Cándida to lie down. Then she swept carefully under the bed and all through the room.

When she finished, she was given water to wash her hands, and then she was given a drink. When she finished everything, she said she was going, and she was given 50 cents in coins and 20 cents' worth of bread, and she left.

She came back again at 6 in the afternoon to give Cándida her sweat bath. Cándida says that the *iyoom* bathed her thoroughly and that only this *iyoom* bathes the patients herself, like this; she washes the head and all the body as if she were bathing a baby. At first, Cándida was embarrassed to be bathed, but the *iyoom* told her that it was always her custom to do so, to leave her patients cleansed. When she finished bathing Cándida, she clothed her and covered her well and put her to bed. (from Lois and Ben Paul's 1941 fieldnotes)

Continuing Care After the Lying-in Period

THE *IYOOM* may continue care of the baby or mother after the 1-week period of seclusion ends, checking on them periodically for some months. Follow-up care is especially likely if there is some residual problem, such as the care needed for a premature infant.

Chona knows how to treat babies who are born prematurely, like three of her granddaughters who were born after 6 months of pregnancy instead of 9. One of them was born "so tiny that her little eyes just seemed painted on and her head was still soft like dough." Her family couldn't wash her for 2 months, until her skull got a little harder. Chona told the baby's mother to feed the baby drop by drop, with the tip of a cloth, because the baby was so premature that she still didn't know how to nurse. The doctors told the baby's mother to send the baby to the hospital on the other side of the lake, but the mother did not follow this advice—she was more confident in Chona's expertise with newborns.

The little preemie did fine and grew to adulthood and now has children of her own.

Usually, at the end of the 1-week ceremony, the *iyoom's* services formally end. If the family offers some ears of corn, bread, ceremonial *atol* drink, or money in thanks, Chona accepts. But a true *iyoom* must not charge for her assistance.

Another *iyoom* recounted learning this requirement—and not to disdain small gifts—in a supernatural journey. Lois and Ben Paul used the pseudonym "Ana" in recording the event, which also illustrates how *iyooma'* learn through supernatural means:

> Once as she was walking along the path to the neighboring village of San Juan la Laguna she suddenly found herself in a huge carpeted chamber inside the hill. On a dais sat a number of deceased midwives completely white from head to toe. "Their hair, clothing, everything was white, white, white, like this," said Ana, holding up a fine china cup. The midwives pointed to a huge table bearing little mounds of corn, beans, salt, coffee, greens, squash, tomatoes, eggs—"everything there is." They told Ana: "These are the things that people will bring as gifts when you are a midwife. Some may give you only a bit of this or that because that is all they have. You must accept whatever they give you with goodness in your heart. You have been chosen to help the women, and you must serve them. Never criticize a woman even if she gives you only a handful of beans."
>
> The scene shifted, and Ana found herself in a grand subterranean chamber. Here she saw fires burning fiercely. In one of the fires sat three deceased Pedrano midwives in positions corresponding to the three stones of the hearth. Ana asked why they were sitting in the fire. The women mournfully replied they were there to burn for eternity. What was their crime? They had thrown away humble gifts of food given them by patients, considering the offerings too small to accept. Each held in her arms the candles she had burned at shrines where she had prayed for the death of patients who had been stingy with their presents. (Paul & Paul, 1975, p. 712)

⁛

AFTER HER SERVICE to the mother and child has formally ended, an *iyoom* may be called in to treat a child or a mother who has become ill.

Chona's spiritual or physical healing skills may be called on outside of pregnancy and childbirth. For example, according to Chona's niece, another relative who had had a difficult pregnancy spent a month in a hospital, and despite an operation and other efforts by the doctor, her face remained very swollen and her mouth pulled off to one side. Her family decided to bring her back to San Pedro. When Chona saw the woman, she told her, "My dear, your face is deformed." Then Chona massaged the woman's scalp and inside her mouth, and told her not to go out that day, not for anything, and to call her the next day. The next day, the woman woke up fine.

An *iyoom* might also be called in to treat a young child for illnesses, including evil eye and a sunken fontanel caused by dehydration from diarrhea (Summer Institute of Linguistics, 1978). Various protections against evil eye have been commonly used, such as tying a loop of red thread around a child's wrist, sometimes with stone beads or small antique Spanish coins (Rosales, 1949). But if a young child falls ill, the *iyoom* might be asked to cure the child, as in this account from a woman recalling her childhood, about 1915 or 1920:

> Once when I had just finished making tortillas all by myself since there was no one to help me, I took my younger sister for a walk. I washed her face, changed her clothes and braided her hair. When I'd fixed her all up, I took her out. . . . I took my baby sister to my aunt's. I thought we'd play there.
>
> When we got there her sister-in-law was there in the house with her and said, "What a pretty little girl! Let me hold her a while. Oh! She's so nice!" Since I was but a child, I didn't think anything about it and gave my little sister to her. That woman really liked my little sister and made a great fuss over her. She kissed her on the cheek.
>
> I didn't realize the woman was pregnant and that it was bad what she did to my sister. So when I got tired of it there I brought my little sister home. It didn't cross my mind whether she'd get sick or not. When we got home she fell asleep and my mother lay her down in the hammock. . . .
>
> Then all of a sudden she burst out crying as if something really hurt her. My mother quickly took her out of the hammock. My little sister was thrashing about as if someone were trying to hold her down against her will. "What's the matter with my little daughter? What have you done to her, girl? Did you drop her? You're the one who took her," she said to me.

"No, I haven't done anything to her," I said.

"Yes, but where did you go with her? Perhaps my little girl got the evil eye."

"I went to my aunt's place. That's the only place I took her. We didn't go anyplace else. When we got there, there was a woman who took the child from me. She held and kissed her. She really liked her," I said to my mother. And then I told her what the woman's name was.

When she heard that she felt terrible and began to scold me: "Why did you do all that to my child? I saw when you took her she was all dressed up. Now my little daughter has the evil eye. You've done it now!" So she must have known that the woman who held my young sister was pregnant. When a woman is pregnant, I guess it's not good if she holds another child. It must have hurt her. But at that time I didn't know that would happen nor did I know that the woman was pregnant.

My sister wouldn't stop crying. It was as if someone were pulling on her legs. "Please go and tell the old lady to come and see my little daughter. When you get there, say, 'Ma'am, my mother says maybe you would come right now to see my younger sister. I don't know what's happened to her.'

So I went off running. When I got there the lady was at home, so I told her what my mother told me to say.

So she said, 'Ay! What's happened to her? Has she a fever?'

But I didn't know, since I was only a child. 'I don't know. That's all I was told,' I said.

'I'll come, my dear.'

'Yes, but "right now," they said. My little sister is really suffering.'

'Now tell your mother I'll come for sure, and not to worry.' The old lady used to treat children when they had diarrhea and vomiting or fever or the evil eye. So that's why my mother sent me to get her.

'Who would give this child the evil eye?' she said.

'Is that what it is, ma'am?' asked my mother.

'It's the evil eye, my friend. If it leaves then she'll rest,' said the old lady. So then she began to prepare medicine and gave it to her. I could scarcely look. I was so scared for my little sister. She really cried in the woman's arms when the lady gave her the medicine. My mother was so worried she couldn't do her housework. . . .

It took a long time for my little sister to get over it. I was so glad when she was better. Even though I hadn't caused it, I was the one who had taken her, and that's why I was sad. And that's how I learned that children got the evil eye. (Summer Institute of Linguistics, 1978, Book 35, pp. 43–57)

The idea of evil eye as well as the treatment with rue (and another treatment with an egg) appear to derive from both European and Mesoamerican sources (Orellana, 1987; Thompson, 1970). The rue plant has Old World origins; it "increases blood flow to the gastrointestinal system, aids in colic, and acts as a stomachic. It may alleviate some of the symptoms associated with evil eye and fright" (Orellana, 1987, p. 235). In Mexico, the European concept of evil eye fit easily with pre-Columbian ideas of diseases called *tlazolmiquiliztli* (*aire de basura*, garbage air) in which innocent people could be harmed by emanations from people who are angry or sullied with sexual passions (Ortiz de Montellano, 1990).

The ways that the *iyoom* and San Pedro families handle the pregnancy, birth, and postnatal care of mother and child provide a revealing illustration of changes and continuities in cultural practices. On the one hand, impressive stabilities tie current practices to those used in Mesoamerica across at least half a millennium. On the other hand, current practices also show dramatic changes emanating from individuals' decisions and inventions. For example, Chona and others of her generation have contributed new ideas, and changes have also come from afar, such as from archaic Spanish medicine and Western medicine.

If we could examine the decisions of each generation with a close-up lens, we could see the dynamic roles of other individuals and the conditions of their lives. We would be able to see each new generation extend and revise the approaches they have had access to seeing or hearing about, in continual processes of learning.

12 ::

Ways of Learning
Across Times and Places

AN *IYOOM* LEARNS the obstetrical and spiritual aspects of her calling by a variety of means. She builds on the expertise developed by prior generations and by other people of her own and other communities. As an adult she can learn from the deliveries of her own children, sometimes with and sometimes without the aid of another *iyoom*. In recent decades, she attends didactic lessons—and sometimes collaborative discussions—with Western medical personnel.

From childhood, an *iyoom* develops with the support of her birth destiny and divine election to the role, and the expectations that go with these. Especially because she is often related to an adult *iyoom*, she has opportunities to learn by overhearing and peeking as the relative discusses a case or tends to a patient. She may hear stories regarding midwives and explanations in the course of everyday events. Ancestor *iyooma'* visit in her dreams, providing professional information, and other professionally related information also comes to her through dreams. In addition, a child destined to be an *iyoom* may engage in play that provides opportunities to practice and explore skills and roles in simulation.

Chona (second from right) chats at a fiesta with Dr. Angélica Bixcul, one of the first Mayans from San Pedro to become a medical doctor with Western training. (Photo © Barbara Rogoff, 2006)

Didactic Medical Instruction or Collaborative Discussion

THE INFLUENCES of "Western" medicine are not necessarily as straightforward in their presentation or in their uptake as may be assumed by those who give courses to midwives. Regarding the courses given to midwives at the public health center in San Pedro, Chona reported, "I watch what the doctor writes, but I don't understand, because I don't know how to read and I don't understand Spanish." Western medical personnel have often used methods that are not well suited to communication when attempting to "train" traditional practitioners (Cosminsky, 1982, 2001a,b).

Brigitte Jordan provided telling examples in her study of courses given to Yucatecan Mayan midwives in Mexico. The courses often took place in an unfamiliar spoken language. And the instructors frequently employed diagrams that do not communicate to people unfamiliar with the conventions of diagrams—such as representing an ovum that cannot be seen as an object that looks like a tennis ball.

During a training course, Jordan asked one of the midwives what she thought about the presentation explaining how a baby starts, showing an ovum surrounded by several spermatozoa. The midwife remarked that it was rather interesting, especially the part about the ball and the little sticks.

> "But," she said with an air of confidentiality, "here in Yucatan we do it differently. *Our* men have a white liquid that comes out of their penis and that's how *we* make babies. Not with little sticks (*palitos*) like the Mexicans and gringos do." (Jordan, 1989, p. 928)

The efforts of the Western medical system to "upgrade" traditional midwifery practice in the Yucatan included no effort to understand the knowledge base used by the midwives. The doctors' ignorance of commonly accepted local information made it difficult for the doctors' information to be accepted by the midwives.

In addition, some of the midwives' knowledge would have enhanced the doctors' medical practice. The doctors could have learned from the midwives' use of steam and massage to aid lactation; cauterization of the umbilical stump with a candle flame to prevent infection in circumstances in which sterilization of tools is difficult; external version to adjust the baby's position by pressing on the abdomen if the baby is not already in the correct head-down position; and inclusion of familiar people during labor (now more common in Western medical settings).

Instead, medical personnel have tried to discourage practices such as external version, claiming that it can harm the fetus (Sesia, 1997).

> According to many biomedical practitioners in the United States and Mexico, the external version carries the risk of detaching the placenta from the uterine walls, provoking a premature birth. Nevertheless, it is noteworthy that U.S. biomedical obstetricians interested in lowering their cesarean rates are beginning to obtain training—often from midwives—in the performance of external versions. (Sesia, 1997, p. 417, citing Hays & Davis-Floyd, personal communication)

In turn, some of the information available to the doctors would have benefited the Yucatecan midwives. For example, the midwives could have learned the importance of not pushing too early during labor and that fertility is greatest at midcycle rather than the days surrounding the woman's period, as was commonly believed (Jordan, 1989).

However, the Western medical personnel's ignorance of local understandings and practices prevented such information from being shared between themselves and the Yucatecan midwives. The usual Western approach is one of hierarchical "delivery" of a curriculum, without the notion of a collaborative sharing of knowledge and worldviews.

The "trainings" of traditional midwives in the Yucatan studied by Jordan included hours of "delivery" of definitions and tests, such as the following:

> Nurse to group: "What is a family?" This is a rhetorical question to which no answer is expected or offered, though nobody would doubt that midwives know what a family is. The nurse provides the answer: "A family is a group of people who live under the same roof and have as a common goal the desire for a better life." Nurse writes definition on the blackboard. There is little response from the audience. Most continue to stare vacantly. Nurse looks expectantly at them, strongly conveying the notion that the definition should be copied. She asks why they aren't writing. A number of reasons are given: "Forgot to bring a notebook." "Do not have a pencil." "Can't write."

Traditional Mayan midwives "waiting out" a lecture, in the Yucatan, Mexico. (Photo from Jordan, 1989, with permission from Elsevier)

The nurse produces some pencils and paper. Then she walks around the room to check on progress, which is elusive. Finally, the entire staff, one physician and two nurses, are engaged in copying the definition on little slips of paper which they give to those midwives who can't read or write. When, mystified, I asked the doctor why he was doing this, he said, "She can't write" as he proceeded to copy. When I pointed out that she couldn't read either, he allowed that that was so, but thought when she goes home, somebody may read to her what he had written down. The midwives are told that they should know what is on the paper because it will be on the final test. Then we go on to the next definition, which is concerned with the question: "What is a home visit?" (Jordan, 1989, p. 927)

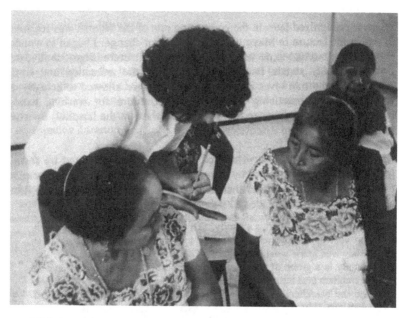

Midwives who cannot write (or read) look on as a nurse copies definitions for them to study (Yucatan, Mexico). (Photo from Jordan, 1989, with permission from Elsevier)

Jordan provided a striking analysis of the shortcomings of the unilateral approach of this training program:

> When the staff asked the midwives if any of them did external cephalic versions or engaged in the traditional practice of cauterizing the umbilical stump of the newborn, none of them admitted to doing it. They all were able to say that in case of breech presentation you refer the woman to the hospital and for treatment of the cord you use alcohol and merthiolate. But when we were alone, swinging in our hammocks at night in the dormitory, and I intimated that I actually knew how to do those things [having learned them from a Mayan midwife] and thought they were good for mother and baby, every one of them admitted that she engaged in those practices routinely. As a matter of fact, a lively discussion and exchange of information about specific techniques ensued.
>
> I would suggest, then, that current teaching methods produce only minimal changes in the behavior of trainees, while, at the same time, providing new resources for *talking about* what they do. In particular, midwives learn how to converse appropriately with supervisory medical personnel, so that when the public health nurse visits to check on them, they can give all of the appropriate responses to her questions. . . . The new knowledge is not incorporated in midwives' behavioral repertoire; it is verbally, but not behaviorally, fixed. (Jordan, 1989, p. 929)

DOCTORS HAVE LONG been critical of the work of Mayan *iyooma'* (see Cosminsky, 2001b). Their opposition to the practice of traditional midwives is widespread and longstanding, and has its basis in professional rivalry and economic concerns. In the eighteenth century, the medical establishment in Mexico and Guatemala began to express concerns about traditional midwives' practice. Their newly hostile attitude derived from their growing interest in including obstetrics as part of their own medical practice (Hernández Sáenz, & Foster, 2001). This attitude can be seen in the writings of Dr. Antonio Villanueva, commenting in 1875 on birth practices in Puebla, Mexico:

> [The kneeling position is] the most common. . . . It is the one used in births attended by midwives, completely ignorant and clumsy. . . . As audacious as they are clumsy, they usually disdain calling for help from a surgeon, resolving by themselves the difficulties

that they encounter, with manifest and irreparable damage to the health and even to the life, of the mother and child. . . .

The families that know to trust themselves to the hands of intelligent doctors [choose] the horizontal position. . . . Only in few, in very few cases, do women take for this supreme act, the only position that is acceptable in that it is the only rational one, the horizontal position. (quoted by León, 1910, pp. 142–143)

The Guatemalan Public Health Ministry's courses required for midwives have condemned many of the traditional practices of the *iyooma'*. The courses denounce the use of the sweat bath, the kneeling or squatting position for giving birth, massage, and cauterization of the cord (Cosminsky, 1982, 1994).

Western medical personnel also try to force *iyooma'* to send their patients to Western clinics. For example, public health officials in a Mayan town near San Pedro demanded that the midwives require their patients to attend the public health prenatal clinics. The midwives reported that their patients refuse to go to the clinics; the women are not supposed to announce that they are pregnant, and they may lack the money or time to travel to the distant clinic (Cosminsky, 1982, 1994).

The public health nurse scolded the midwives, telling them that they should refuse to attend the birth unless the patient attends the clinic—but without offering any information about how a clinic visit would benefit the patient. The authoritarian role taken by the public health nurse conflicts with the midwife–patient relationship, which is one of support by the midwife, not control. Further, suggesting that the midwife threaten not to attend the birth overlooks the *iyoom'*s spiritual calling—it is her sacred duty to attend the birth.

Conflict in the practices of the *iyooma'* and of Western doctors was apparent when anthropologist Elena Hurtado accompanied an *iyoom* to the home of a San Pedro woman in labor about 30 years ago. As the *iyoom* examined the woman, the husband sat on a chair supporting the woman under her armpits and female relatives held the woman's legs, telling her what to do. Then the doctor from the health center knocked on the door (called by a different midwife). The family asked Elena to tell him that everything was fine and that he was not needed. By the time Elena returned to the room, the woman was reclining on her back and the husband was no longer supporting her—only the *iyoom* was near the woman. After Elena told them that the doctor had departed, everyone reverted to their original positions and roles (Hurtado, 2009).

SOMETIMES, collaborative discussions among midwives and Western medical personnel may occur. For example, years back, my then-husband, who is a pediatrician, invited San Pedro midwives to a demonstration to show how U.S. pediatricians resuscitate newborns who don't begin to breathe. He brought to Guatemala a specially designed doll that U.S. medical personnel use to gain practice in infant resuscitation. I was present to help out. A number of midwives attended the meeting, both ones born with the sacred calling of *iyoom*, like Chona, and some who became midwives through medical training.

At first, most of the midwives at the meeting stood aloof and stiff at the edges of the room. They were hesitant about engaging in the conversation, perhaps suspicious of the doctor. Then Chona, usually dignified, broke the ice by teasing my former husband as her "son-in-law," based on her relationship with me as her daughter. (She teased that he should keep a better eye on me because, she warned, I often talk to other men in the streets.) The other midwives warmed up, amused at her teasing. They relaxed and became engaged with the demonstration, and tried out the resuscitation doll with interest.

Salem Magarian (my former husband) shows Chona how to practice resuscitation with the doll. In the background other midwives observe attentively (Rosa Petzey Rocché, in the back, and Jesús Quiacaín Televario, on the right). (Photo © Barbara Rogoff, 1986)

Resuscitation was not a new idea to Chona. In an account from some years before this demonstration, a Pedrano father recalled how Chona resuscitated his lifeless newborn. This was after a difficult delivery in which Chona managed to change the baby's position from transverse by massaging strongly just under the ribcage and shaking the mother.

> The baby was born lifeless, without movement. But the midwife knew what she was about. She had expected this so as soon as the child came as she saw it was lifeless she took it and pulled up on its ears. She really tweaked them hard! But the poor baby didn't respond. It lay like a dead animal. Lifeless! "Ma'am, never mind. It's dead. You'd better look after my wife [who had passed out]," I told her.
> "No, don't say that. Your wife is OK. We need to resuscitate this baby here," she replied. She kept watching the baby, tweaking its ears like I said. Then finally she began to breathe down its nostrils. And believe it or no, after she did this three times, the little one gasped. I was amazed because I'd never seen anything like that before. Then the wee thing gave a yell. (Summer Institute of Linguistics, 1978, Book 45, p. 68)

During the resuscitation demonstration, the midwives and the pediatrician soon began discussing how they do their work, sharing ideas among the midwives and with the pediatrician. Given the rivalries among midwives in San Pedro as well as their suspicion towards Western medicine, this "grand rounds" was an unusual event.

One of the *iyooma'* asked the pediatrician how long he leaves a jaundiced newborn in the sun, a common practice of *iyooma'*. Others asked whether he thought it is more effective to sun a jaundiced baby for a short period once an hour or for a longer time all at once. In U.S. hospitals the same effect is achieved by putting babies under special lights, rather than under the sun, so he had little experience with this and no ready answer. A fascinating and collaborative discussion ensued in which the midwives and pediatrician shared their knowledge and experience in handling this problem using the available resources.

Learning Through Destinies Shared
Across Generations

A KEY FEATURE of the learning environment of San Pedro *iyooma'* is the birth destiny that guides their developmental course—even if they resist it. Often, a young *iyoom*-to-be shares this destiny with an older relative.

When her granddaughter Chonita was born, Chona carefully lifted the little veil from the baby's wet black hair and gave it to Chonita's parents to wash and keep. They safeguarded it in a soft cloth, together with 13 amber-colored chunks of pine incense.[72]

Thus Chona's granddaughter, Chonita, was born with the sign of being an *iyoom* and when she was little, she sometimes overheard adults confiding, with some reverence, that she has the destiny of *iyoom*, the same as her grandmother. In addition she was Chona's namesake and was born on Chona's birthday. What's more, Chona had predicted all this.

Such markers and signs of identity can provide powerful channeling of an individual's development. The influence of expectations held by a person's family and community can be immense, especially if these expectations are held by all. Under such circumstances, a person would have little reason to question the expectation (although he or she might resist, as Chona's mother Dolores resisted being an *iyoom*). Now that people in San Pedro have extensive contact with other communities, the long-held expectations for children's learning and development—and the destiny of an *iyoom*—have become alternatives among many other possibilities rather than "the way things are."

⁙

CHONITA'S CHILDHOOD introduction to her destined role followed the traditions of *iyooma'* that have persisted for centuries, and also deflected from that path in ways that reflect a new era. Like the children in her grandmother's generation, little Chonita was not told where babies come from. Sometimes she was told that foreigners bring babies, or that they are left by the airplanes that fly over San Pedro. When Chonita was about 4 years old, Chona overheard Chonita and her friends saying that I was in San Pedro in order to bring babies to families in San Pedro.

Chonita and Chona, in 1974, about the time that I met Chona.
(Photograph by Santos Quiacaín Pérez)

As with girls in previous generations who were born with the destiny of *iyoom*, Chonita's destiny as *iyoom* became firmer when she became gravely ill later in her childhood. She wasn't eating at all, and the situation looked very serious. After the doctors tried all kinds of medicines that did not help, her parents took her to a traditional shaman.

He prayed to find out what was making her sick, and discovered that her parents had lost the veil that she was born with. Chonita's family looked everywhere for it, and finally found it among some clothes in their old wooden chest. They took care to wrap it up again carefully as they should, with incense. The same day that the veil was found and tended, Chonita started eating again and soon could help her mother again and go back to school.

Chonita was eager to learn Spanish, and she liked being with her friends again, playing hopscotch and sports at recess, in fifth grade. (Photo by Juan Cholotío)

Chonita moved toward her sacred destiny like women had for centuries, following the classic pattern of development of an *iyoom*. At the same time, she had distinctly new opportunities to learn, reflecting her era. She could study Spanish and read, watch and listen in to the activities of her grandmother, and hear Chona's explanations in the context of ongoing events.

Learning Through Observing, Listening in, and Contributing

LEARNING THROUGH BEING PRESENT in family and community events, with opportunities to observe or listen in, has long been a key way of learning in San Pedro. Children—at least during my early visits to San Pedro—had the freedom to move around the town without being under the direct supervision of an adult caregiver. If the small groups of meandering children ran into difficulty, a nearby adult or older child could help them. This allows children an independence to "see what's up" that is rare for middle-class children in the United States.

These youngsters (ages about 3 to 6) noticed my camera as they played in a canoe at the lakeshore, without direct supervision. At a distance down the beach, adults and older children were fishing and washing clothes, and occasionally people walked by on the path to the dock. (Photo © Barbara Rogoff, 1975)

Access to the range of activities of the family and community

UNLIKE IN MIDDLE-CLASS U.S. LIFE, where children are segregated from most adult activities, in San Pedro before schooling became prevalent, children regularly participated in almost the full range of community activities. Although this is diminishing from former times, children in San Pedro still usually have more involvement in the range of their community's life than is common in middle-class communities.[73]

Children were ubiquitous in community events such as this funeral in a Protestant church, when I was first in San Pedro. Children still attend funerals in San Pedro. (Photo © Barbara Rogoff, 1975)

San Pedro was not divided into an adult-world separate from a child-world; for the most part, all ages were included in the community's social and work life. (As schooling has increased, this is changing.)

Opportunities to learn by observing and listening in

ONE OF THE FEW activities from which children were excluded was being present at a birth. But a child in a family that included an *iyoom* might even have occasions to observe or listen in on births, as did Chonita. She stayed at her grandmother's house frequently, so she had the opportunity to listen closely when Chona or other people recounted to visitors how Chona had become an *iyoom*. (Because of Chona's prominence and charisma, and the presence of researchers and other visitors interested in the sacred calling of *iyoom*, Chona is often asked about her life and her profession.)

When she was quite small, Chonita was sometimes able to listen in if Chona took her along at night to a birth. When little Chonita was asleep at Chona's house and the husband of a patient in labor called for Chona in the night and no one else was home, sometimes Chona would have him carry the sleeping young child along to the patient's house. They would put sleeping Chonita to bed in the patient's house. Because houses at that time usually had just one room (with a separate kitchen), this sometimes meant Chonita was in the same room as the birth, which may have been lit by candlelight. Chonita reports that she would keep her eyes closed and pretend to be asleep, but would listen in to what was happening.

When Chonita was a little bigger she sometimes would walk alongside Chona, holding her hand on the way to a birth in the night. Chona welcomed the company, because a woman walking alone at night would run the danger of gossip and of encountering a transforming witch.

Normally, Chonita and children of the pregnant woman's household were not allowed to be present at the birth. If the family did not have a big house with two rooms, they asked a neighbor the favor of keeping the children of the household and Chonita. During the birth, Chona and the mother and other adults spoke quietly, so anyone nearby would not hear. The woman did not scream during the birth. (Chona says, "Their mothers told them, 'Keep quiet. If you scream I'll cut off your ear with a knife.'" In San Pedro it is common and acceptable to make threats without the intention of carrying them out.)

After the baby was born, the adults told the children that they had bought a baby in Guatemala City, and it had come in an airplane, and Chona had brought it because she knows Spanish. (Chona laughed when she told me this, because she speaks almost no Spanish and she understands only a little Spanish.)

Chonita was eager to walk along when Chona visited the pregnant women during the daytime. She accompanied her grandmother on house calls when she was about 5 or 6 years old, to keep Chona company. Chona did not let Chonita see her examination of the pregnant woman—Chonita was supposed to wait outside during the visits.

Another of Chona's granddaughters, demonstrating for me how Chonita accompanied Chona when she was small. If Chona had actually been going to check a pregnant woman, she would have carried her hand-woven shawl elegantly over one shoulder, folded lengthwise. She and other iyooma' *say that without carrying the shawl in that way, "there is no respect." Respect is mutual. Carrying the shawl in this formal manner shows respect on the part of the* iyoom *and also generates respect for this sacred work on the part of others. (Photo © Barbara Rogoff, 1996)*

Although people always shooed Chonita out of the house when a mother was about to give birth, one afternoon when she was about 7 years old, she sneaked in to watch. She stood in a dark corner of the house, not moving at all, peeking through the light plastic curtain hung around the bed.

After the baby was born, Chonita was frightened to see Chona holding a candle flame up to the baby. Chonita ran out of the dark corner where she had been hiding, and shouted to her grandmother not to burn the baby. She didn't know that Chona was using the candle flame to seal off the end of the baby's umbilical cord.

The baby's family was furious with Chonita for being there, but she was glad she had had a chance to see the birth. Chona scolded her at first, but later explained to Chonita what had been happening.

Such explanations are a change from the learning opportunities of *iyooma'* in prior times. For Chona to explain what was happening to Chonita resembles her contributions to changing cultural practices in San Pedro: She informs pregnant women what is happening to them rather than concealing information about the birth process and other "facts of life."

Chonita's knowledge of the work of an *iyoom* thus included opportunities to watch and listen in. However, learning by watching and listening in appears to have been less available to prior generations of *iyooma'*, or at least has been commonly denied by elder *iyooma'*. Their opportunities to observe and listen to births seem to have been largely limited to being present at the births of their own children, before they took on their calling of *iyoom*.

⁞⁞

ALTHOUGH ADULTS in San Pedro claim that the children do not have access to conversations about adult topics, it seems to me that Pedranos underestimate the extent to which their children listen in to and watch surrounding events and conversations. Often children are present and attentive—and ignored—when adults talk about private or adult matters.

For example, when Lois Paul visited a new mother in 1941, children were present as the *iyoom* and the woman's female relatives discussed birth. The women commented that children are not supposed to know where babies come from:

> There was some discussion between the women in zutuhil which they thought I didn't understand about whether I knew where babies come from [Lois did not yet have children]. The midwife told them with assurance that I did because I read books. "Among ladinos and *extranjeros* [foreigners]," she told them, "small children are allowed to watch, *sin vergüenza* (without shame), but among us they are not allowed to know about it." (Paul, 1969, pp. 30–31)

The *iyoom* went on to ask Lois if she thought she could stand labor pains, using a euphemism—"the beating of the *extranjero* [foreigner]"—because of the unmarried girls and children who were present. The *iyoom* graphically imitated how women cry out with labor pains, which keep coming with intensity. She and the other women laughed at this, and the *iyoom* teased Lois that she wouldn't be able to take it.

Surely there is some information available here to the children present, despite—or because of—the attempts at secrecy. The whispered restriction of such information may make it especially interesting to young eavesdroppers.

San Pedro children's traditional almost-universal presence in whatever is happening in the community gives them many opportunities to observe and eavesdrop on many of the events of life.[74] Such access to the range of activities of the community is often accompanied by children pitching in to help.

Learning by pitching in

IF CHILDREN HAVE ACCESS to become involved in the key activities of their community, they can learn by pitching in, collaboratively, from an early age. For example, in the Yucatan, Mexico, Mayan girls in families that include midwives pick up the knowledge and skills of midwifery in daily life. As children, they have many opportunities to learn about peripheral aspects of midwifery. Later, after they have given birth themselves, they continue to learn as they are included in other women's deliveries:

> They know what the life of a midwife is like (for example, that she needs to go out at all hours of the day or night), what kinds of stories the women and men who come to consult her tell, what kinds of herbs and other remedies need to be collected, and the like. As young children they might be sitting quietly in a corner as their mother administers a prenatal massage; they would hear stories of difficult cases, of miraculous outcomes, and the like. As they grow older, they may be passing messages, running errands, getting needed supplies. A young girl might be present as her mother stops for a postpartum visit after the daily shopping trip to the market.
>
> Eventually, after she has had a child herself, she might come along to a birth, perhaps because her ailing grandmother needs someone to walk with, and thus find herself doing for the woman in labor what other women had done for her when she gave birth; that is, she may take a turn with the other women in the hut at supporting the laboring woman, holding her on her lap, breathing and pushing with her. After the baby is born, she may help with the clean-up and if the midwife doesn't have time to look in on mother and baby, she may do so and report on their condition.

Eventually, she may even administer prenatal massages to selected clients. At some point, she may decide that she actually wants to do this kind of work. She then pays more attention, but only rarely does she ask questions. Her mentor sees their association primarily as one that is of some use to her ("Rosa already knows how to do a massage, so I can send her if I am too busy"). As time goes on, the apprentice takes over more and more of the work load, starting with the routine and tedious parts. (Jordan, 1989, p. 932)

Pitching in helpfully to ongoing activities is a primary way of learning in San Pedro. San Pedro children begin early to take on responsibility in the work of the family, especially in former years and still to some extent. They tend younger children and help to maintain the household, and assist in the fields and family businesses. They and their families value their needed contributions.

These little ones contribute a child-size quantity of water and firewood to the family supply. The little girl is coming back with her mother from the lakeshore fetching water and the little boy is coming back with his father from the fields. (Photo on left by Lois and Ben Paul, 1941. Photo on right by John E. Mack, 1976)

A 3-year-old washes the family dishes with her 10-year-old sister. This 3-year-old was also more religious than the rest of her family; in the evenings she went to church on her own, putting on her shawl and walking a short distance to where she joined neighbors in worship. (Photo © Barbara Rogoff, 1975)

This 2½-year-old neighbor delivered Ben and Lois Paul's daily breakfast tortillas, made by her mother next door. (Photo by Lois and Ben Paul, 1941)

An 8-year-old, the photocopy expert in her family's copy store, fills a tricky order, although she has to climb on a table to reach the machine. In the foreground a younger child watches and helps. (Photo © Luisa Magarian, 1998)

THE CULTURAL TRADITION in which children are included in the range of community events and learn by observing, overhearing, and pitching in has been dubbed *learning through intent community participation*. This way of supporting children's development and learning appears to be common in many Indigenous communities of North and Central America (Paradise & Rogoff, 2009; Rogoff, Moore, Najafi, Dexter, Correa-Chávez, & Solís, 2007; Rogoff, Paradise, Mejía Arauz, Correa-Chávez, & Angelillo, 2003).

Learning thorough intent community participation also occurs in non-Indigenous communities—we all learn our first language by listening in and trying to participate. But it is much less prevalent in communities where children are not included in the range of activities of the community.

If children routinely have access to observe and pitch in to the wide range of community activities, there may be little need for adults to organize special child-focused lessons separated from the use of the information. Instead, children may be expected to be attentive to ongoing activities in order to learn and to help out (Briggs, 1991; de Haan, 1999; Gaskins, 1999; Rogoff, 1981; Rogoff et al., 1993).

Keen attention to ongoing events and initiative in learning

SAN PEDRO CHILDREN tend to be keen observers and to listen closely, like 2½-year-old Agustina, on the next page, watching closely how her grandmother bathed her newborn sister.

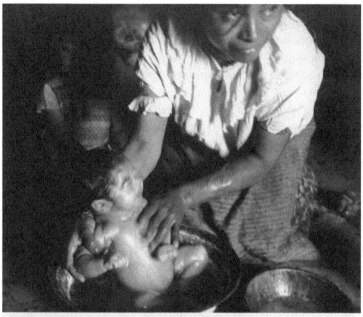

Little Augustina watches alertly as her grandmother and namesake, Agustina Cox, bathes her 2-week-old granddaughter Lucía (in 1941). Little Augustina holds a posture of sustained attention. This grandmother was the woman who washed Chona's veil when Chona was born. (Photo by Lois and Ben Paul)

The attentiveness, initiative, and community inclusion involved in this kind of learning is apparent in an autobiographical account of a San Pedro woman, recalling how she learned to embroider and weave when she was perhaps 6 or 7 years old (about 1915):

My mother could do good embroidery on men's pants. When she used to sew I'd sit down beside her and watch carefully how she did the embroidery. "Girl, move, so I won't poke you in the eye with my needle," she'd say to me. I did that because I liked sewing and wanted to learn how. . . .

Once I found a piece of trousers and began to embroider it. I went to my aunt's who lived in our compound. When I got there with the piece of trousers I was embroidering my aunt really made fun of me. "Come on, my dear. So you've started to embroider. Well, get it done well so that your husband won't get angry." But that's how I taught myself to embroider. I did a design of balancing scales. They don't do that any more. I was really proud when I got one side done. . . .

I used wool that my mother had left over. I'd take the ends of the wool that my mother had extra. And there was a woman in our compound who was always doing embroidery, and there was a lot of odd pieces of wool there. When she went on an errand, I'd stay in the house. "Please look after my child a while. I have to go on an errand."

"No, my mother might get mad at me."

"Yes, girl. I'll just be gone a minute. Your mother won't say anything. And if you stay I'll give you some wool," she'd say to me. The woman persuaded me so I stayed in her house and looked after her child. When her child went to sleep she'd put it in the hammock and then go on her errand. So I'd stay and look after the child. When the mother came back she'd say, "Didn't my child wake up?"

"No, he slept," I'd say.

Then she gave me my wool, and I'd be so happy. There was red, green, blue. She gave me lots of colors. She'd always do that when I looked after her child. And the wool she gave me wasn't just small bits and pieces. They were long strands. I'd save it all. My mother would give me wool, too. Then I'd use it in the trousers I was embroidering, and that's how I taught myself.

I'd just got nicely started embroidering the trousers when my aunt saw it. "Oh, you are doing that so well. You didn't think so, but I'm going to tell your mother that you can do the embroidery on the trousers for my little son," she said to me. She really liked my embroidery. But it was just for fun I had done it, not for real. When she said that to me I was overjoyed. But I didn't really believe I was to do the embroidery on her son's trousers. I just thought she was teasing me. Playing with me. But it was true what she said to me!

Right then my mother arrived and she said to her, "Oh! Your daughter embroiders well."

"What embroidery is she doing?"

"Haven't you seen it? Come and see!"

"Well, I sure didn't realize the child was doing it!"

"Is it all right if she does some for my boy?"

"OK. Let her do it. She's doing good work," my mother said.

So I was given a little pair of trousers and some wool. My mother showed me and explained to me how to do it. At first it was OK for me to embroider a piece of trousers, but it wasn't on the real thing. So my mother said to me, "When you embroider you use a thread of the weaving [of the trouser fabric] as a guide so that it will come out straight. And you count stitches in the weaving to keep your embroidery even, so that it stays the same size. Sometimes some of the weaving the people do is crooked and this will affect the embroidery. So if the weaving is like that, you don't stay on the same thread as a guide, but as it bends you choose another thread so that your row of embroidery won't follow the weaving but will be straight." But at first I didn't know that's what you had to do when you embroidered, or even that some weaving was crooked.

So I began to embroider the little trousers. When I finished one row I was so happy I'd done a good job. It was straight and even. Then my mother started me on the next row. I put two rows on each leg. I did it well and no one had to reprimand me. My aunt was very pleased when she saw it, and had no criticism of it. So that's how I embroidered my first trousers.

There were other designs I didn't know how to do. All I learned was how to do chains and balancing scales. I put scales on these trousers, and they turned out so well. The other designs I learned as I watched my mother sew.

When I found old trousers lying around, I'd unpick the embroidery and see how it was done. That's how I learned how to do other designs such as rings, bales of hay, fish and jugs. I was content when I learned how to do all the embroidery designs.

[My aunt then offered to make me a beautiful blouse.] "I'd like you to do some embroidering in exchange for the blouse now that you can do that kind of work," she said to me. . . . So that's how I began to embroider trousers. I earned some money which bought my blouse. But that was of my own volition. My father or mother didn't tell me to do it.

And I really liked to watch the women weave. I wanted to do it too. When I went baby-sitting, I'd sit close to the one who was weaving and watch how she did it. I saved all the ends of the threads because I wanted to weave. When I saw that I had a lot of thread I started to figure out how to do it. I looked for some sticks which I stuck in the ground to make an apparatus to measure out my threads for weaving. . . . After I had them all measured as to the right length, I set up my weaving.

But it wasn't real weaving, it was just for fun. But it turned out good, just like a boy's little sash. I did that because I was just a child, and besides I had to baby-sit as well. I finished one and started the other. It kept me busy and I looked after my young brother at the same time. I did two or three strips like belts.

I'd just gotten nicely started when a lady came in to visit my mother and she saw them. "My dear, what is that? Is it a tie for an apron?" she asked.

"No, it's just something I've done for fun," I said.

"Oh, you're kidding! You did it, did you? You sure did a good job! Why don't you let me have it, my dear. I'll buy it from you."

"Ho! What do you want to buy that for?" my mother asked.

"It's useful to me. It'll be good for apron ties."

"Well, if it's useful take it if you like it," my mother told her. The lady took four of them, and paid me five cents for each one. I was overjoyed when she gave me twenty cents. I'd never had that much money before. (Summer Institute of Linguistics, 1978, Book 35, pp. 64–84)

::

AMONG SOME Indigenous people of Mexico, observation is so effective that sometimes people pick up a new skill without any practice, such as learning to drive by "spying" on bus drivers when riding buses (Chamoux, 1992). Similarly, Guatemalan Mayan adults learned to use a footloom by watching an experienced weaver for some weeks, asking no questions and receiving no explanations, and then simply began to weave (Nash, 1967).

The attentiveness of San Pedro children (and adults) has been noted in several research studies. Pedrano toddlers and mothers attended skillfully to more than one event at a time, without interruptions of one event by another, more often than middle-class European American toddlers and mothers (Chavajay & Rogoff, 1999; Rogoff, Mistry, Göncü, & Mosier, 1993).

In another study, San Pedro children watched closely how their sister or brother made a toy with a research assistant, even though they were not addressed and were not led to expect that they would have the chance to make the same toy. They were simply told they would have the chance to make a different toy in a few minutes and given an object to play with while they waited. Pedrano children from relatively traditional families watched more intently than Pedrano children whose mothers had extensive experience in Western schooling. However, both of these groups of Pedrano children observed more closely than European American middle-class children. The San Pedro children learned more from the opportunity to observe—they needed less help when they were unexpectedly given the opportunity to make a toy like their sister or brother had, a week later (Correa-Chávez & Rogoff, 2009).[75]

Children in San Pedro (top) and California (bottom) watched intently (or not) as their sibling was taught how to construct a mouse that runs on a spool with a rubber band. (Photos courtesy of Maricela Correa-Chávez)

In addition to watching closely, San Pedro children have the opportunity to pick up information and ways of doing things seemingly by osmosis, by simply being around and involved. They have the chance to be part of the rhythms and routines of everyday community life, so they can attune themselves to ideas, values, information, and ways of doing things by being part of life as it is lived. Their expectations are formed by seeing how things happen on a routine basis. This is unlikely to occur for children who are segregated from many of the activities of their community.

Nowadays in San Pedro, children are less likely to be present for such a wide range of everyday community life, because most of them attend school on a daily basis for many years. They are less involved in their family's work than previous generations, instead spending time in school and doing homework. It remains to be seen whether their opportunities and interest in learning by observing and listening in to ongoing events will be reduced in the near future.

Girls doing homework on the front stoop. (Photo © Luisa Magarian, 1998)

Narratives and
Explanations in the Course of Action

IN ADDITION TO learning by observing surrounding activities, Pedrano children have opportunities to hear stories and explanations. The stories may occur as their elders reminisce about the old days, an uncle returns from a trip with adventures to tell, a friend recounts a tale, or a neighbor tells their mother about the complications that occurred during the birth the night before. In addition, gossip is a central form of entertainment, sharing news and information, and political action in San Pedro.

This child caregiver, the toddler, and even the baby pay rapt attention to the older girls' tale. (Photo by Lois and Ben Paul, 1941)

Explanation is often part of learning through intent community participation, as commentary in the context of an ongoing activity. This is unlike the kind of Western medical explanation *out* of the context of shared activity that was offered in the Yucatecan midwife "training" classes critiqued by Jordan.

An example of explanation in the context of ongoing activity appeared in the account above of the girl who wanted to learn to embroider, when her mother explained how to use the lines of woven cloth to guide her stitches. The lengthy explanation occurred in the context of the girl's efforts to embroider and was immediately useful in that context. Here is the explanation again (italicized), and its context:

So I was given a little pair of trousers and some wool. My mother showed me and explained to me how to do it. At first it was OK for me to embroider a piece of trousers, but it wasn't on the real thing. So my mother said to me, "*When you embroider you use a thread of the weaving [of the trouser fabric] as a guide so that it will come out straight. And you count stitches in the weaving to keep your embroidery even, so that it stays the same size. Sometimes some of the weaving the people do is crooked and this will affect the embroidery. So if the weaving is like that, you don't stay on the same thread as a guide, but as it bends you choose another thread so that your row of embroidery won't follow the weaving but will be straight.*" But at first I didn't know that's what you had to do when you embroidered, or even that some weaving was crooked.

So I began to embroider the little trousers. When I finished one row I was so happy I'd done a good job. It was straight and even. Then my mother started me on the next row. (Summer Institute of Linguistics, 1978, Book 35, pp. 72–75)

In the midst of an activity, comments can be offered in reference to events as they unroll. For example, a mother can tell a weaving daughter, "Sit back a little more," and thereby let the daughter know that she needs to maintain more tension on the loom threads (attached to the backstrap passing around her hips) to be able to make straight edges on the belt she is beginning to weave. If the same information were to be given *out* of the context of weaving, a comprehensible explanation would need to provide much of the context in words that would otherwise be available in the shared context of ongoing activity.

This mother and daughter can both refer to the ongoing process in which the child is engaged in situations like that portrayed in this drawing from the Codex Mendoza of 1541–42, showing an Aztec mother kneeling as she teaches her daughter to grind corn and to weave. The scroll emanating from the mother's mouth symbolizes speech; the mother also gestures with her hands. Her explanations would build on the shared information available in the ongoing activities.

The two tortillas above each drawing signify that the girl is in the stage when a girl would commonly eat two big tortillas—a contrast to measuring development in terms of years since birth or in terms of level of schooling (e.g., "preschoolers," "middle-schoolers"). (Image courtesy Bodleian Library, University of Oxford; Shelfmark: MS. Arch.Selden.A.1, fol. 60r)

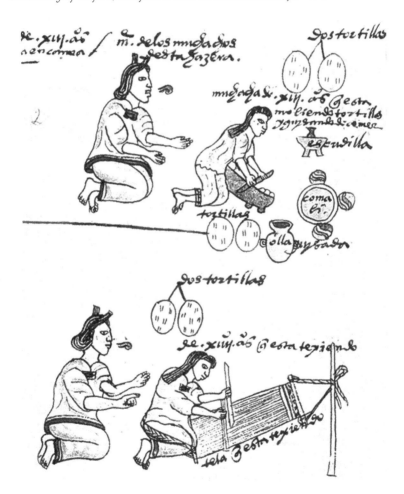

Thus, within shared activity, narratives and explanations are ordinarily used to extend communication. In Brigitte Jordan's study with traditional midwives in the Yucatan, Mexico, midwives and birth assistants used narratives and explanations to discuss possible diagnoses and consider different courses of action. They brought up similar previous cases and together pondered the extent to which prior cases applied to challenges of the case at hand. In contrast with communication isolated from the activity to which it refers, their talk was in the context of action and supported it:

> In the traditional system, to know something is to know *how to do it*, and only derivatively to know *how to talk about it*. Talk is never primary. . . .
>
> There is some evidence that information learned [solely] in the verbal mode is used again in the verbal mode, in talk, and is unlikely to be translated into other behavior. What is generated, then, is a new way of talking, rather than a new way of doing. For example, one midwife began to refer to the uterus as the "prolapso" after she had attended a training course. This term probably came from a discussion of "prolapsed uterus," but it is noteworthy that the midwife had not acquired any way of dealing with this complication. What the course had provided for her was simply a fancier and more prestigious way of talking. . . .
>
> What I observed in working with midwives who had attended training courses is that they had learned how to talk to representatives of the official health care system. They had learned what kinds of things were "good" and what kinds of things were "bad." They had become exposed to an ideology which they knew was powerful, which commanded resources and authority, and to which they could now better accommodate. Specifically, they had learned new ways of talking, new ways of legitimizing themselves, new ways of presenting themselves as being in league with this powerful system, which, however, had little impact on their daily practice. (Jordan, 1989, pp. 928–929)

Although many aspects of life in San Pedro can be learned through hearing explanations and observing, Chona declares that her knowledge did not come to her through such sources. She reports that she did not see an actual birth (other than that of her own first child) before she did her first delivery. Furthermore, she claims that when she was a child, she did not hear discussions of birth, because children were more respectful and obediently left the room when adults discussed adult matters. Chona says that her knowledge and skills came to her from her divine destiny and her dreams.

Learning via Dreams

A CHALLENGE for me, in describing Chona's learning, and that of other *iyooma'*, is to make sense of learning through dreams. In my own upbringing, dreams are regarded as peripheral experiences that occur while one sleeps, not communication within a metaphysical realm, with a reality of their own. They are not seen as a way of entering and tuning in to a reality of the ancestors, spiritual figures, and the spirits of the mountains, the rocks, the forests, water, and the other creatures of the earth and the celestial sphere.

In San Pedro, dreams are often regarded as travel of the spirit or important communication with the dreamer, regarding otherwise hidden meanings and portending or announcing events such as illness of a relative. They provide guidance in one's life direction.

So, from my U.S. researcher background, how would I explain learning through dreams? I like Lois Paul's (1975) suggestion that dreams give simulations of events and skills. She suggested that in their dreamwork, Pedrana *iyooma'* are able to role-play the obstetric and ritual practices that they will carry out, using this simulation as apprenticeship.

In addition, dreaming provides opportunities to make connections, building on prior experience and ideas of daily waking life and also those of the imagination and other dreams. Dreams can foster flexibility in thinking and consolidation of ideas in new ways. Research indicates that sleep enhances learning and memory and encourages insight into solutions to problems (Gómez, Bootzin, & Nadel, 2006). According to research by Harvard neurologist Jeffrey Ellenbogen, sleep increases people's frequency of connecting related ideas by 33%, even though people are not aware of this process (Berlin, 2008).

This opening-up is sometimes reported as the source of creative discoveries, such as chemist August Kekule realizing that benzene was structured as a ring, based on a dream of a snake eating its own tail. Another such account is that of Elias Howe inventing the automated sewing machine, based on a dream of being attacked by warriors whose spears had holes in the sharp end, unlike the centrally placed eyes of the needles in his original model (Berlin, 2008; Browne, 1988).

Dreaming seems often to provide an opening-up that may allow connections to be made both within the dream itself and also in later waking efforts to understand them. In a community in which dreams are seen as important, it is not just the dream itself but individual and group efforts to understand the dream that may provide opportunities to make new connections—that is, to learn.

Spiritually selected individuals such as Chona have an especially important relation with dreams. They have been expected to get lost in daydreams as children, and to learn through dreams as their destiny calls—being visited by ancestor *iyooma'* or other spiritual figures. Such relation to dreaming is beyond that of ordinary Pedranos. And of myself.

::

HOWEVER, I HAD an experience once that may help to understand learning through dreams. I was illustrating a picture book (*The Hen that Crowed*), and was working on a draft with the book editor. She had told me to design the illustrations so that they are in motion, like a movie, across the pages of the book. I had learned a technical rule of thumb, that the design of a page should move the eye from left to right, with the composition unbalanced toward the right, so that readers would keep going in the book, being led to turn to the next page. I understood this rule of thumb, but I couldn't get my mind around the idea of the illustrations being a movie. I thought of them more like still pictures.

But then, on one of my trips to Guatemala, I picked up amebic dysentery. With a high fever, unable to move, I lay on my stomach in a stupor in the hot afternoon, sweating and hallucinating. Out of nowhere, I saw the images that I had been drafting for the book, and they began to move as in a moving picture, from left to right across the turning pages of the book. Even in my weak state, I realized that the visual image I had seen was extremely important, and I roused myself to make sure to remember it. I was able to fix this idea in my mind and later use it. This insight was extremely important for my progress in illustrating the book.

My dream-like state allowed me to make new connections, building on information and ideas that I had some access to but did not understand. So maybe that is one aspect of learning through dreams.

::

BUT MISSING from my own experience is the spiritual aspect, the role of destiny connecting Chona and other *iyooma'* with spiritual ancestors

through dreams, and the continuity of their responsibilities with generations of spiritual practitioners and of sacred practices. This spiritual
aspect is important.

In addition, however, I would speculate that the opportunities and
connections provided by dreams also build on information and ideas
accessible in everyday life. As a child and young woman, Chona had
numerous sources of knowledge that could have informed her dreams.
She may have had access to some aspects of her great-aunt's practices as
an *iyoom* through overhearing, in addition to Doña Josefa telling her,
"You, dear child, if you live to grow up, you will do like I do, going from
house to house like I do now." She heard stories and legends and gossip,
some about prominent *iyooma'* like Doña María Puac and about special
destinies. She had experience with her own children's births, with an
iyoom and alone, and the birth experiences of her friends and relatives.

Doña María Puac, a prominent iyoom *who was practicing by the time
Chona was a young woman, and whom Chona now says "delivered" me. That
would have been some years after the Pauls took this photo of her. (Photo by
Lois and Ben Paul, 1941)*

IT WOULD NOT be surprising for individuals in San Pedro, or anywhere else, to be unaware of all the various sources of their learning. Most of us have little knowledge of where we learn things (Dunbar, 1995; Munroe & Munroe, 1997; Sommerville & Hammond, 2007). This would be especially true with informal/casual repeated everyday experience and secondhand learning through other people's experience.

In addition, the idea of keeping track of life events may be one that has special importance to academics—especially developmental psychologists—but not to many others. In some nonliterate societies, detailed memory of history is held by a local *griot* or specialist, but such historical recall may not be a priority for everyone else. Most of us may focus our attention on living our current days. Indeed, memory itself is a construction in the present. There is plentiful evidence of memory shifts in people's recall of historical events, as people reconstruct past events based on their current reality, taking into account potential future considerations.

Furthermore, for sacred practitioners such as *iyooma'*, the credential that distinguishes them from everyday individuals or trained *practicantes* is their connection with the divine, through their birth destiny and their visits by spiritual ancestors through dreams. Acknowledging everyday experience or instruction would undermine the *iyoom*'s credibility and indeed her efficacy. A good part of any healer's efficacy comes from the belief of the patient in the power of the treatment. Some of the power of Chona's role comes from being divinely selected and prepared supernaturally.

Similarly, in the Yucatan, traditionally, and still in remote hamlets, "midwives told about dreams during which they received their calling and learned everything they know from 'goddesses' (*diosas*)." The stories of midwives' supernatural selection and knowledge served to legitimize and credential their role. In the Yucatan, this has largely been replaced by stories that midwives tell about Western medical training, revealing the changing power structures from Mayan spiritual to Western medical sources of knowledge (Jordan, 1989).

Stories of dream instruction and divine selection are likely to provide information regarding the *iyoom*'s role and practices for children like Chonita who may be listening in—especially because such stories are often told in hushed voices expressing awe. Pedranos accord great importance to dreams and recount ordinary ones; the dreams of an *iyoom* carry special importance.

::

THE EXPLANATIONS that I might give for the learning of an *iyoom*, as a developmental psychologist from the United States, are likely to be at odds with the stance of a sacred Mayan professional, whose explanations focus on sacred destiny and spiritual guidance. I recognize that my efforts so far to explain may be more like "explaining away."

A more complete account of the role of dreaming in learning to be a healer, including spiritual and intuitive aspects, is given by a native North American healer:

> It is through dreams that we get our calling. . . . It is through dreams that we get our spiritual knowledge, power objects, doctor tools, and acquire certain forms of knowledge to become Native healers. (Lake, 1991, p. 27)
>
> An ancestor, ghost, animal, spirit, force, power, or the Great Creator talks to us in dreams. They tell us that we have been chosen to be a certain kind of medicine person, and they give specific instructions on how to use their medicine and power. (p. 40)
>
> Perhaps the most difficult thing about dreams is believing in them. At first when you hear dream allies or spirits talking to you, you might think it is your imagination going crazy. Your conscious, rational mind will do everything to block it out, so you must be persistent. To become a medicine man or woman, you must have faith in the Great Creator, the dreams, the spirits, the good powers, and in yourself. (p. 41)
>
> Most people in Western society (including nontraditional Natives) primarily think on the conscious level. They have not been taught about the other parts of the mind–brain complex, and most of them have never experienced that there is more to reality than the physical dimension. But dreams, spirits, unconscious archaic symbols, and intuitive/psychic forms of reality and knowledge do not compute with the logical intellect. Hence when average persons encounter something "psychic" or mystical in a dream, for example a talking animal, bird, ghost, or guardian spirit, their minds do not know how to handle or process it. . . . They have spent most of their lives stimulating, developing, and using the conscious mind; hence the subconscious mind is forbidden territory. It does not exist for them. To ignore it, they believe, is the best way to deal with it. (p. 30)

An account of a San Pedro bone healer's development similarly integrates the spiritual aspects of dreaming and the connection of ideas and information from everyday life. San Pedro's sacred bone healers are widely renowned; injured people travel from other countries for treatment with San Pedro bone healers. Their treatment of fractures and dislocations is regarded as much more successful and rapid than what is available in Western medicine (Paul, 1976). Dreaming was important in the beginning of Francisco Sunú's profession as bone healer, in the early 1900s:

> When I started in as bone healer I didn't know a thing about it, nor did I really want the job. . . . I didn't enter the profession for the money, but when I became a man a very clear dream kept recurring to me. In my dream a man suddenly appeared standing before me. We didn't speak to each other. I just watched him. He wasn't very old. As I watched, his flesh disappeared, leaving just his bones in a heap. "Now why did he do that?" I mused. "I've never seen anything like that happen to a person." Then I realized I must have been dreaming.
>
> As I kept watching and wondering about it, I heard a voice. I could see nothing, but the voice said, "You are looking at all of a person's bones without flesh. Now set the bones in place." So I began to arrange them although I really didn't know how. I had no idea where to start, or how they went together. But I thought I'd better try since I had been told to do it. So I picked up a bone and tried to find what went with it. I finally found it and put a leg together, then the foot. I paid very careful attention to what I was doing and how all the bones went together. When that was done I then put the other leg and foot together. That wasn't so hard!
>
> "Now what'll I do?" I thought to myself since I had been told to put all the bones together. So I started on the arm. When I finally got it done I put the second one together, too. I was able to put the whole body together, but it wasn't easy! The rib cage was a unit, and so was the skull. I could see the sockets, so then it wasn't hard to assemble. I put the legs and arms on and then the head, and it was finished. It wasn't so hard! It was like putting a doll together.
>
> Then I heard a voice saying, "Now you can do it. You obeyed what I told you to do. You weren't afraid to touch the bones and you figured out by yourself how to assemble them. I now charge

you to help people young or old in the town who have fractures. Don't stay home. You've had your training, now go! I can see you'll do a good job." I had no idea who was talking to me. I couldn't see where the voice was coming from, but it was very clear. As I was wondering whether or not to answer, I woke up. . . .

Eventually I forgot about it. My work occupied my attention. But then I began to dream again, and every dream was about setting bones. There'd be dreams about children who fell and who had me set them, and dreams about adults who had me set their bones. So that set me thinking, and I said to my wife, "Gal, I've been dreaming a lot lately, but every time it's about me healing bones."

"Huh! I wonder what that means?" she replied.

[Francisco then found an object that he thought was a plaything.] I kept on dreaming about setting bones, but I wasn't told what to use. . . . One night at bed-time when I knelt down beside my bed I said to God, "Lord, you know all the dreams I've had about bone-healing, well, I want to ask you what I should use to set the fractures. If it is your will that I set bones, show me what to use."

In the dream I met a man somewhere who said to me, "You want to know what to use for setting broken bones. Well, you already have it though you didn't realize it, and so you weren't treating it as anything special. . . . So take it from your children and use it, and you'll see whether or not it'll help in setting bones.". . .

Several times in my dreams I was told to use my ability to help people since I could now. So one morning I began thinking. I told my wife some of it. I didn't know how to start in this new calling. If I offered my services the people might laugh at me and not believe me. And all this time in my dreams I was being told to get out and help people. I knew I was a bone-healer now, since I had my "tool". . .

[Then his wife took a fall and broke her leg, and he set the fracture.] The leg was better in two weeks and my wife could walk again. . . . Later on I dreamed again and was told, "See, you can set bones. Now, don't refuse to help young or old that come to you for help." (Summer Institute of Linguistics, 1978, Book 45, pp. 1–24)

Clearly, I am on thin ice in trying to "explain" learning through dreams. I have no doubt, though, that dreams can be a very important source of learning. They can build on the ideas and information available in everyday life, as people learn by observing, listening, and pitching in to their communities' activities. In addition, children's imagination and play gives them opportunities—perhaps resembling some of those available in dreaming—to expand and connect their understanding and skills.

Learning Through Simulations in Play

IN SAN PEDRO, children's play has often emulated the work and social life of the community, giving children the opportunity to simulate more mature roles in this context. Such simulations give children a chance to act in ways that stretch their development (Vygotsky, 1978).

The main playmates in San Pedro are other children, especially siblings and cousins. Mothers have not regarded playing with children as part of their role; in fact, a number of them laughed with embarrassment when I asked them if they played with their toddlers (Rogoff et al., 1993). Play is the domain of children—and sometimes of a lighthearted uncle or grandparent who will play with a small child when work is done.

This sequence shows an older sister playing with her baby brother, helping him wrap a baby doll appropriately for carrying in a shawl, and getting him to kiss the doll. The little sister also helps the baby brother nurture the doll. (Photos by Lois and Ben Paul, 1941)

In the following sequence, 7-year-old Graciela Cotuc sets up a play weaving loom for her 2½-year-old sister Magdalena and helps Magdalena operate it—which the little one does with surprising skill. Even when she mugs for the camera, her hands skillfully hold the sticks in position to keep the loom together. (Photos by Lois and Ben Paul, 1941)

CHILDREN'S OPPORTUNITIES to be part of community life are a powerful source of learning, as they can observe and overhear almost the whole range of community activities, except birth and a few other activities from which children are excluded. Their play often shows their developing skill and provides a medium for trying out what they are learning.

Children can be part of ongoing discussions and endeavors as they become ready to contribute, with the support of other people who may provide them explanations, *consejos* (advice), and meaningful narratives. In dreams, people can consolidate their ideas and experiences and bring them into new relations, in a creative process of abstraction from their individual everyday lives and the collective ideas and experiences of their community.

The dynamic destinies and developments of communities are based on the processes of learning as well as on the routine practices of individuals and generations. At the same time, the changes and continuities of communities' ways contribute to the life-course opportunities and constraints of individuals' routine practices and their learning—individuals' destinies and developments.

13 ::

Traditions and Transformations

ALTHOUGH CHONA STILL carries herself like a younger woman—she dresses smartly, wears her hair free, and walks tall—she recently told me she is tired and doesn't deliver babies much anymore. In younger years, she often delivered a baby about every 3 days, and had many prenatal and postnatal visits associated with each birth. She was responsible for almost half of the births in San Pedro, and many in the neighboring town of San Juan as well.

In her early 80s, she hesitates to take on more patients, but when I visit, a family may come to her door, kiss the back of her hand, and ask if she would please deliver their baby. She does, until recently even walking to the neighboring town of San Juan if needed for a delivery. At 83, she is tired and it is difficult for her to walk, and she tries to decline requests to deliver babies. But she gives in on occasion, sometimes going to people's houses in San Pedro or San Juan, and sometimes agreeing to deliver a baby in her home.

(Photo © Barbara Rogoff, 1987)

Chona hopes that Chonita and some other young women who are born to be *iyooma'* will carry on this sacred role that has helped mothers and infants for centuries. However, the way that the destiny of an *iyoom* plays out is new with each generation, and differs with each individual's life circumstances and choices.

Destinies and Developments in the Course of Individual Lives

CHONITA NOW LIVES in a city several hours away. For some years, she worked helping care for abandoned children, and now she is raising her own children. Chona was the *iyoom* for Chonita's first child, and the second was born in a clinic closer to where Chonita lives.

To date, although Chonita has participated in several deliveries, she is not working as an *iyoom*. This is consistent with the traditional development of an *iyoom*, who takes on the calling towards the end of her childbearing years. However, even if Chonita does not ever follow her destined calling, I do not have the impression that she or Chona are as concerned about her welfare as people might have been in years past. Chona says that for some women born as *iyooma'* who refuse their work, nothing happens, whereas others get sick—"It depends on God."

⠿

THE CHANGEABLE NATURE of destiny in light of individuals' circumstances can be seen in Chona's relationship with a 17-year-old from the United States. This young woman wrote about Chona's advice about the young woman's own destiny:

> All who see Chona in the street kiss her hand to show their respect. However, when we meet, she draws me to her in a sturdy embrace. I am like a granddaughter to her; she gives me advice for how I should live my life. "Don't marry till you're thirty," she tells me. . . . She gives me a cloth, saying that when I marry I must use it to keep the tortillas warm that I make for my husband. Most of all she wants to help me grow with the strength and courage to fulfill the destiny for which I was born.
>
> I was apparently born with a birth sign meaning that I would have the sacred profession of midwife, according to Chona and Doña Elena, the wise deaf and blind shaman who blessed me with incense and incantations to the Mayan and Christian saints. Because I was delivered by doctors following different medical traditions than the sacred Mayan midwives, the birth sign (the amniotic sac that supposedly formed a veil over my head) was never seen.
>
> Despite my skepticism, the responsibility of having a destiny frightens me. Chona tells me most young women who have this destiny would prefer an easier life. Some are afraid to be out at night and to help other women through the pain and fears of childbirth. . . . But when one of their family becomes very ill they usually accept what they must do and begin their life's work. Chona's mother, who was also destined to be a midwife, succumbed to her fear and never fulfilled her destiny, dying at an early age.
>
> I don't know what I'll be doing next year, let alone in 30 years. Questions of my future race through my head, along with the

ever-present shadow (or perhaps I should say light) of my destiny. I don't believe that being a Mayan sacred midwife is the only way I can fulfill my destiny. But the thought of having a destiny at all is mind-boggling. I hope to find a way to make my life worthwhile, to do something good for my community and the world. Chona assures me that that would fulfill my destiny.

Chona's affectionate counsel to the young woman illustrates the combination of destiny and development in the life of an individual:

> You are born to be an *iyoom* like me. But you were not born in San Pedro, your life is different than mine. You will fulfill your destiny as an *iyoom*, but it will be in a different way than a San Pedro *iyoom*. (Anonymous, 1996)

Individuals Contributing to Transformations of Cultural Practices

THE CHANGES AND CONTINUITIES in the lives of these individuals, as well as in the town of San Pedro itself, show the dynamic mutual relation of individuals' actions and communities' cultural practices. As a prominent midwife and leader, Chona has contributed changes to San Pedro's practices and life, just as changes in San Pedro and elsewhere have contributed to transformations in Chona's life and practices.

Some of the changes in San Pedro's obstetrical practices to which Chona has contributed include the use of the lying-down position for the moment of giving birth; patience and encouragement of the woman in labor rather than urging and scolding the woman; and the practice of having only the woman's husband present at the birth rather than many relatives. Of course, Chona has also contributed to San Pedro's obstetrical practices by continuing the use of many other birth practices.

As an individual, Chona has also contributed to San Pedro's ways beyond her role in changing and maintaining obstetrical practices of San Pedro. Due to her prominence, Chona is sometimes asked to speak at important public events. At such events, as well as more private events, she speaks out for justice, especially fair treatment of girls and women. Chona's niece, Virginia Concepción Pérez Juárez, who has a post in the municipal office of communication and social programs, said:

> Whenever Chona is asked to collaborate in public events, she does. She goes, even though it's difficult for her to walk now. She takes

the microphone at community "town hall" events, and speaks straight. She is very courageous.

She speaks out for rights: "Girls or boys—we are all equal, and we all have the same rights." Sometimes during a delivery, a father may complain that she brought a baby girl. She explains that it's not the midwife that determines the baby's gender, and explains how girls and boys are created. She tells him, we are all equal. (Personal communication, August 2008)

Chona makes a point with Nobel Laureate Rigoberta Menchú, during the inauguration of the new "Intercultural Learning Center." Menchú addressed the celebration in English and Spanish in addition to a Mayan language, as she urged Pedranos and Pedranas to build on the traditional Mayan ways represented by the Tz'utujil language, as well as Guatemalan national ways represented by Spanish and international ways represented by English and the Internet. (Photo © Barbara Rogoff, 2006)

CHONA ALSO makes use of her many ties to the youth of San Pedro to encourage young people when they are experiencing difficulties. She tries to steer people to a healthy, productive life. Chona's niece, Concepción, said that Chona has changed San Pedro through the *consejos* [counsel] that she gives to the children and young people, especially if they are straying, taking drugs or drinking, or having other problems:

> For example, sometimes young people are going astray, and the parents don't do anything about it—sometimes the parents don't call the youngster's attention to their behavior. Chona counsels them. She likes to talk with them, and gives them talks that they never have with their parents.
>
> Chona sits out on the front stoop across the street from her house, and it looks like she's just relaxing. But when people kiss her hand and greet her, sometimes she pats the spot next to her, inviting them to have a seat. She's not just passing time. Talking with her is like psychotherapy. Someone comes to sit with her and she begins to counsel them, gives them therapy and help. She says, "I brought you into the world—and for what? You need to make something of your life, be a good person."
>
> She is so positive, and so fair. She talks and jokes with everyone, little kids, elders, everyone, and she's kind to everyone. She always has a "flower" for each person—she tells me, "You are so pretty." And wealth doesn't matter to her—she treats everyone the same, whether they live in a house made of cane or drive fancy cars.

In such ways, as a prominent individual, Chona has contributed to both continuities and changes in the cultural practices and functioning of her community—and indeed, of other communities than San Pedro, as can be seen in the accounts in this book and the potential impact of the book itself. Likewise, other prominent individuals, such as Nobel Laureate Rigoberta Menchú and Chona's former suitor, former Guatemalan Vice President Mario Monteforte Toledo, have made notable differences of one kind or another in their communities and the world.

But what about less prominent individuals?

Whether or not the acts of our lives are marked and recorded together with our names, our everyday decisions and unnoticed habits are the material of cultural practices. Each of us, in carrying on or adapting or rejecting the cultural practices of our communities, participates in transformations as well as stabilities in the cultural practices of our communities, at the same time that our participation in the practices of our communities constitutes our own development.[76]

The importance of everyday unpublicized acts is central to a commentary on changes in San Pedro by my colleague Marta Navichoc Cotuc:

> Many children now are getting sick because they were not received by an *iyoom*. If nobody keeps their birthsign, children with a special birth destiny get sick. The *practicantes* don't know about this, so when they deliver a baby that has a special destiny, they don't save the birthsign.
>
> Many people now have doubts about Mayan culture.
>
> Others say that it is important. But in practice? Many waver.
>
> It is Pedranos ourselves who are changing San Pedro, not just the gringos, by our acts. It's a matter of what we do, not a matter of what we say. Many people want to conserve Mayan ways, but they don't put it into practice, they just talk. If we don't stick with the *iyooma'*, this practice and knowledge will be lost. *The world is constructed of the acts of each one of us.* (August 2008)

Developments and Destinies of Communities

THE CONSTELLATION of ways of San Pedro has changed dramatically across Chona's lifetime (and beyond), while many practices continue. The ways of San Pedro are a dynamic combination of transformations and continuities across days and years and millennia.

For the current generation of children and youth in San Pedro, life has transformed from what Chona and even Chonita grew up with. Since I met Chona over 35 years ago, television has arrived and now most households have access to shows from the United States and Mexico on a daily basis. Most of the younger people now speak the national language, Spanish, in addition to the Mayan language, and some speak English. Some have emigrated to the U.S. and many consider doing so. Extensive schooling—organized according to Western ways—has become the norm, with almost all children attending for a number of years and many continuing on to become teachers themselves or completing other professional degrees. Tourism has ballooned since the Pan-American Highway was built in the 1950s (Brumfiel, 2006), as visitors from around the world have taken note of the beauty of Lake Atitlán, surrounded by picturesque volcanoes and Mayan towns.

Along with the greater contact with the outside world have come some problems that did not exist in prior generations. Some of the visitors come seeking the drugs that have become available thanks to other visitors. Now some Pedranos have succumbed to the economic attraction of selling drugs, primarily to the visitors.

Until a few years ago, San Pedro did not have police, and that also attracted some unsavory visitors who mistakenly thought that without police there was no social control. Police simply were not necessary in San Pedro until recently. Local people regulated themselves, for the most part acting in accord with local norms.

Even if Pedranos considered acting outside the norms, they generally held to approved behavior out of concern that "people would talk" if they acted in a way that diverged from the usual. In communities like San Pedro, there is plentiful daily social interaction with neighbors over many years, with multiple links across families such as shared worship, land disputes, work groups, intermarriage, illness, and trouble. Thus one's reputation has great consequences, and being watched and potentially gossiped about induces conformity to approved behavior (Martini, 2004).

When I lived in San Pedro in the 1970s, I found this form of social regulation puzzling. People sometimes asked my advice on a family problem, and if my suggestions fell outside usual ways, the advice-seeker would respond that he or she could not follow that course of action because "people would talk." I was also surprised at how often people would stand and watch what I thought were private events, if they occurred in public or could be seen through an open door.

This woman and child are interested in knowing what preparations for the town fiesta are being made within this tent by merchants from another town. (Photo © Barbara Rogoff, 1975)

The concern that "people would talk" began to make sense to me as I considered that the opinion of one's neighbors matters deeply if one's town is virtually one's whole world. In my early days in San Pedro, there was limited travel to or knowledge of regions away from the Lake Atitlán region by many Pedranos. Most Pedranos' identification was as Pedranos, not as Mayans or as Guatemalans. Some people seemed to think that the United States was a town on the other side of Guatemala City. Most people from San Pedro married other people from San Pedro, as they had for centuries, and the reputation of one's family made a huge difference for one's life chances and the social relations and opportunities of one's children.

So now it is a striking change that many Pedranos follow U.S. politics, some Pedranos live in the U.S. and a number have visited there, and the children see visitors from other countries on a daily basis in the burgeoning restaurants and Spanish schools by the lakeside. Some San Pedro children and youth have picked up the use of drugs, and some gangs have appeared.

Chona and many other Pedranos worry about the struggles of the current generation of young people, noting that they run into dangers that did not exist before. In a conversation with my longtime research associate Marta Navichoc, Chona commented that young people now get into trouble and experience challenges that are new with this generation (such as drugs, gangs, violence,[77] AIDS, and more casual contact among young women and men).

Marta commented that in former times, young people did not feel mixed up like they sometimes do now. She noted with some puzzlement that people say it is because they are going through "the stage of adolescence." But, she remarked, she was that age 30-some years ago, and young people then were not confused—"*we* didn't have adolescence!" Chona agreed that this is new; adolescence was unheard of in her generation too. There was simply no reference to the existence of such a stage in prior times.[78] When I asked Chona what she thought it was due to, she said, "They see it on television."

∷

A 23-YEAR-OLD Pedrana university student in Guatemala City speculated in 2003 that the troubling behavior of some of the youth, such as drug use, stems from a loss of concern that "people will talk." When I asked her (via e-mail from the United States!) why she thought this traditional form of social control had diminished, she responded:

> I think that people now have changed a lot since many aren't in San Pedro. They go to study now in Quetzaltenango or in the capital. Also, a lot of tourists from all over the world now live in San Pedro; some Pedrana women have foreign husbands. In the past the different customs seemed strange but now it is normal, perhaps that influences it too. Also, television and popular music.
>
> Something else very important is that the town is very big, there are many people and we don't know everyone. For example, I don't know all the people. Sometimes I see them in the capital and I don't know them, though my sister tells me they are from San Pedro, or sometimes I tell her they are from San Pedro but she doesn't know some. So they could do a lot of things. There are no longer close relations among people from town. In the past it was expected for everyone to greet each person as one passed them in the street even if they weren't known, but now not everyone speaks to each other, greeting each other. Now it is different.

:::

IN SAN PEDRO, the increased contact with other places has contributed to many changes—both those that are welcomed and those that are criticized. Indeed, San Pedro represents a prime case of the collision, fusion, and resistance among different cultural logics referred to by Tally and Chavajay (2007) as *glocalization*.

The uncertainty of change is reflected in the observations of a leading citizen of a Mayan town in Yucatan, Mexico. In 1948, Don Eus was one of the few people in his village who read the newspapers printed in the city. He read and interpreted national and international news for others in the village. He figured out how to find reports of the price of corn on the Chicago Board of Trade in the newspaper and noticed that the price of corn in Mérida, the closest city, related to those quoted prices; he used this information in his own plans to buy or sell corn. Don Eus argued that it is not enough to learn to read, as some in his village had—it is important to actually use books. At the same time, he was concerned that people are not necessarily better off if they read books:

He notes that in the city, where there are so many books, there are also many troubles. "In the city people are always talking about their problems, wondering how to solve them. Out here, even if we do not use books, we have some way to solve every difficulty. In the old days, there could have been no books, and yet people knew what to do in every situation." It seems to him that, although books are there to help one solve problems, where there are many books, there also are many problems. Nevertheless, he continues to read, and, when printed matter along the lines of his practical interests comes to his hand, he spends long periods of time with it, going through it and thinking about what he reads. (Redfield, 1950, p. 145)

::

THE LIVES of Chona and her town—like the rest of the world—exemplify the dynamic as well as continuing nature of cultural and individual ways and the relatedness as well as distinctions among us.

Chona hopes that the wisdom of the ages is retained, even as many aspects of Mayan life change. As one of San Pedro's most knowledge-able childrearing experts, she is concerned about the loss of traditional ways, though she also embraces many new ways.

Although she used to laugh at the idea of paper talking, Chona now chuckles at the change in her perspective and her interest in this practice that used to seem so odd to her. Now she is eager for this book to talk to future generations, helping to preserve the knowledge that might other-wise be lost. Some changes contribute to continuities.

::

WHAT IS TODAY regarded as "traditional" is based on the everyday decisions, adaptations, struggles, preservations, and inventions of pre-vious generations, yielding a sort of cultural "destiny" for current gen-erations. The way that current generations receive their communities' "destinies" continues the dynamic process, as living people decide, adapt, struggle with, preserve, and invent the ways of today, in a con-tinuing sort of development.

This sort of development is not toward a fixed and knowable end-point, toward a single predestined apex of human capacity and ways, as earlier theorists of human development such as Jean Piaget or Lev Vygotsky assumed. Nor is this sort of development "progress" toward the cultural ways of the dominant communities, as earlier theorists of culture change such as Lewis Henry Morgan posited.

Instead, the combination of destinies and development on which this book focuses is a dynamic process in which each generation and individual builds on prior ways available to them—accepting, rejecting, recombining them. While adjusting to new circumstances, people engage in a creative and open process with an unknowable future. Unknowable, that is, except that it is certain that future generations will continue to build on prior ways available to them. Our generation's inventions and patchwork solutions to today's issues become tomorrow's cultural traditions, along with whatever our generation carries forward from people who lived before.

⁛

Three-year-old Bacilio, wearing traditional San Pedro pants, takes off on his hand-carved toy airplane. Behind him, in the road in front of his house, maguey fibers for rope-making are drying.

Bacilio did take off; as of 2009, he lives in North Carolina.

(Photo © Barbara Rogoff, 1975)

Interesting Notes ⠶

1. Another woman a few years younger than Chona told me that her father said, "No, daughter, you aren't going to go on in school. You are very intelligent and clever, and you know how to work. But your long-eared burro sisters are going to go to school; they are foolish. They need to be smarter and more cooperative."

Similar considerations appeared in a Mayan community in Chiapas, Mexico, where a man replied to a question about whether parents sent their smartest children to school: "'The stupid ones go to school so the teacher can make them smart.' Parents bring up their smart children themselves" (Greenfield, 2004, p. 66).

2. According to Ben Paul, who studied San Pedro as an anthropologist in 1941.

3. I was skeptical that Chona was always well-behaved and recently asked her, "Didn't you ever get into trouble?"

> "No, I was always well-behaved. I was afraid of being beaten by my father."
>
> "Didn't you ever do anything mischievous when you were off with your friends?"
>
> "No, when I went out to do an errand, I always had to come straight home."

4. Chona's light complexion was regarded as more beautiful than darker skin tones like her sister Susana's. A preference for light complexion in San Pedro was noted in Rosales' 1938 fieldnotes (published in 1949), which also reported that white people are weaker than dark ones and that in earlier times, the old people claimed that light-skinned people were lazy and pretentious, whereas dark-skinned women and ugly ones were hard-working.

5. See Redfield (1950) for another account of the introduction and role of schooling in changes in a Mayan community (in Yucatan, Mexico).

CHAPTER 2

6. My colleagues and I, and other scholars, have developed related ideas about culture in a number of publications. For example, my 2003 book on *The Cultural Nature of Human Development* examined how individuals contribute to cultural change and how cultural practices contribute to the development of individuals. Other related work includes Bruner, 1986; Cole, 1996; Dewey, 1916; Eisenhart, 1995; Engeström, 1990; Erickson, 1982, 2004; Goodnow, 1990; Gutiérrez, Baquedano-López, & Tejeda, 1999; Heath, 1991; John-Steiner, 1985; Lave & Wenger, 1991; Ochs, 1988; Schieffelin, 1991; Wertsch, 1991.

7. At least 90% of all children worldwide were spending some time in school by the 1990s (Meyer et al., 1992).

8. Mesoamerica encompasses a cultural region extending from Central Mexico through much of Central America.

9. The importance of investigating historical change to understand cultural and developmental processes has become increasingly apparent in the social sciences, including developmental psychology. (See, for example, Keller & Lamm's 2005 analysis of historical changes in parenting in recent generations in Germany, and Elder, Modell, & Parke, 1993; Elder, 2002; Pillemer & White, 2005.) Analyses of culture contact are also growing, along with analyses of relations between immigrant communities and their sending communities (including the ground-breaking volume by Greenfield & Cocking, 1994).

10. See Redfield (1950) for an account of the adoption of Protestantism by some factions of a Yucatecan Mayan town in the 1930s.

11. Openly nursing in public seems less common now than in the 1970s, and some women lay a cloth over their breast as they nurse a baby. The change is perhaps due to fewer babies being born, the much greater use of brassières and slips, and the awareness of foreign ideas about breasts (from television and movies). When I commented to a Pedrano friend in his 40s that perhaps the breast belonged to babies before, and now the breast belongs to men too, he responded:

> Exactly. In my lifetime, breasts have become a sex object for men; before, they belonged to babies. Women no longer wash at the lake with nothing on above the waist, like they did when I was a child. Now, breasts have a sexual connotation—even brassières are hidden now. But even now, if a woman is nursing, the breast doesn't have a sexual connotation, it's just feeding a baby.
>
> I'm going to tell you a story—it's a true one. There was a little kid who was 4 years old and he was still nursing [which sometimes occurred with lastborn children]. He and his mother were out in public and the boy said, "Mom, Mom, I'm thirsty. Give me the breast." She was embarrassed because the boy was already big, so she said, "Hush. Wait til we get home." But the boy continued, "Mom, please, please, I'm really thirsty. Give me the breast." A man nearby noticed that the boy wanted something and asked, "What does he want?" The mother murmured with embarrassment, "He's still nursing and he wants the breast." The man replied, "Go ahead, give it to him." The mother protested, "But he's already 4 years old and he still wants the breast." The man grinned and said, "That's OK, I'm 55 and I'm still at the breast—my wife's."

CHAPTER 3

12. In a much earlier out-migration, a number of Pedrano families moved to their lands on the coastal side of the volcano San Pedro, forming the town of San Pedro Cutzán.

13. A survey of midwives who had participated in a training program in Guatemala found that only about 18% of the Mayan midwives spoke Spanish (alone or in addition to a Mayan language) and only a slightly higher percentage had attended school or knew how to read (Hurtado & Sáenz de Tejada, 2001).

14. Interestingly, the name *Tz'utujil* itself is derived from the sacred corn plant—it means a person of the maize flower (Christenson, 2001).

15. Currently, several Western doctors practice in San Pedro. Before our arrival, contact with Western doctors was limited to periodic visits from out-of-town doctors or via costly and difficult travel by Pedranos to the hospital or doctors' offices on the other side of the lake. There were a few local pharmacies at the time we arrived in San Pedro, where the pharmacists performed some medical procedures, such as injections. When Pedranos make use of Western medicine, it is often in addition to use of some traditional approaches, including herbal medicines and the services of bone healers, midwives, and shamans.

CHAPTER 4

16. Of 24 babies born about 1990 to San Pedro mothers whom I interviewed, 3 were born in a hospital or clinic and the remainder were born at home; 14 were attended by an *iyoom* and 7 were attended by a Pedrana *practicante* with midwife training. In rural Mayan communities in general, an estimated 90% of births are attended at home by a Mayan midwife (not specified whether *iyoom* or *practicante*; Hurtado & Sáenz de Tejada, 2001). Worldwide, at the turn of the 21st century, about 60% to 80% of births occurred in the home, attended by a midwife (Jordan, 1999).

17. "Western" medicine refers to the medical practices of the medical establishment of the United States and Western Europe. In general, the term "Western" is used to refer to practices of colonial nations rather than referring geographically to the direction "west."

18. Skepticism of secular training of midwives has been widespread in Southern Mexico and Guatemala (Cosminsky, 2001a).

19. Doña Jesús said that the doctors don't permit the practice of heating the umbilical stump; the *practicantes* just use talc.

20. I asked *iyoom* Dolores Cumatz if the photos I have in the book are fine to include; she said, "Yes, indeed; the problem is when the woman's private parts are shown."

21. The life of written words can be seen in an incident in which spiritual guides ("daykeepers," *ajq'ijab'*) prayed with incense smoke over old documents when they were being read, in the neighboring Tz'utujil town of Santiago Atitlán. The necessity of prayer was explained in terms of disturbing the ancestors who had written the documents, for "to read the words of one who is dead is to make that person's spirit present in the room and give him a living voice" (Christenson, 2001, p. 4).

22. The Pauls' fieldnotes from 1941 are an amazing resource. They are publicly available on microform in Harvard's Tozzer Library, where I read them before my first trip to San Pedro. The original hardcopy notes are in the Stanford University library archives. (The fieldnotes are also available in microform in 11 other university libraries, last I knew.)

CHAPTER 5

23. The idea that Pedranos routinely refer to as *nahual* seems to be referred to in some other parts of Mesoamerica as *tonal*. These terms sometimes are used to refer to distinct but related ideas, such as having animal spirit companions or being a transforming witch or a shaman.

24. A twentieth-century example of the animosity of many Catholic priests towards Mayan spiritual practices occurred in the neighboring town of Santiago Atitlán, where Maximon, an ancient local deity, has long been part of Easter observances (Christenson, 2001). In 1912, a Catholic bishop who regarded Maximon as a "pagan idol" tried to have Maximon's wooden image burned, but the priest was driven out of town himself.

In 1950, a priest became furious when he saw the image of Maximon receiving offerings on the porch of the church during Easter Week. He went for his pistol and threatened to destroy the wooden image of Maximon, yelling that the local people were idolaters and savages, and shooting. He threatened not to say Mass unless the people of Santiago Atitlán ceased worshiping Maximon, but a local group told him that Maximon would curse him with insanity if he did not desist. A compromise was reached, but weeks later, the priest brought another priest and his Father Superior to attack the image of Maximon with a machete, chopping off its head and taking two of Maximon's ancient masks. (One of the masks appeared in the Musée de l'Homme in Paris; it was returned to Santiago Atitlán in 1979.)

25. The vitality of Mayan culture has also been noted in the governance structure of Mayan towns: "The means by which a subordinated but vigorous culture yields, changes form, yet in the end captures the institutions of the dominant culture and molds them to its own pattern are well worth the scientist's attention" (LaFarge, 1947, p. 148).

26. This pattern has also been noted in other Central American settings. About 59% to 69% of Highland Mayan healers reported that their families included other healers; the proportion is even higher among Yucatecan Mayan and Zapotec healers (98% and 88%, according to Lipp, 2001; see also Huber & Sandstrom, 2001; Hurtado & Sáenz de Tejada, 2001).

27. Both Gaspar's and Concepción's mothers were named Chona, according to Marcos' son Erasmo. Chona says she was named for her grandmother Concepción's younger sister. Another sister of Concepción was Josefa Yojcom, a famous San Pedro *iyoom*—the *iyoom* who assisted when Chona was born.

28. In the Mam town of San Pedro Sacatepequez, Guatemalan Mayan women are more rapidly switching to Western dress, often citing the greater cost as a reason despite the fact that the repeated cost of replacement is so much higher that over the long term, it costs almost 10 times as much to use Western dress compared with the traditional *corte* and *huipil* (Ehlers, 1990; see also Greenfield, 2004). The change of apparel contributes to paradoxes of identity, such as those that appear in the annual competition for *Reina Indígena* (Indigenous Queen), sponsored by the elite professionals of the town. Selected teenage girls sashay into the town hall in traditional costumes and dance a traditional dance, praised by the emcee as examples of "our beautiful Mam race"—although none of them can speak any Mam and they had to borrow or rent the clothing that was widely used by their mothers and almost universally used by their grandmothers.

29. My assistance was an ordinary aspect of mutual help that is common within families. Chona and Josué felt that it was important to add that in this case, it was especially needed, as Josué was left without a father as an infant, due to his father (Juan Chavajay Batz) being "disappeared," never to return, in the time of the violence in the early 1980s.

30. Alcohol has been both a cause and a consequence of the hardships of Indigenous life. The Pulitzer Prize-winning anthropologist LaFarge observed in 1947 that in the Cuchumatán Mayan village Santa Eulalia, in the Northwestern highlands of Guatemala:

> The Conquest and the changes it brought about in the Indians' ways of life took a heavy toll of their spare vitality and cheerfulness. . . . Their lot is hard, they are a conquered people, and occasional bouts of drunkenness do them good. When they drink they become jovial and tend to treat Ladinos as equals; then they become morose, dance, and lament the dead. Finally, they fall into a coma. Afterward they sober themselves and return to work.

... When partway drunk, an Indian will sell his soul for more liquor; upon this the *finca* [plantation] system is based. (p. 7)

Not only have men under the effects of alcohol sold off their land, often under disadvantageous terms, they have also been more easily taken advantage of and indentured to plantation service.

31. Some women who were born with the birthsigns for both *iyoom* and shaman have chosen to carry out only the work of shaman, because an *iyoom* has to be responsible for two lives at a time (Antmann, personal communication, August 2008).

32. Continued life is not assumed in San Pedro. For example, it is common for people who are planning to meet again after one of them takes a trip to add to their plans, "if God lends us life." When I have departed San Pedro after living there for a while or visiting, people sometimes remark, "I may be dead when you return." Sometimes they extend the uncertainty to me, "One never knows what will happen."

However, when I first lived in San Pedro, the uncertainty of life was sometimes regarded as not as applicable to North Americans, who were occasionally reputed not to die. This reflected, in an exaggerated form, the accurate information that infant mortality was much less, and longevity, enough food, and medical intervention were much greater among North Americans than Pedranos.

33. The state of Sololá had a maternal mortality rate estimated in 1995 to be 446 per 100,000 live births, according to the U.S. Agency for International Development.

34. There may also have been the danger of accusations of witchcraft in Dolores' day, and subtle forms of ostracism, as reported more widely for the region (Cosminsky, 2001a).

35. This may no longer be the case, as Chavajay (personal communication, August 2008) reports that children are held down for vaccinations.

36. The features of recruitment of San Pedro shamans and *iyooma'* are similar to those identified as classic recruitment patterns of sacred Mayan professionals, entailing "divine election" through birthsigns, severe and intractable illness, and supernatural dreams (Tedlock, 1982; see also Cosminsky, 2001a; Hurtado & Sáenz de Tejada, 2001).

In a vivid dream, the individual is informed by a spirit being— saint, angel, Keeper of the Game, Sun and Moon, ancestral curer— that she or he will receive the divine gift to cure illnesses. . . .

Although the person may resist the calling, refusal results in worsening sickness or death" (Lipp, 2001, p. 103).

Midwives generally experience premonitory dreams and illnesses between the ages of eight and fifteen, although some are well into adulthood when this happens. Their call comes from *tamatinime*, all-knowing supernatural guardians of nature who appear to people in the form of lightning bolts, snakes, little children, and old people in traditional clothing. (Huber & Sandstrom, 2001, p. 159)

CHAPTER 6

37. Josefa Yojcom continues to be remembered as an important midwife. She was born March 15, 1890 (Cetinea Taa' Pi't Kortes Ong, 2007), and according to Chona, died when Chona was about 12 (thus, about 1937).

38. Evil eye was described as "an affliction attributed to persons who have 'strong vision'" in Tlayacapan, a Central Mexican town where people formerly spoke Nahuatl:

When such a person admires a child and experiences envy—a hot emotion—looking at the child will cause it harm. Children are more vulnerable to the evil eye than adults because their blood is "weak," "sweet," or "cool." The physically attractive child is especially apt to attract the glance of a covetous adult and so is more likely to suffer the sickness. By contrast, ill-tempered children, whose blood is more like that of adults, and unattractive children are less affected . . . .

One sometimes sees men passing time on their doorsteps before entering their houses. They are delaying entrance because they do not want to convey an *aire* [similar to evil eye] to an infant indoors. By resting for a few moments, they cool down, which motivates any *aire* to leave. (Ingham, 1986, pp. 164–165)

39. Similar protection of girls from knowing about sex until they were married and about menstruation, pregnancy, or birth until they experienced these has also been noted in a number of other Mesoamerican communities: a Mayan community in Chiapas, Mexico, as of the early 1960s; a Mayan community in Yucatan, Mexico, as of the 1930s; and working-class Cuernavaca before the 1970s (LeVine, 1993; Nash, 1970; Redfield & Villa Rojas, 1934).

40. Likewise, girls in Eastern European Jewish *shtetls* of years gone by were not told about menstruation in advance: "When she first begins to menstruate, if she tells her mother it will probably be with tears of fright, since any forewarning is unlikely. 'I thought I was going to die. I didn't know what was wrong with me. . . . The only thing I could think of was that I was very sick or something like that.'" (Zborowski & Herzog, 1952, p. 347).

CHAPTER 7

41. President Ubico "wanted representatives of all the Mayan tribes exhibited at his fair" (Perera & Bruce, 1982, p. 37), to celebrate the seventh anniversary of his dictatorship.

42. Monteforte Toledo went into exile in Mexico when Guatemala's democratic government was overthrown by U.S. actions in 1954.

Gore Vidal recalled that his friend Mario Monteforte Toledo, as Vice President of Guatemala in the late 1940s, had told him, "We don't have much longer you know. . . . Your government has decided to seize Guatemala." Vidal replied, "Oh, come on, we just got Germany, we just got Japan, what are we going to do with Guatemala? It's not worth our while!" Toledo answered, "It's worth the while of the United Fruit Company and they control these things" (Elizalde, 2007).

43. Lakeshore courtship ceased as boys and girls were allowed more casual contact when the previously separate boy's school and girl's school were combined (about 1956) and the necessity of fetching water from the lake was removed when water was piped into neighborhood taps in San Pedro in 1958 (Paul & Paul, 1963).

44. In precolonial times, it was usual for the leaders of a lineage to arrange marriages in some Mayan regions; in 1515 Spain commanded that Indians could marry whom they wished, taking this role away from the leaders and parents (Orellana, 1984). In the Mayan town of San Pedro Sacatepéquez, parents arranged a daughter's marriage until the 1930s (Ehlers, 1990).

45. The Pauls' 1941 fieldnotes indicate that Marcos' father, Gaspar Pérez of San Juan, died about the same time as his wife, Concepción Yojcom, who was from San Pedro and had eloped to San Juan. According to stories, Concepción died due to "black magic" done by people who envied her for having miraculously found great wealth. Gaspar is also said to have died due to black magic, in his case because of some land.

After the parents' death, Marcos and his brother were raised by relatives in San Pedro—Josefa Yojcom, his mother's sister, who was the *iyoom* who delivered Chona.

46. The epidemic of 1520 preceded the arrival of the invading Pedro de Alvarado in Guatemala (in 1523). The diseases were probably introduced by ambassadors sent from Mexico. The epidemic, which is likely to have been measles or perhaps smallpox accompanied by plague or typhus, is estimated to have killed about a third of the population (Orellana, 1987).

Smallpox was a key ally of the Spanish *conquistadores*. It was known in Central Mexico as *cocoliztli* (infernal sickness); Spanish soldiers intentionally spread it with the use of contaminated rags (Le Clézio, 1993).

The epidemics were widespread—"the most brutal demographic catastrophe in history" (Bonfil Batalla, 1996, p. 81). In central Mexico, the Indigenous population is estimated to have dropped from 25.2 million in 1518 to 1.4 million in 1605. According to Bonfil Batalla, it wasn't until well into the 1900s that the population of México (by then largely de-Indianized) reached a similar size to the population that had inhabited the region at the arrival of the Spanish.

47. On several other occasions, Chona told me that little Marcos died of measles. Traditional Mayan and Western medical interpretations of the causes of death may coexist.

CHAPTER 8

48. The heart was regarded as the location of thought and feeling in ancient Mexico; among the ancient Quichés of Guatemala, memory, willpower, and reasoning as well as the soul were located in the heart (Orellana, 1987; see also Hayes-Bautista, 2004). In San Pedro, the Tz'utujil word for *heart* is the same as the word for *spirit* or *soul*.

CHAPTER 9

49. With Chona's permission, I have substituted Chona's name for the pseudonym used in Lois Paul's publications, here and in other quotations.

50. Lois Paul elaborated in unpublished notes:

> The penitents are on their knees for hours, sometimes through the night while the air grows thick with the smoke of incense, candles

flicker hypnotically in the darkness, and libations of rum are drunk as well as poured on an 'altar' for the hosts of spirits whom the shaman summons in his repetitive and endless litanies. (in Lois' file of miscellaneous material on women and midwives, 1974–75, p. 10)

51. Licensing of traditional Guatemalan midwives began with regulations drawn up in 1953; training courses overseen by the Ministry of Health began to be required in 1955 (Cosminsky, 2001b).

CHAPTER 10

52. I wonder if calling twins "saints" relates to the holy Hero Twins who played a prominent role in creation, in the scripture of the *Popol Vuh* (Christenson, 2001). There is a little evidence to support this, from a Mayan village in Yucatan, Mexico. As of the 1930s in Chan Kom, making fun of having twins was thought to bring the risk of becoming the parent of twins oneself, as I experienced. At the same time, the older people in Chan Kom regarded twins with particular respect, referring to them as "god children" and giving a small gift if a twin visited the older person's house (Redfield & Villa Rojas, 1934). In the state of Morelos in central Mexico, where some small towns retain Nahua influence, beliefs about twins are linked to dual deities (such as Ometéotl-Omecíhuatl, Quetzalcóatl-Xólotl; Mellado, Zolla, & Castañeda, 1989).

53. Paul and Paul (1952) noted that this was widespread in many Mayan communities of Guatemala and Mexico of the 1940s.

54. Plentiful evidence indicates that stress experienced by a pregnant woman has long-lasting negative effects on the fetus (Kaiser & Sachser, 2009).

55. Foster (1960) cited numerous features common throughout Latin America that he claimed derived in large part from Spain: the Spanish language, of course; the Catholic religion; feast days, fiestas, and *cofradías*; marriage rules and death rites; many farming, fishing, and craft practices; the grid plan in which towns were arranged around a plaza ringed by the church, government buildings, and market; the social class system; the legal dominance of men in family structure; governance based on personal relationships with the "right people"; and the importance of dignity and face.

56. Protecting the baby from the effects of an eclipse or of the moon (both pre- and postnatally) includes using other reflective surfaces, such as placing scissors open in the form of a cross or a receptacle with water near the bed or other sleeping place, in the state of Morelos in central Mexico (Mellado, Zolla, & Castañeda, 1989). In San Pedro it has been common for mothers to leave crossed *machetes* or a bowl of water under the hammock of a sleeping baby as protection against various supernatural dangers, especially if they are out of the room where the baby is sleeping.

57. Similar competition and envy characterizes the relation among midwives in some other locales. Midwives may avoid cooperation out of fear of being blamed for problems that are not their responsibility (Huber & Sandstrom, 2001). Chona reported that for the first 10 to 12 years that she practiced, other midwives were angry and gossiped about her; after that, their anger dissolved and sometimes they called her to help in a delivery. Across her career, Chona estimates that two midwives worked together for about six or seven cases she was involved in. These cases involved difficult births, such as a baby presenting in transverse (sideways) position.

58. This method has also commonly been used in central Mexico (León, 1910).

59. Women change clothes modestly at the lakeshore. After bathing in their 7-yard wraparound skirt, they put a fresh skirt around themselves loosely and drop the damp clothes to the ground. (Clara demonstrates this in the photo that follows.) Then the clean skirt is tucked tight around the waist and fastened with a long hand-woven belt.

(Photo © Barbara Rogoff, 1976)

60. Administration of opossum tail was not mentioned in my conversations with San Pedro *iyooma'*. I did not investigate other obstetrical medications used currently in San Pedro, and few were spontaneously mentioned by Chona or other *iyooma'*. However, Dolores Cumatz, an elderly *iyoom*, mentioned that if the birth is delayed, it is necessary to massage the woman with hot lotion or oil. Previously there was a pomade used called *mulienta*, but it isn't available anymore, so she simply uses caper pomade. There are also some medicinal teas that one of the *iyooma'* reported using to facilitate a birth. The woman's family may prepare chamomile tea or strong coffee for her when she is having labor pains, and for after the birth.

CHAPTER 11

61. The photo that follows shows the same renowned shaman ("Taa' Kuu," Domingo Chavajay) who was shown at a hillside altar in the 1941 photo in Chapter 6, in his later years (in 1976). Each day when I climbed the street in front of his little shop, he would tease me about marrying him, and I would banter in return. On this day, he had boasted that he'd been eating raw eggs in preparation for our wedding night, and his wife Manuela teased him in turn, calling out to me not to believe him, that he wasn't good for anything anymore.

(*Photos © Barbara Rogoff, 1976*).

62. According to the Pauls' genealogical records, Chona and Juana are related several generations back. Juana's maternal grandparents were María Mejicana and José Antonio González, who were Chona's maternal great-grandparents. Many such kin relations are found throughout San Pedro.

63. However, in the past few years, there has been a resurgence of interest in the Mayan calendar and traditional Mayan spiritual practices among parts of the population. (At the same time, Mayan spiritual practices are also opposed by some segments of the population, especially by many Protestants but also some Catholics.) Nonetheless, more Pedranos now know their *nahual* from the Mayan calendar than was the case a generation ago. Now some Pedranos are interested in knowing about the destiny connected with their *nahual*—whether their day prepares them to be a teacher or a doctor or what kind of character they are prone to have, what kind of life will be theirs, and how they will do in love. There seems to be more open consultation with the Mayan day-keepers by some Pedranos now than was the case a generation ago.

64. The birthsigns might have some connection with medieval European traditions, such as the belief that babies born with the caul (a piece of the amniotic sac) had special destinies, perhaps including the "grace" to cure (Paul & Paul, 1975).

65. Transforming witches are found in other Indigenous regions as well. For example, in Tlayacapan (a town in central Mexico where Nahuatl was formerly spoken), a person who is a *nagual* changes into a domestic animal to scare people, steal things, or threaten or harm people (Ingham, 1986).

66. Of 23 San Pedro families who had babies about 1990, 60% swaddled their babies.

67. In Yucatecan Mayan birthing practices, the placenta is regarded as the *compañero* (companion) of the baby, not as simply an "afterbirth." The time between the emergence of the baby and the birth of the placenta is the most perilous part of the delivery for the mother, given the dangers of hemorrhage. "Baby and *compañero* are believed to be mystically connected, so that the fate of the *compañero* influences the fate of the child. For this reason, there are traditional rules about disposing of it" (Jordan, 1993, p. 107).

68. In 1995, 35% of 66 midwives in 60 small rural Guatemalan communities reported routinely using the sweat bath with mothers after birth. Most of the midwives were Mayan; 36% reported that they learned to attend pregnant women through divine calling (Goldman & Glei, 2000).

69. I recently learned that a person's spirit can become separated from the person due to an accident or injury. Some Pedrano friends who are skeptical about many traditional Mayan ideas (saying that they are "just beliefs") told me that it is sometimes necessary to beat the place where an accident or injury occurred, to get the spirit to return to the person.

The family recounted that they had had to call in a specialist to get the spirit to return to a boy in the family (I'll call him Juan) who had not recovered from an accident. Juan had recovered physically after medical treatments but could not focus on his studies and stayed in bed all day.

The specialist prayed and sprinkled water and beat the spot in the street where the accident had occurred, addressing the boy's spirit by the boy's name, while the boy was at home in bed: "You don't belong here, Juan, there is too much traffic. Go home, Juan." At that moment, Juan, home in his bed, began sweating and asked for water, which is the usual reaction when the spirit returns. From then on, he regained his energy and could focus on his studies.

After hearing this, I asked other Pedranos about spirits getting separated from people. Several Pedranos told me that often when people fall, they make sure that their spirit returns to them by beating the spot where they fell. My "nephew" Josué Chavajay told me that his research shows that although many traditional beliefs are no longer given credence, this one is not questioned and is followed by Protestants as well as Catholics.

Chona and some of her family members told me that the spirit has its own life. When the spirit returns to the body, the person experiences a sharp intake of breath. Chona told me that when she falls, she picks up her own spirit by hitting the spot five times, saying, "Come, come, I'm still here." She hits nearby rocks as well, so that the living being that is the rock will give up the spirit in case it has settled there. She hits all around so the spirit won't settle there. It can even go into a person who is passing by.

A few days later, I fell on some stairs. Although I did not get hurt, I gave myself a scare, as I had come very close to falling about 3 meters down from the stairs. I picked myself up and walked on a few steps, but I noticed that I felt strange. Then I remembered this precaution, and went back and hit the stair where I had fallen, five times. My neighbors laughed, knowing what I was doing, and I indeed felt better. Colleagues who work in other parts of Mesoamerica report that the same or a similar precaution is widely used.

70. See also Huber and Sandstrom (2001) and Fuller and Jordan (1981).

71. The symbolic importance of the *muxu'x* (pronounced approximately mooSHOOSH) is shown in a press report about the visit of former U.S. President G.W. Bush to a sacred Guatemalan Mayan site. Protesters were concerned that this man who fomented wars and repealed laws protecting the environment was contaminating hallowed ground. They shouted the rhyme, "Bush, Bush, here is not your *muxu'x*" (Durbin, 2007, p. 3). The article explained that burial of the *muxu'x* near the home symbolizes the blood-tie between the person and the land.

CHAPTER 12

72. The number 13 is a spiritually important number, identifying cycles in the sacred calendar; pine incense has been burned ceremonially since ancient Mayan and Aztec times.

73. Observations of the daily activities of 3-year-olds from San Pedro found that they had substantially greater opportunities to observe adult work than did 3-year-olds from two middle-class European American communities. The middle-class children's days in turn more often involved specialized child-focused activities such as lessons, play with adults, scholastic play, and freestanding conversations with adults on child-related topics (Morelli, Rogoff, & Angelillo, 2003).

74. See also Ward (1971).

75. Similar results have been found with children from Mexico whose families likely have experience with Indigenous practices (Correa-Chávez, Rogoff, & Mejía Arauz, 2005; López, Correa-Chávez, Rogoff, & Gutiérrez, 2010; Mejía Arauz, Rogoff, & Paradise, 2005; Silva, Correa-Chávez, & Rogoff, 2010).

CHAPTER 13

76. Frye (1996) similarly pointed out that:

Each of us is constantly reinventing and reassimilating our cultures, the stories we tell about our conventions and habits, through innumerable individual interactions. The construction of culture occurs at every social level and across borders of all kinds — between individuals, between groups and communities, between those imagined communities known as nations.
(1996, p. 9)

Frye provided an amusing example of cultural interchange across generations and nations. He recounted the history of the only surviving "Nahuatl" surname in a Mexican town where the residents spoke the Nahuatl language (indigenous to central Mexico) until the 1840s. It is the name Quixtiano, which is now spelled Quistián. This was the Nahuatl term for "Christian," a name meaning "Spaniard." It was originally a nickname in colonial times, presumably connected to a person's appearance or background (for example, "Pedro de Santiago, el quistiano" which referred to an individual who lived in 1736 [p. 218]).

77. The violence includes not only the political violence in which dozens of Pedranos were kidnapped, never to return (Paul, 1988), but also family violence. I was told by personnel of several San Pedro municipal offices in 2008 that family violence has increased recently.

The official of the Municipal Office for Women accounted for the increase in this way: Formerly, husbands and wives helped each other and appreciated each other's contribution to the family with mutual respect, but that is less common now; currently the attitude is more that either the husband or the wife is boss and that is why family violence has become more common.

This pattern of change has been documented in another Guatemalan Mayan town, San Pedro Sacatepéquez:

> The Mayan productive system where couples are interdependent and mutually supportive, is still characteristic of many *Sampedrano* homes. At the same time, however, development is moving the urban population away from traditional modes of production and toward modern employment and increasing levels of female dependency. In line with this cultural dichotomy, *Sampedrano* marriages lie somewhere between the mutual complementarity and relative equality of marriages among traditional Mayan peasants and the full-blown *machismo* that characterizes marriages of middle-class *ladinos* in which men maintain dominance through female economic dependence. (Ehlers, 1990, p. 6)

This pattern also resembles the change in Aztec gender roles in the centuries after the arrival of the Spanish to what is now Mexico, from complementary or parallel roles to a more patriarchal system (Burkhart, 1997; Kellogg, 1995).

78. See also Redfield (1950).

(Photo © Barbara Rogoff, 1975)

Acknowledgments ⠓

Barbara: I am grateful for the forces of the universe that brought me the privilege of learning from the people of San Pedro. Warmest thanks especially to the children and the *iyooma'* of San Pedro—especially Chona Pérez González—and to Chonita Chavajay Quiacaín and Josué Chavajay Quiacaín. My deep appreciation to Lois Paul and Ben Paul for their wisdom and generosity over the years. *Maltyoox* to Marta Navichoc Cotuc for advice, guidance, and assistance with this project and many others over the past three decades.

Sincere appreciation also to Beatrice Whiting, Jerry Kagan, Shep White, Michael Cole, and Sylvia Scribner for their roles in my initial work and continuing education in San Pedro. Thanks especially to Chona's family for their good-natured welcome to their family, to Bobby and Janie Paul for sharing their parents with me, and to the people of San Pedro who enthusiastically greeted my inclusion of their words and images in this book.

The transformations of this book owe a great deal to the information and wise advice on drafts provided by Karrie André, Cathy Angelillo, Tom Barbash, Joan Birch, Joan Bossert, Rebeca Burciaga, Jim and Judy Butler, Pablo Chavajay, Sheila Cole, Maricela Correa-Chávez, Sheila Cosminsky, Pablo Cox Bixcul, Melanie Donovan, Sally Duensing, Mark Duvall, Elaine Fulwood, Cynthia García-Coll, Elena Gonzáles, Pedro Rafael González Chavajay, Lori Handelman, Elizabeth Knoll, David Magarian, Luisa Magarian, Salem Magarian, Valerie Magarian, Theresa May, John Modell, Melinda Porter, Dolores Quiacaín Pérez, Linda Quiacaín Pérez, Juana

Rocché, Maura Roessner, Evelyn Schlatter, Meryl Selig, Josh Wagner, Helen Wang, David Weitzman, and several anonymous reviewers.

∷

Chona: I thank Benjamin and Luisa (Lois) Paul, for their writing, which has allowed me to relive these moments of my past. I thank Barbara and Salem because I feel that they gave great importance to my work and valued the sacrifices that I have made. I am sure that in future generations, people will know all that we have written, and by means of this book they will know about my life and my work. My words will not die, even though I will. I also thank my father, because he knew that I would be an *iyoom*, and God, María, and Santa Ana.

∷

Chonita: I want to thank the *corazón del cielo y de la tierra* [the heart of heaven and earth], from my culture and form of viewing the world, for my having encountered people like Barbara, Ben, and Lois—involved people who make the efforts to investigate and make known the development, changes, growth, and renewal of the value of the cosmovision of the Tz'utujil Mayan culture. To my grandma, *Mama Tiit*, who has been for me a model of community social service and willingness to serve the most needy people, dedicating a whole life to mother-infant care of a highly vulnerable population.

∷

Josué: I deeply appreciate the honor that Barbara has provided by including me in such an interesting project, which has awakened my interest in the social sciences. The effort to fill a few pages with the words of experience of my grandmother and give life to this work was well worth it.

To give shape in black and white to the vast knowledge of my grandmother is a fitting tribute to her many years of service. *Maltyoox Mama Tiit.* The ancient knowledge that is deposited in the spoken spark, today is transcribed so that time does not lead it to oblivion. After all, our psyche is formed from our ancestry.

I must also mention my father, Juan Chavajay, whose smile was extinguished by the war and returned the day that my son Milan was born. Still, his dreams and concerns are with us. Thus I can say that his legacy survives. I cannot leave out the father who raised me, Ventura Quiacaín, who left us only recently.

And no matter where I am, I will always carry with me the Tz'utujil essence, like the magical breeze of the lake and the mystery of the mountains. . . .

References ❖

Batz, L. (1991). *Las cofradías de San Pedro La Laguna, Sololá*. Guatemala: CENALTEX [Centro Nacional de Libros de Texto y Material Didáctico "José de Pineda Ibarra"] Ministerio de Educación.

Behar, R. (1993). *Translated woman: Crossing the border with Esperanza's story*. Boston: Beacon.

Berlin, L. (2008, Sept 27). "We'll fill this space, but first a nap." *New York Times*. Technology section. http://www.nytimes.com/2008/09/28/technology/28proto.html?th&emc=th

Bonfil Batalla, G. (1996). *México profundo: Reclaiming a civilization*. Austin: University of Texas Press.

Briggs, J. (1991). Expecting the unexpected: Canadian Inuit training for an experimental lifestyle. *Ethos, 19*, 259–287.

Brown, R. M. (1998). A brief cultural history of the Guatemalan Highlands. In S. Garzon, R. M. Brown, J. B. Richards, & W. Ajpub' (A. Simón) (Eds.), *The life of our language: Kaqchikel Maya maintenance, shift, and revitalization* (pp. 44–61). Austin, TX: University of Texas Press.

Browne, M. W. (1988; August 16). The benzene ring: Dream analysis. *New York Times*. Science section. http://query.nytimes.com/gst/fullpage.html?res=940DE4DF113BF935A2575BC0A96E948260&sec=&spon=&pagewanted=1

Brumfiel, E. M. (2006). Cloth, gender, continuity, and change: Fabricating unity in anthropology. *American Anthropologist, 108*, 862–877.

Bruner, J. (1986). *Actual minds, possible worlds*. Cambridge, MA: Harvard University Press.

Burkhart, L. M. (1997). Mexica women on the home front: Housework and religion in Aztec Mexico. In S. Schroeder, S. Wood, & R. Haskett (Eds.), *Indian women of Early Mexico* (pp. 25–54). Norman, OK: University of Oklahoma Press.

Calvert, K. (2003). Patterns of childrearing in America. In W. Koops & M. Zuckerman (Eds.), *Beyond the century of the child: Cultural history and developmental psychology* (pp. 62–81). Philadelphia: University of Pennsylvania Press.

Cetinea Taa' Pi't Kortes Ong. (2007). *Homenaje a las comadronas*. San Pedro la Laguna, Guatemala: Cetinea Taa' Pi't Kortes Ong.

Chamoux, M.-N. (1992). *Trabajo, técnicas y aprendizaje en el México indígena*. Mexico: Centro de Investigaciones y Estudios Superiores en Antropología Social.

Chavajay, P. (2006). How Mayan mothers with different amounts of schooling organize a problem-solving discussion with children. *International Journal of Behavioral Development, 30,* 371–382.

Chavajay, P. (2008). Organizational patterns in problem solving among Mayan fathers and children. *Developmental Psychology, 44,* 882–888.

Chavajay, P., & Rogoff, B. (1999). Cultural variation in management of attention by children and their caregivers. *Developmental Psychology, 35,* 1079–1090.

Chavajay, P., & Rogoff, B. (2002). Schooling and traditional collaborative social organization of problem solving by Maya mothers and children. *Developmental Psychology, 38,* 55–66.

Christenson, A. J. (2001). *Art and society in a Highland Maya community: The altarpiece of Santiago Atitlán*. Austin, TX: University of Texas Press.

Chudacoff, H. P. (1989). *How old are you? Age consciousness in American culture*. Princeton, NJ: Princeton University Press.

Cole, M. (1996). *Cultural psychology: A once and future discipline*. Cambridge, MA: Harvard University Press.

Correa-Chávez, M., & Rogoff, B. (2009). Children's attention to interactions directed to others: Guatemalan Mayan and European American patterns. *Developmental Psychology, 45,* 630–641.

Correa-Chávez, M., Rogoff, B., & Mejía Arauz, R. (2005). Cultural patterns in attending to two events at once. *Child Development, 76,* 664–678.

Cosminsky, S. (1982). Knowledge and body concepts of Guatemalan midwives. In M. A. Kay (Ed.), *Anthropology of human birth* (pp. 233–252). Philadelphia: F. A. Davis.

Cosminsky, S. (1994). Childbirth and change: A Guatemalan study. In C. P. MacCormack (Ed.), *Ethnography of fertility and birth* (pp. 195–219). Prospect Heights, IL: Waveland.

Cosminsky, S. (2001a). Maya midwives of Southern Mexico and Guatemala. In B. R. Huber & A. R. Sandstrom (Eds.), *Mesoamerican healers* (pp. 179–210). Austin, TX: University of Texas Press.

Cosminsky, S. (2001b). Midwifery across the generations: A modernizing midwife in Guatemala. *Medical Anthropology, 20,* 345–378.

de Haan, M. (1999). *Learning as cultural practice: How children learn in a Mexican Mazahua community*. Amsterdam: Thela Thesis.

Demarest, W. J., & Paul, B. D. (1981). Mayan migrants in Guatemala City. *Anthropology UCLA, 11,* 43–73.

Demos, J., & Demos, V. (1969). Adolescence in historical perspective. *Journal of Marriage and the Family, 31,* 632–638.

Dewey, J. (1916). *Democracy and education*. New York: Macmillan.

Dunbar, K. (1995). How scientists really reason: Scientific reasoning in real-world laboratories. In R. J. Sternberg & J. E. Davidson (Eds.), *The nature of insight* (pp. 365–395). Cambridge, MA: MIT Press.

Durbin, A. (2007). Bush unfit to step on sacred ground. *Report on Guatemala, 28*, 2–3.

Duque Arellanos, V. (1999). *Forjando educación para un nuevo milenio: Desafíos educativos en paises multiculturales*. Guatemala: Fundación Rigoberta Menchú Tum.

Ehlers, T. B. (1990). *Silent looms: Women and production in a Guatemalan town*. Boulder, CO: Westview.

Ehrenreich, B., & English, D. (1978). *For her own good: 150 years of the experts' advice to women*. Garden City, New York: Anchor Press/Doubleday.

Eisenhart, M. (1995). The fax, the jazz player, and the self-story teller: How do people organize culture? *Anthropology & Education Quarterly, 26*, 3–26.

Elder, G. H. (2002). Historical times and lives: A journey through time and space. In E. Phelps, F. F. Furstenberg, & A. Colby (Eds.), *Looking at lives: American longitudinal studies of the twentieth century* (pp. 194–218). New York: Russell Sage Foundation.

Elder, G. H., Modell, J., & Parke, R. D. (Eds.). (1993). Children in time and place. New York: Cambridge University Press.

Elizalde, R. M. (2007, 21 February). Republic vs. Empire: The rise and fall of the USA: An interview with Gore Vidal (part 1). *The Guardian*. http://www.cpa.org.au/garchve07/1308vidal.html

Elmendorf, M. L. (1976). *Nine Mayan women: A village faces change*. Cambridge, MA: Schenkman Publishing Co.

Engeström, Y. (1990). *Learning, working and imagining*. Helsinki: Orienta-Konsultit Oy.

Erickson, F. (1982). Taught cognitive learning in its immediate environments. *Anthropology & Education Quarterly, 13*, 149–180.

Erickson, F. (2004). *Talk and social theory*. Cambridge, UK: Polity.

Few, M. (2002). *Women who live evil lives: Gender, religion, and the politics of power in colonial Guatemala, 1650–1750*. Austin, TX: University of Texas Press.

Flores, O. (n.d.). Guillermo Prieto. http://ocw.udem.edu.mx/cursos-de-profesional/historia-del-mexico-independiente/12guillermoprieto.pdf

Foster, G. (1960). *Culture and conquest: America's Spanish heritage*. Chicago: Quadrangle Books.

Frye, D. (1996). *Indians into Mexicans: History and identity in a Mexican town*. Austin, TX: University of Texas Press.

Fuller, N., & Jordan, B. (1981). Maya women and the end of the birthing period: Postpartum massage-and-binding in Yucatan, Mexico. *Medical Anthropology, 5(1)*, 35–50.

Gaskins, S. (1999). Children's daily lives in a Mayan village. In A Göncü (Ed.), *Children's engagement in the world* (pp. 25–81). Cambridge, England: Cambridge University Press.

Gaskins, S. (2003). From corn to cash: Change and continuity within Mayan families. *Ethos, 31*, 248–273.

Goldman, N., & Glei, D. A. (2000, December). *Evaluation of midwifery care: A case study of rural Guatemala. Measure: Evaluation working paper*. Chapel Hill, NC: Carolina Population Center.

Gómez, R. L., Bootzin, R. R., & Nadel, L. (2006). Naps promote abstraction in language-learning infants. *Psychological Science, 17,* 670–674.

Goodnow, J. J. (1990). The socialization of cognition: What's involved? In J. W. Stigler, R. A. Shweder, & G. Herdt (Eds.), *Cultural psychology* (pp. 259–286). Cambridge, England: Cambridge University Press.

Greenfield, P. M., & Cocking, R. R. (Eds.). (1994). *Cross-cultural roots of minority child development*. Hillsdale, NJ: Erlbaum.

Greenfield, P. M. (2004). *Weaving generations together*. Santa Fe, NM: School of American Research.

Guatemala Human Rights Commission/USA. (2009, March). *El Quetzal, 2,* 10.

Gutiérrez, K. D., Baquedano-López, P., & Tejeda, C. (1999). Rethinking diversity: Hybridity and hybrid language practices in the third space. *Mind, Culture and Activity, 6,* 286–303.

Gutiérrez, K., & Rogoff, B. (2003). Cultural ways of learning: Individual traits or repertoires of practice. *Educational Researcher, 32,* 19–25.

Hayes-Bautista, D. (2004). *La Nueva California: Latinos in the Golden State*. University of California Press.

Heath, S. B. (1991). "It's about winning!" The language of knowledge in baseball. In L. B. Resnick, J. M. Levine, & S. D. Teasley (Eds.), *Perspectives on socially shared cognition* (pp. 101–124). Washington, DC: American Psychological Association.

Hernández, D. J. (1994, Spring). Children's changing access to resources: A historical perspective. *Society for Research in Child Development Social Policy Report, 8,* 1–23.

Hernández Sáenz, L. M., & Foster, G. M. (2001). Curers and their cures in Colonial New Spain and Guatemala. In B. R. Huber & A. R. Sandstrom (Eds.), *Mesoamerican healers* (pp. 19–46). Austin, TX: University of Texas Press.

Hofling, C. A. (1993). Marking space and time in Itzaj Maya narrative. *Journal of Linguistic Anthropology, 3,* 164–184.

Huber, B. R., & Sandstrom, A. R. (2001). Recruitment, training, and practice of indigenous midwives: From the Mexico—United States border to the Isthmus of Tehuantepec. In B. R. Huber & A. R. Sandstrom (Eds.), *Mesoamerican healers* (pp. 139–178). Austin, TX: University of Texas Press.

Hurtado, E. (2009). (http://www.usaid.gov/our_work/global_health/home/News/women/health_hurtado.html)

Hurtado, E., & Sáenz de Tejada, E. (2001). Relations between government health workers and traditional midwives in Guatemala. In B. R. Huber & A. R. Sandstrom (Eds.), *Mesoamerican healers* (pp. 211–242). Austin, TX: University of Texas Press.

Ingham, J. M. (1986). *Mary, Michael, and Lucifer: Folk Catholicism in Central Mexico*. Austin, TX: University of Texas Press.

John-Steiner, V. (1985). *Notebooks of the mind: Explorations of thinking*. Albuquerque: University of New Mexico Press.

Jordan, B. (1978). *Birth in four cultures: A crosscultural investigation of childbirth in Yucatan, Holland, Sweden and the United States*. Montreal, Canada: Eden Press Women's Pub.

Jordan, B. (1989). Cosmopolitical obstetrics: Some insights from the training of traditional midwives. *Social Science & Medicine, 28*, 925–944.

Jordan, B. (1993). *Birth in four cultures: A crosscultural investigation of childbirth in Yucatan, Holland, Sweden, and the United States* (4th ed.). Prospect Heights, IL: Waveland.

Jordan, B. (1999). Childbirth cross-culturally. In H. Tierney (Ed.), *The women's encyclopedia vol 1: Views from the sciences* (2nd ed., pp. 220–224). Westport, CT: Greenwood Press.

Kaiser, S., & Sachser, N. (2009). Effects of prenatal social stress on offspring development. *Current Directions in Psychological Science, 18*, 118–121.

Keller, H., & Lamm, B. (2005). Parenting as the expression of sociohistorical time: The case of German individualisation. *International Journal of Behavioral Development, 29*, 238–246.

Kellogg, S. (1995). *Law and the transformation of Aztec culture, 1500–1700*. Norman, OK: University of Oklahoma Press.

Knoke de Arathoon, B. (2005). In J. P. LaPorte, B. Arroyo, & H. E. Mejía, (Eds.), *XVIII Simposio de Investigaciones Arqueológicas en Guatemala, 2004* (pp. 1–13). Guatemala: Museo Nacional de Arqueología y Etnología.

LaFarge, O. (1947). *Santa Eulalia: The religion of a Cuchumatán Indian town*. Chicago: University of Chicago Press.

Lake, M. G. (1991). *Native healer: Initiation into an ancient art*. Wheaton, IL: Quest Books.

Lave, J., & Wenger, E. (1991). *Situated learning: Legitimate peripheral participation*. Cambridge, England: Cambridge University Press.

Le Clézio, J. M. G. (1993). *The Mexican dream: Or, the interrupted thought of Amerindian civilizations*. Chicago: University of Chicago Press.

León, N. (1910). *La obstetricia en México [Obstetrics in México.]* México: Tipografía de la Viuda de F. Diaz de León.

LeVine, R. A. (1980). A cross-cultural perspective on parenting. In M. S. Fantini & R. Cardenas (Eds.), *Parenting in a multicultural society* (pp. 17–26). New York: Longman.

LeVine, S. (1993). *Dolor y alegría: Women and social change in urban Mexico*. Madison, WI: University of Wisconsin Press.

Linde, C. (1993). *Life stories: The creation of coherence*. New York: Oxford University Press.

Lipp, F. J. (2001). A comparative analysis of Southern Mexican and Guatemalan shamans. In B. R. Huber & A. R. Sandstrom (Eds.), *Mesoamerican healers* (pp. 95–116). Austin, TX: University of Texas Press.

Lipsitt, L. P. (2003). Crib death: A biobehavioral phenomenon? *Current Directions in Psychological Science, 12*, 164–170.

López, A., Correa-Chávez, M., Rogoff, B., & Gutiérrez, K. (2010). Attention to instruction directed to another by U.S. Mexican-heritage children of varying cultural backgrounds. *Developmental Psychology, 46*, 593–601.

Loucky, J. P. (1974). *Unpublished field notes from San Juan la Laguna*. University of California, Los Angeles.

Loucky, J., & Moors, M. M. (Eds.). (2000). *The Maya diaspora*. Philadelphia: Temple University Press.

Magarian, L. (1996). A question of my destiny. *The Trident*, student newspaper of Santa Cruz High School.

Magarian, S. (1976). *Morbidity and mortality in mothers and children in San Pedro la Laguna, Sololá, Guatemala*. Unpublished manuscript, Harvard Medical School.

Martin, L. (1994). Discourse structure and rhetorical elaboration in Mocho personal narrative. *Journal of Linguistic Anthropology, 4*, 131–152.

Martini, M. (2004). Family development in two island cultures. In J. L. Roopnarine & U. P. Gielen (Eds.), *Families in global perspective* (pp. 120–147). Boston: Allyn & Bacon.

McClain, C. (1975). Ethno-obstetrics in Ajijic. *Anthropological Quarterly, 48*, 38–56.

Medical Economics Staff & Gruenwald, J. (Eds.). (2000). *Physician's Desk Reference for herbal medicines*. Medical Economics.

Mejía Arauz, R., Rogoff, B., & Paradise, R. (2005). Cultural variation in children's observation during a demonstration. *International Journal of Behavioral Development, 29*, 282–291.

Mellado, V., Zolla, C., & Castañeda, X. (1989). *La atención al embarazo y el parto en el medio rural mexicano [Attending pregnancy and birth in rural México.]* Mexico City: Centro Interamericano de Estudios de Seguridad Social.

Menchú, R. (1983). *I, Rigoberta Menchú: An Indian woman in Guatemala*. London: Verso.

Miller, M. E., & Taube, K. A. (1993). *The gods and symbols of ancient Mexico and the Maya: An illustrated dictionary of Mesoamerican religion*. New York: Thames and Hudson.

Monteforte Toledo, M. (1948). *Entre la piedra y la cruz*. Guatemala: Editorial "El Libro de Guatemala."

Morelli, G., Rogoff, B., & Angelillo, C. (2003). Cultural variation in young children's access to work or involvement in specialised child-focused activities. *International Journal of Behavioral Development, 27*, 264–274.

Mosier, C., & Rogoff, B. (2003). Privileged treatment of toddlers: Cultural aspects of individual choice and responsibility. *Developmental Psychology, 39*, 1047–1060.

Munroe, R. L., & Munroe, R. H. (1997). Logoli childhood and the cultural reproduction of sex differentiation. In T. S. Weisner, C. Bradley, & P. L. Kilbride (Eds.), *African families and the crisis of social change* (pp. 299–314). Westport, CT: Bergin & Garvey.

Najafi, B., Mejía Arauz, R., & Rogoff, B. (2005, September). *Cultural continuity and transformation in the practice of indigenous Mexican traditions*. International Society for Cultural and Activity Research, Seville Spain.

Nájera-Ramírez, O. (1997). *La fiesta de los Tastoanes*. Albuquerque: University of New Mexico Press.

Nash, J. (1970). *In the eyes of the ancestors: Belief and behavior in a Maya community*. New Haven: Yale University Press.

Nash, M. (1967). *Machine age Maya*. Chicago: University of Chicago Press.

Ochs, E. (1988). *Culture and language development: Language acquisition and language socialization in a Samoan village*. Cambridge, England: Cambridge University Press.

Orellana, S. L. (1984). *The Tzutujil Mayas: Continuity and change, 1250–1630*. Norman, OK: University of Oklahoma Press.

Orellana, S. L. (1987). *Indian medicine in Highland Guatemala: The pre-Hispanic and colonial periods*. Albuquerque: University of New Mexico Press.

Ortiz de Montellano, B. R. (1990). *Aztec medicine, health, and nutrition*. New Brunswick, NJ: Rutgers University Press.

Paradise, R., & Rogoff, B. (2009). Side by side: Learning through observing and pitching in. *Ethos, 37*, 102–138.

Paul, B. D. (1950). Life in a Guatemalan Indian village. *Patterns for modern living. Division 3, Cultural patterns*. Chicago: The Delphian Society.

Paul, B. D. (1976). The Maya bonesetter as sacred specialist. *Ethnology, 15*, 77–81.

Paul, B. D. (1988). Operation of a death squad in San Pedro la Laguna. In R. M. Carmack (Ed.), *Harvest of violence: The Maya Indians and the Guatemalan crisis* (pp. 119–154). Norman, OK: University of Oklahoma Press.

Paul, B. D., & Demarest, W. J. (1984). Citizen participation overplanned: The case of a health project in the Guatemalan community of San Pedro la Laguna. *Social Science & Medicine, 19*, 185–192.

Paul, B. D., & Johnston, J. (1998). Arte étnico: Orígenes y desarrollo de la pintura al óleo de los artistas mayas de San Pedro la Laguna, Guatemala. *Mesoamérica, 36*, 423–440.

Paul, B. D., & Paul, L. (1952). The life cycle. In S. Tax (Ed.), *Heritage of conquest: The ethnology of Middle America* (pp. 174–192). Glencoe, IL: Free Press.

Paul, L. (1969, June). *The changing role of the midwife in San Pedro la Laguna*. Unpublished manuscript.

Paul, L. (1974–75). Unpublished manuscript notes from file of miscellaneous material on women and midwives.

Paul, L. (1975). Recruitment to a ritual role: The midwife in a Maya community. *Ethos, 3*, 449–467.

Paul, L., & Paul, B. D. (1963). Changing marriage patterns in a Highland Guatemalan community. *Southwestern Journal of Anthropology, 19*, 131–148.

Paul, L., & Paul, B. D. (1975). The Maya midwife as sacred specialist: A Guatemalan case. *American Ethnologist, 2*, 707–726.

Perera, V., & Bruce, R. D. (1982). *The last lords of Palenque: The Lacandon Mayas of the Mexican rain forest*. Berkeley: University of California Press.

Pillemer, D. & White, S. H. (Eds.). (2005). *Developmental psychology and social change*. New York: Cambridge University Press.

Pratt, C. (1948). *I learn from children: An adventure in progressive education*. New York: Simon & Schuster.

Redfield, R. (1950). *A village that chose progress: Chan Kom revisited*. Chicago: University of Chicago Press.

Redfield, R., & Villa Rojas, A. (1934). *Chan Kom: A Maya village*. Chicago: University of Chicago Press.

Reina, R. E. (1966). *The law of the Saints: A Pokomam pueblo and its community culture*. Indianapolis: The Bobbs-Merrill Co.

Richards, M. (1997). *The rainmaker: A Tz'utujil Maya story from Guatemala* (Angelika Bauer, illus.) Litoprint.

Richards, M. (2003). *Atlas Lingüístico de Guatemala*. Guatemala: Editorial Serviprensa.

Richman, A., Miller, P., & LeVine, R. (1992). *Developmental Psychology, 28*, 614–621.

Rodríguez Rouanet, F. (1969). Prácticas médicas tradicionales de los indígenas de Guatemala [Traditional medical practices of the Indians of Guatemala.] *Guatemala Indígena, 4*, 52–86.

Rogoff, B. (1981). Adults and peers as agents of socialization: A Highland Guatemalan profile. *Ethos, 9*, 18–36.

Rogoff, B. (2003). *The cultural nature of human development*. New York: Oxford University Press.

Rogoff, B., & Angelillo, C. (2002). Investigating the coordinated functioning of multifaceted cultural practices in human development. *Human Development, 45*, 211–225.

Rogoff, B., Correa-Chávez, M., & Navichoc Cotuc, M. (2005). A cultural/historical view of schooling in human development. In D. Pillemer & S. H. White (Eds.), *Developmental psychology and social change* (pp. 225–263). New York, NY: Cambridge University Press.

Rogoff, B., Mistry, J., Göncü, A., & Mosier, C. (1993). Guided participation in cultural activity by toddlers and caregivers. *Monographs of the Society for Research in Child Development, 58*(8, Serial No. 236).

Rogoff, B., Moore, L., Najafi, B., Dexter, A., Correa-Chávez, M., & Solís, J. (2007). Children's development of cultural repertoires through participation in everyday routines and practices. In J. Grusec & P. Hastings (Eds.), *Handbook of socialization* (pp. 490–515). New York: Guilford.

Rogoff, B., Paradise, R., Mejía Arauz, R., Correa-Chávez, M., & Angelillo, C. (2003). Firsthand learning through intent participation. *Annual Review of Psychology, 54*, 175–203.

Rogoff, B., Sellers, M. J., Pirotta, S., Fox, N., & White, S. H. (1975). Age of assignment of roles and responsibilities to children: A cross-cultural survey. *Human Development, 18*, 353–369.

Rosales, J. de D. (1949). *Notes on San Pedro la Laguna*. Microfilm collection of manuscripts on Middle American cultural anthropology, No. 25. Chicago: University of Chicago Library.

Sahagún, Fa. B. de. (1963). General history of the things of New Spain (Florentine Codex), Book 2: Earthly things. In C. E. Dibble & A. J. O. Anderson (Eds. and trans.), *Monographs of the School of American Research and The Museum of New Mexico*, No. 14, Part 12. Santa Fe, NM: School of American Research and University of Utah.

Sahagún, Fa. B. de. (1969a). General history of the things of New Spain (Florentine Codex), Book 6, Rhetoric and moral philosophy. In C. E. Dibble & A. J. O. Anderson (Eds. and trans.), *Monographs of the School of American Research*, No. 14, Part 7, Santa Fe, NM: Twenty-sixth chapter, pp. 149–150.

Sahagún, Fa. B. de. (1969b). General history of the things of New Spain (Florentine Codex), Book 6, Rhetoric and moral philosophy. In C. E. Dibble & A. J. O. Anderson (Eds. and trans.), *Monographs of the School of American Research*, No. 14, Part 7, Santa Fe, NM: Twenty-seventh chapter, pp. 151–158.

Sahagún, Fa. B. de. (1969c). General history of the things of New Spain (Florentine Codex), Book 6, Rhetoric and moral philosophy. In C. E. Dibble & A. J. O. Anderson (Eds. and trans.), *Monographs of the School of American Research and The Museum of New Mexico*, No. 14, Part 7. Santa Fe, NM: School of American Research and University of Utah, Twenty-eighth chapter, p. 159.

Sahagún, Fa. B. de. (1969d). General history of the things of New Spain (Florentine Codex), Book 6, Rhetoric and moral philosophy. In C. E. Dibble & A. J. O. Anderson (Eds. and trans.), *Monographs of the School of American Research and The Museum of New Mexico*, No. 14, Part 7. Santa Fe, NM: School of American Research and University of Utah, Thirtieth chapter, Thirty-first chapter, pp. 167–173.

Sahagún, Fa. B. de. (1969e). General history of the things of New Spain (Florentine Codex), Book 6, Rhetoric and moral philosophy. In C. E. Dibble & A. J. O. Anderson (Eds. and trans.), *Monographs of the School of American Research and The Museum of New Mexico*, No. 14, Part 7. Santa Fe, NM: School of American Research and University of Utah, Thirty-second chapter, pp. 175–177.

Sahagún, Fa. B. de. (1969f). General history of the things of New Spain (Florentine Codex), Book 6, Rhetoric and moral philosophy. In C. E. Dibble & A. J. O. Anderson (Eds. and trans.), *Monographs of the School of American Research and The Museum of New Mexico*, No. 14, Part 7. Santa Fe, NM: School of American Research and University of Utah, Thirty-third chapter, pp. 179–182.

Sahagún, Fa. B. de. (1969g). General history of the things of New Spain (Florentine Codex), Book 6, Rhetoric and moral philosophy. In C. E. Dibble & A. J. O. Anderson (Eds. and trans.), *Monographs of the School of American Research and The Museum of New Mexico*, No. 14, Part 7. Santa Fe, NM: School of American Research and University of Utah, Thirty-sixth chapter, pp. 197–199.

Sahagún, Fa. B. de. (1969h). General history of the things of New Spain (Florentine Codex), Book 6, Rhetoric and moral philosophy. In C. E. Dibble & A. J. O. Anderson (Eds. and trans.), *Monographs of the School of American Research and The Museum of New Mexico*, No. 14, Part 7. Santa Fe, NM: School of American Research and University of Utah, Thirty-seventh chapter, Thirty-eighth chapter, pp. 201–207.

Schieffelin, B. B. (1991). *The give and take of everyday life: Language socialization of Kaluli children.* Cambridge, England: Cambridge University Press.

Sesia, P. M. (1997). "Women come here on their own when they need to": Prenatal care, authoritative knowledge, and maternal health in Oaxaca. In R. E. Davis-Floyd & C. F. Sargent (Eds.), *Childbirth and authoritative knowledge: Cross-cultural perspectives.* Berkeley: University of California Press.

Silva, K., Correa-Chávez, M., & Rogoff, B. (2010). Mexican-heritage children's attention and learning from interactions directed to others. *Child Development, 81,* 898–912.

Sitler, R. K. (1994). *Through Ladino eyes: Images of the Maya in the Spanish American novel.* (Unpublished dissertation). University of Texas at Austin. www.stetson.edu/~rsitler/CV/DISSERTA.doc

Sommerville, J. A., & Hammond, A. J. (2007). Treating another's actions as one's own: Children's memory of and learning from joint activity. *Developmental Psychology, 43,* 1003–1018.

Smith, C. A. (1990). *Guatemalan Indians and the state, 1540 to 1988.* Austin, TX: University of Texas Press.

Sullivan, T. D. (1969). Embarazo y parto: Costumbres, supersticiones y técnicas prehispánicas de los aztecas y su supervivencia en México [Pregnancy and birth: Prehispanic customs, 'superstitions' and techniques of the Aztecs and their survival in Mexico]. *Anuario Indigenista, 29,* 285–293.

Summer Institute of Linguistics, Central America Branch (1978). *Tzutujil anthropology volume.* Photocopies of 1145 pages of fieldnotes collected by Jim and Judy Butler, during their several decades of missionary work in San Pedro. Transmitted to Ben Paul January 29, 1978, with permission for use in publications.

Tally, E., & Chavajay, J. (2007). Multiplicidad y antagonismo en torno a la Mayanización en San Pedro la Laguna [Multiplicity and antagonism about Mayanization in San Pedro la Laguna]. In S. Bastos & A. Cumes (Eds.), *Mayanización y vida cotidiana: La ideología multicultural en la sociedad guatemalteca [Mayanization and daily life: Multicultural ideology en Guatemalan society]* (Vol. II, pp. 496–531). Guatemala: FLACSO, CIRMA, Cholsamaj.

Tedlock, B. (1982). *Time and the Highland Maya* (rev.ed.). Albuquerque: University of New Mexico Press.

Thompson, J. E. S. (1970). *Maya history and religion.* Norman, OK: University of Oklahoma Press.

Tuy Navichoc, Saqiiq'-Felipe de J. (1999). Interview with Naan Jesús Iyoom (Rosaria Quiacaín Televario), "The Art of Being *Iyoom.*" In P. Petrich (Ed.), *Técnicas del Lago Atitlán I* (pp. 185–191). Quetzaltenango, Guatemala: CAEL/MUNI-K'AT.

Urrieta, L., Jr. (2003). *Las identidades también lloran*: Identities also cry: Exploring the human side of Indigenous Latina/o identities. *Educational Studies, 34,* 147–168.

Vygotsky, L. S. (1978). *Mind in society.* Cambridge, MA: Harvard University Press.

Ward, M. C. (1971). *Them children: A study in language learning.* New York: Holt, Rinehart & Winston.

Wertsch, J. V. (1991). *Voices of the mind: A sociocultural approach to mediated action.* Cambridge, MA: Harvard University Press.

Zamora Acosta, E. (1976). Apuntes para una etnografía de la población del lago Atitlán en el siglo XVI [Notes for an ethnography of the population of Lake Atitlán in the 16th century]. *Ethnica, 12,* 149–172.

Zborowski, M., & Herzog, E. (1952). *Life is with people: The culture of the shtetl.* New York: Schocken.

Quotation Credits ⠿

Quotes from Paul and Paul (1975) reproduced by permission of the American Anthropological Association from *American Ethnologist* Volume 2(4), pp. 707–726, 1975. Not for sale or further reproduction.

Quotes from Paul (1975) reproduced by permission of the American Anthropological Association from *Ethos* Volume 3(3), pp. 449–467, 1975. Not for sale or further reproduction.

Quote from B.D. Paul and L. Paul, "The life cycle" (p. 177). In *Heritage of Conquest*, edited by Sol Tax. Copyright © 1952 by the Free Press. Copyright renewed © 1980. Reprinted with permission of Free Press, a Division of Simon & Schuster, Inc. All rights reserved.

Quotes from Jordan (1989) were published in *Social Science & Medicine*, 28(9), Jordan, B., Cosmopolitical obstetrics: Some insights from the training of traditional midwives, pp. 925–944, Copyright Elsevier (1989).

Quotes from Lake (1991) published by Quest Books, copyright 1991 by Theosophical Publishing House. Reproduced with permission of Theosophical Publishing House in the format Other book via Copyright Clearance Center.

Quote from Sesia (1997), copyright 1997 by University of California Press—Books. Reproduced with permission of University of California Press—Books in the format Other book via Copyright Clearance Center.

Index ❖

age
    confusion about, 144
    recording life events *vs.*, 144
    tortillas *vs.*, 144, 267, *267*
Agudelina, kitchen of, 54, *54*
aire (cold air), 218–19, *219*, 300n38
aj'iitz (sorcerer)
    birthsign of, 206
    death of, 206–7
ajq'iij ("day-keeper"), *203*, 306n63
    birthsigns and, 201–3, 205
alcohol
    evangelical Protestantism against, 96
    Indigenous people and, 96, 298n30
    iyoom and, 147
    land ownership and, 96, 298n30
    Pérez Yojcom, Marcos, and, 91–92,
      95, 98
amniotic membrane. *See* birthsign(s)
ancestors
    of Chona, 89–91
    combinations of, 89–91
    cultural practices *vs.*, 85–91
    deceased *iyooma'*, 103
    of González Navichoc, Dolores,
      89–91

Angelillo, Cathy, 95, *95*
attentiveness
    in learning by observing, 257–58,
      258, *262*, *263*
    to stories, 265, *265*
author, *45*, *47*. *See also* research
    Chona as mother of, 49, 57–61
    dreams of, 270
    family story about, 57–61
    library founded by, 60
    namesakes of, 169, *169*
    permission for, 66
    sitting on floor, 50, *50*, 57
    spirit separation and, 307n69
    teacher as identity of, 38
Aztecs. *See also* Florentine
    Codex
    babies' purification by, 225
    formal speeches to midwives by,
      173–75
    prayers of, 213, 225
    purification/naming
      ceremony, 222
    sweat baths and, 216
    teaching girls, 267, *267*
    umbilical cords and, 212

Catholicism and, 77, *77–79, 79*
for families loosing babies, 229–30
girls in, 78, *78*
incense for, *122,* 122–23, 226,
    302n50, 308n72
involving the moon, 164
by *iyoom,* 220–31, *221–23, 225*
maatz' and, 83–84, *83–84*
by Pérez Yojcom, Marcos, 123, 158
for postpartum, 221–22, *221–22,* 224
in San Juan, 230
by shamans, *122, 122,* 158, 206, *206,*
    302n50
for umbilical cord around neck, 220
Chavajay, Antonio, 12, *12,* 186
Chavajay, Domingo, *122, 122,* 202,
    302, 305n61, *306*
Chavajay, Francisco, 81, *81*
Chavajay, Josué, 66, 68–69, 90, *94, 95*
    assistance for, 94, 298n29
    on spirit separation, 307n69
Chavajay, Pablo, 95, *95,* 203–4, *204*
Chavajay Petzey, Marina, 227, *227*
Chavajay Quiacaín, Chonita, 66,
    90, 247
    attending births as child, 250, 251
    baby's spirit for, 170–71
    birthsign of, 245, 246
    Chona and, 245–47, *246,* 250–52
    Chona's delivery prediction
        for, 170
    destiny/development of, 281–82
    ignorance of, 245
    illness of, 246–47
    as *iyoom,* 71, *71,* 245, 246, 282
    learning by observing by, 249–52
    opportunities for, 247
    son of, 170–71
    work of, 281
Chávez, Nicolás, 79–80, 211
childbirth, 185–200, *187*
    adults present at, 185
    ajq'iij and, 201–3, *203,* 205, 306n63
    bathing newborn after, 211, 214,
        222, *222*
    beliefs about, 63–64, 75
    "buying babies" *vs.,* 107–9

cesarean sections for, 184
children at, 117, *117,* 250, 251
children's knowledge of, 107–11
of Chona, 75, 190–93, *191*
by Chona alone, 192–93
colonization and, 163
death and, 99, 135–39
folk remedies for, *197,* 197–98,
    305n60
González, Rafael, on, 196–97,
    211–12, 230–31
husbands at, 185–86, *186,* 190–91,
    191, 196–97
husband's ignorance of,
    112–13, 284
location of, 63, 296n16
Mayan calendar and, 76–77,
    201–2
modesty and, 64
newborn care after, 210–14, 218–20,
    219, 224–26, *225*
pain of, 252
Pérez Yojcom, Marcos, and,
    190–91, *191*
perineum in, 215–16
placentas and, 192–95, 211, 212,
    307n67
positions for, 241–42
prayers during, 198–200
preferred attendants for, 62–63
premature, 180, 231–32
primipara's ignorance of, 111–13,
    190–91
in San Juan, 156, 161, 280
shamans and, 201–2, *202*
silence during, 250
with sleeping children, 117, *117*
as taboo subject, 109–13
traditions/new ways and, 109–11
young adults' knowledge of,
    110–13, 118
child mortality, 137–38, 302n47
    Chona's children and, 135–36,
        139–41
    from epidemics, 136
    grief and, 136
    reduction in, 140–41

children (Mayan). *See also* boys;
　　Chona's children; girl(s)
　childbirth and, 107–11, 117, *117*
　at childbirths, 117, *117*, 250, *251*
　chores of, 225, 253–57, *254–56*
　at community events, 249, *249*,
　　308n73
　dangers for, 24–25, *24–25*, 106, 140,
　　300n38
　death of, 135–41, 302n47
　eavesdropping, 107, 252–53
　family size and, 25
　at funerals, 249, *249*
　health of, 25, 135–41, 302n47
　ignorance of pregnancy among,
　　107–10, 118, 245, 250–52
　independence of, 248, *248*
　infant mortality and, 109, 113, 136
　language lessons from, 46
　learning by observing for, 248–53,
　　257–64, *258, 263*, 308n73, 309n75
　maternal mortality and, 109
　in midwives' families, 253–54
　mothers' schooling and, 30
　observing adult work, 308n73
　older, breastfeeding for, 294n11
　parents' schooling and, 30–31
　play of, 24–25, *24–25*, 28–30, *28–30*,
　　248, *248*, 276–79, *277*
　pregnancy's displacement for,
　　169–70
　respect from, 107, 110
　sexual intercourse near, 116–18
　taboo subjects for, 107–18
　traditions/new ways and, 109–11
　vaccinations for, 99–100, 299n35
　work of, 6–7, *7*, 25–27, *26–27*
children (U.S.)
　child-focused activities of, 308n73
　family size and, 21
　health of, 21
　history and, 20–21
　school for, 20–21
　skills of, 21
　work for, 20–21
chipilez, 170
Chi-Tzunún-Choy, 40

chocolate, 215, *215*
Chona, *134*. *See also* iyoom / iyooma'
　adolescence of, 114
　advice from, 282–85
　aging of, 280
　ancestors of, 89–91
　announcement of, 155, *155*
　appearance of, 59
　as author's mother, 49, 57–61
　average deliveries by, 161
　on baby's spirit, 170
　as beauty queen, 124–25
　birth predictions by, 160, 170–71,
　　189, 245
　birthsigns of, 8, 75, 155
　books and, 4, 5, 9, 62, 66–69
　breastfeeding and, 34, *34*, 135, *135*
　Catholic church and, 76–77, 96
　chair for, 49–50, *50*
　childbirths alone for, 192–93
　children's death for, 135–36,
　　139–40, 302n47
　choice of husband for, 131–32
　Chonita and, 245–47, *246*, 250–52
　destiny/development and, 8–9,
　　18–19, *19*, 161
　destiny's acceptance and, 142–43,
　　150, 153–58, 282–83, 302n49
　dreams of, 118–20, 156–57, 269, 271
　early labor and, 188
　encouragement from, 189
　evangelical Protestantism and,
　　82, 96
　family's occupations of, 8, 228
　first delivery for, 147, 152, 153–55
　first interview with, 48–49
　first menstruation for, 114
　folk remedies of, 167
　gentle treatment by, 188–90
　gestures of, 48–49
　husband of, 59, 131–32, 157,
　　190–91, *191*
　illness of, 122–23, 143, 156, 158
　information from, 112
　iyooma of, 75, 105–6
　Magarian, Salem, and, 243, *243*–44
　maternal mortality and, 99

evil eye, 106, 140, 300n38
  ceremonial bath protecting against, 222, *222*
  iyoom and, 233–35
  pregnancy and, 233–35
  protections against, 233
  rue plant protection against, 222, 235
explanations
  learning from, 265–69, *267*
  supernatural, 147–48

family history and origins, 89–91
family size, 21, 25
family's occupations, 8, 228
family violence, 309n77
Favorite Old Man, 69–70, *70*
Florentine Codex, 52, *52*, 80, *174*, 200
  on bathing baby, 223, *223*
  formal speeches in, 173–75
  newborn bath and, 213
  newborns and, *212*, 212–14
  opossum-tail medication in, *197*, 197–98
  pregnancy in, 175–76
  on prenatal massage, 178–79, *179*
  soothsayers and, 202, *202*
  umbilical cord and, 226–27
formal speech
  for celebrations, 172, *172*
  as cultural practice, 171–75, *172*, *174*
  for *iyoom* requests, 171, 173–75
Foster, George, 177, 221, 303n55
Frye, D., 85, 309n76
funerals, children at, 249, *249*

genocide, 86
  out-migration and, 44
  against Tz'utujil Mayans, 44, 72, 86, 309n77
girl(s)
  Aztecs teaching, 267, *267*
  boys and, 114
  in ceremony, 78, *78*
  chores for, 6–7, *7*, 26, *26*, 108, *108*, 254–56, *254–56*, 267, *267*

ignorance about menstruation for, 111, 114, 300n39, 301n40
  ignorance about sexual intercourse for, 114–18, 300n39
  learning embroidery, 259–61, 266
  learning weaving, 29, *29*, 261, 266–67, *267*
  marriage age for, 133–34
  play for, 25, *25*, 28–29, *28–29*, 119, *119*, 259–61
  water and, 254, *254*
  weaving and, 29, *29*, 51, *51*, 261, 266–67, *267*, 278, *278*
glocalization, 290
González, Cándida, 196–97, 211
González, Juan Fermin, 117, *117*
González, Rafael, on childbirth, 196–97, 211–12, 230–31
González Chavajay, Pedro Rafael, 186, *186*, 196
González Mejicano, Chema, 89–90
González Navichoc, Dolores, *83*, 84, 120, *154*
  ancestors of, 89–91
  death of, 98, 156
  destiny and, 83, 92, 98–99, 154
  fears of, 98–99
  illness of, 92
  Ladino, Spanish, Mayan ancestry, 89
  reputation of, 99, 299n34
  Susana on, 98

healers. *See also* Chona; shaman
  bone healers, 274–75
  Native American healer, 273
higher education, discrimination and, 88
hospital visits, 182, *182–83*
  death and, 183–84, *184*
Howe, Elias, 269
how to do *vs.* how to talk about, 239, 241, 268
human development. *See* development, child
Hun Hunahpu (Mayan deity), 81
Hurtado, Elena, 242

Mayan language. *See* Kaqchikel;
　　Tz'utujil
Mayan people. *See also* San Pedro
　　Aztecs and, 52
　　Latino and, 15, 87–88
　　Monteforte Toledo and, 128
Mayan spiritual practices
　　Catholicism and, 77, 77–78,
　　　79–82, 164
　　Catholic priests against, 77, 80,
　　　297n24
　　religion and, 306n63
Mead, Margaret, 74
memory, 272
　　in research discrepancies,
　　　145–46, *146*
men. *See also* husband(s)
　　work of, 54–55, *55*
Menchú, Rigoberta, 35, 185, 284, *284*
menstruation
　　girls' ignorance about, 111, 114,
　　　300n39, 301n40
　　Paul, Lois, on, 111
　　as taboo subject, 114
Mesoamerica, 294n8
midwives. *See also iyoom, iyooma';*
　　practicante midwives
　　Aztecs formal speeches to, 173–75
　　children in families of, 253–54
　　competition among, 304n57
　　divine calling for, 174–75, 307n68
　　formal acceptance by, 174
　　humility of, 174–76
　　learning by participation for,
　　　253–54
　　limitations of, 174–76
　　narratives/explanations from, 268
　　patron deity of, 76, 76–77, 164–66,
　　　165, 200
　　prejudice against, 86–87
Monteforte Toledo, Mario, 87–88
　　book by, 87–88, 126–28
　　as Chona's suitor, 126, *126*
　　exile for, 301n42
　　Lacandones and, 125–27
　　as Ladino, 87–88
　　leadership of, 128

and Mayans, 128
　　Vidal and, 301n42
Morgan, Lewis Henry, 291–92
mother(s). *See also* childbirth;
　　postpartum; pregnancy
　　of author, Chona as, 49, 57–61
　　of Chona, 82–84, *83*, 89–92, 95, 154,
　　　154, 156
　　clothing for nursing, 155, *155*
　　lessons on nursing, 33–34, *34*
　　school and language lessons of, 30
muxu'x (umbilical stump), 308n71
　　care for, 218–19
　　occupations and, 226–27
　　placement of, 227, 228
　　practicante midwives and, 296n19
　　preservation of, 226–29

nahual, 8–9, 76–77, 90, 220, 306n63
　　destiny/development and, 8–9
　　interest in knowing, 306n63
　　tonal vs., 297n23
Nahuatl (language), 39, 170
　　as official language, 47–48
namesake (*k'axeel*), 170–71, 245
namesake, of author, 169, *169*
Native American healer, 109–10, 273
Navichoc Cotuc, Marta, 109–10,
　　286, 289
　　babies' source and, 109–10
　　on children/childbirth, 109–10
North Americans. *See also*
　　United States
　　longevity for, 299n32
number 13, 200, 308n72

observing, learning by, 248–53,
　　257–64, *258, 263*, 308n73, 309n75
obstetric medications, 305n60
obstetric skills, 305n60
　　of Chona, 157, 160, 170, 180, 182,
　　　188–90
　　from divine, 157, 159
occupations
　　babies and, 222–24, *223*, 226–27
　　changes in, 227, 227–28
　　in Chona's family, 8, 228

placenta (*compañero*), 192–93
  care of, 211, 212, 307n67
  expulsion techniques for, 194–95,
    197–98
  patience for, 194
Pop, Agustín, 208–9
  meeting, 37–38
Popol Vuh, 220, 303n52
postpartum
  binding mother's abdomen in, 214
  ceremony for, 221–22, *221–23*, 224
  coals under bed during, 219, 229
  gifts and, 214–15
  for Spanish, 221
  sweat baths for, 215–17, *217*, 307n68
power objects
  for bone healer, 275
  for Chona, 157–58
  for *iyooma'*, 104, 157–58, 167
practicante midwives, 149–50, 286
  iyoom vs., 63–64, 66, 149–50
  languages of, 295n13
  literacy of, 295n13
  modesty and, 64
  money and, 64
  muxu'x and, 296n19
  numbers of, 62
  respect and, 64
  secular training of, 19, 63, 296n18
  umbilical cords and, 63
Pratt, Caroline, 21
prayers
  of Aztecs, 213, 225
  during childbirth, 198–200
  Chona and, 198–200
  Cumatz, Dolores, on, 199
  by *iyoom/iyooma'*, 198–200, 214
  Mayan *vs.* Catholic, 198, 199–200
  nahual and, 76–77
  Quiacaín Televario, Jesús, on,
    198–99
pregnancy
  breech babies during, 180–82, *181*
  ceremony in, 164
  children's detection of, 169–70
  children's ignorance of, 107–10,
    118, 245, 250–52

  Chona's detection of, 170
  clothing and, 110
  desires during, 176
  eclipses and, 177, 304n56
  evil eye and, 233–35
  external version in, 157, 178–80, 238
  in Florentine Codex, 175–76
  food cravings during, 175–77, 178
  foods to avoid during, 177
  foreigners' knowledge of, 252
  hospital visits during, 182–83,
    182–83
  iyoom's work during, 178–82
  local references to, 111
  positioning baby during, 178–79,
    179, 180, *181*
  prenatal massage for, 179–80,
    179–80
  prenatal visits during, 180
  primipara's ignorance of, 111–13,
    178, 252
  protecting, 175–78, 303n53
  respect for, 110, 118
  Spain and, 177
  stress on fetus during, 176, 303n54
  sweat baths during, 178–79, *179*, 216
  as taboo subject, 109–13
  transverse babies during, 180, 182
  viewing eclipses during, 177,
    304n56
  young adults' knowledge of,
    110–13, 118
prejudice. *See* discrimination against
  Mayans
Prieto, Guillermo ("Fidel"), 86–87
Puac, María, 59, 160, 195–97, 271, *271*
Puzul, Teresa, 90

Quiacaín Chavajay, Felipe, 12, *12*
Quiacaín Pérez, Abraham, 90,
  151, *151*
Quiacaín Pérez, María Lidia
  ("Linda"), 90, 151, *151*
  family stories from, 94, 95, 97–98
  at lunch celebration, 94, 95, 97–98
  on Pérez Yojcom, Marcos, 97–98
  religion of, 97

San Pedro la Laguna, Guatemala
(*continued*)
  colonialization and, 163
  congregation by Spanish, 40–43,
    41–43
  drugs in, 287, 289
  evangelical Protestantism in, 32, 82,
    96–97, 198
  family violence in, 309n77
  genocide and, 206, 309n77
  history of, 40–44, *41–43*
  library for, 33, 60, *60*
  out-migration from, 44, 295n12
  political role in, 32–33
  population of, 40, 41, 42, 43
  reputation in, 287, 289
  romanticizing, 33, 39
  school in, 5–6, 10–12, *11*
  social control in, 287, 290
  television in, 68, 286
  tourism and, 286–87
  U.S. and, 14, 289
San Pedro Sacatepéquez, 309n77
Santa Ana, 76, *76*, 200
Santiago (saint), 79
Santiago Atitlán, 16–17, 79, 164–66,
  206, 296n21, 297n24
scholars, related, 294n6
school(s), 264, *264*, 286
  changing relation to, 5
  Chavajay Petzey, Marina, and,
    227, *227*
  Chona's childhood without, 5–6
  as depriving of skills, 6
  girls and, 6, 10, 293n1
  grade expansion in, 10
  hiding from, 5–6
  higher education, 88
  intelligence *vs.*, 6, 293n1
  language and, 5, 11, 22
  mothers and, 30
  in other cities, 44
  out-migration and, 44
  parents and, 5–6, 30–31
  participation in, 5–6, 10, 294n6
  in San Pedro, 5–6, 10–12, *11*
  Susana and, 5–6

  for U.S. children, 20–21
  work *vs.*, 6
sexual intercourse
  avoidance of, for *iyooma'*, 101–2
  breasts and, 294n11
  Chona and, 118
  dream about, 118
  girls' ignorance about, 114–18,
    300n39
  husbands and, 101–2, 114–16
  near children, 116–18
  repulsion and, 115–16
  shock and, 114–16
  as taboo subject, 114–18
  young adults and, 114–18
shaman, 246–47
  and acceptance of divine calling
    for, 103–4
  birthsigns and, 80, 104, 203, *203*, 205
  ceremonies by, 122, *122*, 158, 206,
    206, 302n50
  Chavajay, Domingo, as, 122, *122*,
    305n61, *306*
  Chavajay, Francisco, as, 81, *81*
  childbirth and, 201–2, *202*
  destiny of, 105, 299n36
  iyoom/iyooma' and, 150, 299n31
  Mayan calendar and, 201–2
  painting of, 206, *206*
  Pérez Yojcom, Marcos, as, 91,
    156, *158*
  Rocché González, Juana, as, 203,
    203
SIDS. *See* sudden infant death
  syndrome
Siiwaan Tinaamit (beings of nature), 123
Sisay, Juan, 206, *206*
skills. *See also* obstetric skills
  non-obstetric healing skills, 233–34
  without practice, 261–62
  school endangering, 6
  of U.S. children, 21
skin color, 5, 7, 294n4
social status
  Mayan identification and, 85
  racial classification for, 84–85
  tribute and, 85

Spanish. *See also* Catholicism; Ladino
    in Castellanización class, 11, *11*
    Latin American heritage from,
        303n55
    against Mesoamerican spiritual
        practices, 77, 80
    Phillip III and, 47–48
    postpartum quarantine and, 221
    Tz'utujil and, 5, 11, 48, 67–68, 286
    Tz'utujil Mayans and, 39–40
    usefulness of, 10
    Yojcom, D., as, 90
spiritual concepts, 32, 157, 242,
        296n21. *See also* deities; *nahual*;
        prayers
    aj'iitz and, 206–7
    babies' spirits in, 170–71, 220,
        307n69
    cross and, 81
    of destiny, 102–5, 299n36
    of "divine election," 102–5, 299n36
    of dreams, 269
    four directions in, 220, 229
    of heart, 302n48
    spirit separation in, 307n69
    spirits' instruction and, 105, 232
    tamatinime as, 299n36
spiritual guides (*ajq'ijab'*), 296n21
stillborn, 210
    resuscitation of, 244
sudden infant death syndrome
        (SIDS), 220
Sunú, Francisco, 274–75
Susana
    clothing of, 17, *17*
    culture of, 16–17, *17*
    eloping, 132
    on González Navichoc, Dolores, 98
    nature of, 6
    school for, 5–6
    story from, 90
swaddling
    of baby born with cord around
        neck, 220
    cultural change and, 210–11,
        307n66
sweat baths, *217*

Aztecs and, 216
discontinuation of, 216–17
Indigenous people and, 215–17
postpartum, 215–17, *217*, 307n68
during pregnancy, 178–79, *179*, 216

taboo subjects
    babies' source as, 107–9
    for Mayan children, 107–18
    menstruation as, 114
    pregnancy/childbirth as, 109–13
    sexual intercourse as, 114–18
talk about *vs.* practice, 241, 286
teachers, 195
    author identity, 38
    language and, 5, 11
    Pedranos as, 11, *11*
    unemployment for, 44
television, 68, 286
Teotihuacan, 39
Toltec Chichén Itzá, 39
tonal, nahual as, 297n23
traditions
    in cultural communities, 32
    discrimination against, 22, 242
    European, 306n64
    of respectfully greeting
        elders, 19, *19*
    transformations and, 280–92, *281*,
        284, *288*, *292*
    weaving and, 29
traditions/new ways, 36
    children/childbirth and, 109–11
    in cultural constellations, 22–23
    as norm, 23
    in U.S., 22
transforming witch (*q'iisoom*)
    acceptance of, 210
    activities of, 209–10, 307n65
    birthsign of, 209
twins
    conception and, 167–68, *168*
    respect for, 168–69, *169*, 303n52
    as "saints," 168, 303n52
Tz'utujil (Mayan language), 39
    culture and, 15–16
    English borrowed terms, 48